Economic Development
and American Foreign Policy
1943-62

Economic Development and American Foreign Policy

1943–62

DAVID A. BALDWIN

THE UNIVERSITY OF CHICAGO PRESS

CHICAGO AND LONDON

Library of Congress Catalog Card Number: 66-20597

THE UNIVERSITY OF CHICAGO PRESS, CHICAGO & LONDON
The University of Toronto Press, Toronto 5, Canada

© *1966 by The University of Chicago. All rights reserved. Published 1966*
Printed in the United States of America

And if you lend only where you expect to be repaid, what credit is that to you? Even sinners lend to each other if they are to be repaid in full.

LUKE 6:34

Preface

The need for an interdisciplinary approach to international affairs has been highlighted during the postwar years by the establishment of several departments and schools of international relations. In the field of research, however, the response to this need has been relatively limited. For several years I have advocated closer co-operation between economists and political scientists in the study of international relations. This book attempts to demonstrate the usefulness of integration of these two disciplines in international studies. The topic of foreign aid was chosen because of its importance as a current public issue and because of its obvious interest to members of both disciplines. There are many pitfalls in the no man's land between two disciplines, and one of these is wandering aimlessly across the terrain. One must have a focus, and the focus of this book is provided by political science. More specifically, the book is organized around some basic principles of systematic foreign policy analysis developed by political scientists during the last twenty years. These principles can be summarized as follows. It is desirable to:

1. Substitute probabilistic language for deterministic language.
2. Distinguish between real environments and those perceived by policy-makers.
3. Distinguish between the nation-state and the policy-makers who act on its behalf.
4. Distinguish between policy-making analysis and capability analysis.
5. Use functional approaches instead of legalistic ones.
6. Emphasize the domestic, as well as the foreign, influences on foreign policy.
7. Avoid careless use of the concept of "national interest."

Although the book is undoubtedly oriented more toward political science than economics, the approach has enabled me to bring in ideas developed by economists interested in international economic policies. The book seeks to illuminate the blind spots in discussions of foreign aid by both political scientists and economists. In doing so, it has inevitably developed its own blind spots. I leave to others the judgment as to whether the price of the illumination has been too high.

My intellectual debts are many. The most obvious ones are owed to colleagues who read drafts of the manuscript and offered helpful criticism. They include Robert E. Asher and Andrew Westwood of the Brookings Institution, Raymond F. Mikesell of the University of Oregon, Michael K. O'Leary of Syracuse University, and Harold Sprout of Princeton University.

In addition to these, I should acknowledge debts to several former teachers who greatly influenced the way I think about international affairs. These include Inis Claude, Jr., of the University of Michigan; Walter Laves of Indiana University; Edgar S. Furniss, Jr., of Ohio State University; Jacob Viner, Gardner Patterson, and Harold Sprout, all of Princeton University.

The manuscript was prepared during my tenure as a Research Fellow at the Brookings Institution in 1964–65. I am grateful to Brookings for this opportunity. The Brookings Institution bears no responsibility, however, for the views expressed in this book. I should also like to thank *World Politics* for permission to use portions of my article, "The International Bank in Political Perspective," which appeared in the October, 1965, issue.

For her patience, encouragement, and editorial advice during preparation of this book I thank my wife, to whom I dedicate this book.

DAVID A. BALDWIN

_____ Contents

I. Introduction 1

II. Prelude to Point Four 8

III. Point Four: Reconsideration: 1949–53 72

IV. The Soft Loan Experiment: 1954–57 117

V. Adoption and Refinement of Soft Loans: 1958–62 . 191

VI. Concluding Remarks 243

Selected Bibliography 273

Index 287

I

_____ Introduction

ECONOMIC DEVELOPMENT AND
FOREIGN POLICY

When future historians look back on the twentieth century, they may not think of it in terms of three wars, two hot and one cold; instead they may regard it as the century of economic development. What judgment history will pass on American foreign policy during this century we can only guess, but we can be certain that policies concerned with foreign economic growth will figure prominently in the history books. For a variety of reasons and in various ways the United States has sought to improve economic conditions in some of the poorer areas of the world during the postwar period. This is a study of how and why America has gone about promoting economic development in underdeveloped areas.

One technique used by the United States to stimulate economic growth has been much discussed—foreign aid. Other techniques have been overshadowed by the eye-catching foreign aid program, and the impression is thereby given that the American desire to spur economic growth developed simultaneously with the aid program. Economic development as a goal of United States foreign policy, however, emerged during the early 1940's, and policies for pursuing this goal evolved to some extent independently of what is usually considered the "foreign aid program." Since much attention has been given to studying foreign aid and the several uses to which it has been put, there is widespread misunderstanding of the panoply of techniques used by the

United States to pursue one of the goals of foreign aid—economic development.

We are concerned here with American attempts to influence events outside national boundaries, and thus we are concerned with foreign policy. If we are to discuss techniques of statecraft we should have in mind at least some rudimentary concept of what foreign policy is and how it is made. It us useful to define foreign policy as the scheme or pattern of ends and means explicit or implicit in a state's actions and reactions vis-à-vis other states or components thereof.[1] Given this definition, we shall consider foreign policy-making as a process in which governmental officials make decisions based on their perceptions of the international milieu and the domestic situation. Although such a simple conception of foreign policy-making may seem primitive, it is highly sophisticated compared with most studies of foreign aid, which usually ignore the foreign policy context.

Within this broad context of American foreign policy aimed at promoting economic development, we shall focus on America's most important foreign aid technique, soft lending. The central analytical question in the following pages is how and why the United States came to adopt soft lending as "the instrument of primary emphasis—the single most important tool"[2] for stimulating economic growth in poor nations. In answering this question it will be necessary to survey the alternatives available to policy-makers and to analyze the process by which they chose one set of alternatives and rejected others.

SOME PRELIMINARIES

Many techniques of American foreign policy involve movement of capital among nations; therefore it is useful to be aware of the various ways in which this can be accomplished. Figure 1 illustrates a number of channels through which capital can be moved. Any attempt by the American government to facilitate the move-

[1] Harold Sprout and Margaret Sprout, *Foundations of International Politics* (Princeton, N.J.: Van Nostrand, 1962), p. 108.

[2] "Foreign Aid: Message of the President to the Congress," *Department of State Bulletin,* April 10, 1961, p. 511.

ment of capital through one of these channels will be considered a technique of statecraft.

The term "soft loan" is not self-explanatory. Although the literature on foreign aid often uses the term "soft loan," it is rarely defined. Anyone reading widely in this literature encounters such apparent synonyms as "fuzzy loans," "political loans," "especially risky loans," "local currency loans," "soft currency loans," "foreign currency loans," "long-term low-interest loans," and "gift loans." These terms are usually undefined also, and they are frequently used interchangeably with "soft loan." Since there are differing opinions as to how "soft loan" should be defined and since the

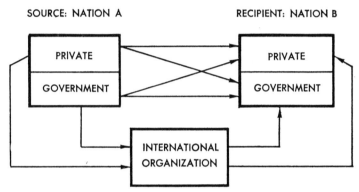

Fig. 1.—Channels for transfer of capital from nation A to nation B

differences are significant for an understanding of soft lending as a technique of statecraft, it is unwise to leave the term undefined.

If we could emblazon a single sentence on the mind of the student of foreign aid, this would be as useful as any: "Money has but one fundamental purpose in an economic system: to facilitate the exchange of goods and services."[3] Much of the confusion in the discussion of soft lending has resulted from a failure first to keep this primary function of money in mind and second to recognize that there is more than one way to define "money." There are both legal and functional definitions of "money," and economists themselves are not all agreed on the "best" definition.[4] The definition of "money" is especially impor-

[3] Lester V. Chandler, *The Economics of Money and Banking* (4th ed. rev.; New York: Harper & Row, 1964), p. 4.

[4] See *ibid.*, pp. 12–16.

tant in analyzing soft loans because of the prevalence of a tendency to define them as loans repayable in "local currency." The terms "local currency," "soft currency," "foreign currency," and "inconvertible currency" are often used interchangeably. The term "local currency" usually connotes that the currency is inconvertible; otherwise the term "foreign exchange" is used. In other words, "local currency," by either implicit or explicit definition, is severely limited in the degree to which it can fulfil the primary function of money—facilitating the exchange of goods and services. If we are using a functional definition of money, we may not want to refer to such "local currency" as "money." The literature on foreign aid treats us to the spectacle of one scholar explaining that local currencies are "merely money,"[5] while another is explaining that they are "not money for our purposes."[6] A third scholar fails to define "local currencies" but assures us that they are a "potentially useful instrument" of statecraft if the United States policymakers know how to use them.[7] He overlooks the fact that experience is not likely to increase the usefulness of something which is *by definition* useless.

The discussion of soft loans is further confused by the fact that the term "local currency loan" has been used in at least three different ways: (1) to refer to dollar loans repayable in inconvertible currency; (2) to refer to loans in foreign exchange, and repayable in same, for the purpose of financing indirect foreign exchange costs of a project resulting from the fact that local expenditure on labor or domestically produced equipment will usually give rise to an increased demand for imported consumer goods or raw materials; and (3) to refer to a loan of the borrowing nation's own currency which is repayable in same.[8] In the following analysis the term "local currency" will be defined as currency which is

[5] Harlan Cleveland, "The Fits and Starts of Foreign Aid," *The Reporter,* April 16, 1959, p. 27.

[6] Edward S. Mason, "Foreign Money We Can't Spend," *Atlantic Monthly,* May, 1960, p. 80.

[7] John D. Montgomery, *The Politics of Foreign Aid* (New York: Praeger, 1962), p. 256.

[8] The first of these, the most common, is often used to describe the activities of the Development Loan Fund. The latter two are described in International Bank for Reconstruction and Development, *Fifth Annual Report, 1949–1950,* pp. 10–11.

not legally convertible into dollars; and unless otherwise indicated, a functional definition of money will be used. Also, the terms "foreign currency" and "soft currency" will be used as synonymous with "local currency."

Several definitions of "soft loan" are currently in use; they include the following: (1) A soft loan is any loan repayable in local currency.[9] In this definition it is usually implied, but seldom stated, that the loan was initially made in foreign exchange and is repayable in less useful currency. (2) A soft loan is any loan which is either repayable in inconvertible currency or which is repayable in dollars at lower rates of interest or over a longer period than loans from "conventional" lending agencies such as the World Bank or the private capital market.[10] (3) Soft loans are loans repayable in local currency and include loans made initially in the borrowing nation's own currency.[11] (4) Soft loans are loans with regard to which the borrower is likely to fail to meet the conditions of repayment agreed upon at the time the loan was made. In the everyday jargon of commercial banking the term "soft loan" is a derogatory term which is used to refer to unwise loans from the point of view of the private commercial banker. The connotation is that "hard loans" are made by "hard-headed" businessmen (good) and that "soft loans" are made by "soft-headed" businessmen (bad). Testifying on behalf of the First National Bank of Chicago in the International Development Association hearings, one man noted that "in conventional private or government finance, a soft loan is a self-evident contradiction

[9] For example, see Robert L. Heilbroner, *The Great Ascent: The Struggle for Economic Development in Our Time* (New York: Harper Torchbooks, 1963), p. 113.

[10] For example, see Robert E. Asher, *Grants, Loans, and Local Currencies: Their Role in Foreign Aid* (Washington: Brookings Institution, 1961), p. 14. A rather odd variation of this definition is provided by James A. Robinson, who defines soft loans as having "longer terms of repayment" and "lower rates of interest," without indicating what it is that the terms of repayment are longer than or what the interest rates are lower than. *Congress and Foreign Policy-Making* (Homewood, Ill.: Dorsey Press, 1962), p. 85.

[11] For example, see H. Bradford Westerfield, *The Instruments of America's Foreign Policy* (New York: Crowell, 1963), pp. 366–68. Although it is not entirely clear, it appears that Raymond F. Mikesell would also include loans made initially in local currency in a definition of soft loans. See Raymond F. Mikesell (ed.), *U.S. Private and Government Investment Abroad* (Eugene: University of Oregon Press, 1962), p. 293.

in terms."[12] Although his formal logic may have been faulty, his implication was clear—soft loans are bad business. Traditionally, "soft loans" have been regarded as "unbusinesslike," that is, unwise from the point of view of one who is trying to make money by lending it. By and large this connotation has been retained by the various definitions of "soft loan" that have been formulated. Arguments for such loans have usually focused on the reasons for giving loans which admittedly would not be made by private commercial bankers. A few definitions, however, do not carry this connotation. Professor Crabb, for example, claims that "soft loans" are not loans of "doubtful validity"[13]—despite the fact that the term often connotes that such loans are of doubtful validity *by normal banking standards*. Also, the third definition described above does not always carry the connotation of "unbusinesslike" activity. Making a loan in rupees and being repaid in rupees is, after all, not an inherently "unbusinesslike" act; but making a loan in dollars and accepting repayment in rupees which cannot be spent is something else. If we would stray no more than necessary from the traditional common-sense notion of "soft loans," we must reject the third definition. This study assumes that it is desirable to have technical definitions conform as closely as is feasible with common-sense notions.

A "soft loan," then, as the term is usually used, implies that such a loan is in some sense "easier" on the borrower than a normal commercial loan. We can break the elements of a loan into four parts: (1) Time is an aspect of all loans. A loan can be "softened" by allowing the borrower to have a "grace period," during which payments on interest and principal are suspended, before he has to begin repaying the loan. It may also be "softened" by allowing repayment over a longer period of time than is normally the case, over fifty years instead of fifteen, for example. (2) The nature of the currency in which the loan is initially made is important in defining a loan. Any definition of a soft loan should specifically state whether loans made initially in inconvertible currency are to be included. Such a specific statement would, of course,

---

[12] U.S., Congress, House, Committee on Banking and Currency, *Hearings, International Development Association Act,* 86th Cong., 2d sess., 1960, p. 62.

[13] Cecil V. Crabb, Jr., *American Foreign Policy in the Nuclear Age* (Evanston, Ill.: Row, Peterson & Co., 1960), p. 415.

be unnecessary if everyone assumed that loans were initially
made in foreign exchange. As was noted above, however, this
assumption is unwarranted. (3) All loans carry an interest rate—
even if this is zero. A loan can be "softened" by lowering the
interest rate below that which would be charged by conventional
lending institutions[14] for a given loan. (4) The nature of the
currency in which repayment is made should also be specified in
defining a soft loan. Loans may be "softened" by allowing repayment in inconvertible currency. The economic effects of such action resemble those of an outright grant.

None of the definitions of "soft loans" currently in use adequately accounts for the foregoing four components of a loan.[15]
As used in this study, "soft loans" will be defined as follows: A
soft loan is one made initially in foreign exchange (or in real
goods or services) carrying one or more of the following conditions: (*a*) longer time period for repayment than is normal in
the commercial capital market, (*b*) lower interest rate than could
be obtained from conventional lending institutions, and (*c*) repayment in inconvertible currency. The terms "soft loan" and
"unconventional loan" will be used synonymously. The terms
"hard loan" and "conventional loan" will both be used to refer
to loans made initially in foreign exchange and repayable in same
at rates of interest and over time periods which are normal in the
commercial capital market.

[14] Conventional lending institutions are defined as all private commercial banks
and the International Bank.

[15] The best discussion of problems in defining a soft loan is in Mikesell, pp. 275–
77. Mikesell's definition, however, fails to specify the nature of the currency in which
the loan is initially made and thus leaves open the possibility of a loan in rupees,
repayable in rupees, at commercial interest rates, with a conventional maturation
period, being called "soft."

II

Prelude to Point Four

In 1964 the United States Mutual Defense and Development program called for 67 per cent of the economic aid funds to be expended in the form of loans, most of which were soft loans.[1] The bulk of these loans would have been described as "unsound," "bad," or "unbusinesslike" in the 1940's, and they would have been rejected as techniques of statecraft by the informed public, Congress, business leaders, and the executive branch. What follows is a description of the process by which the United States came to adopt a technique of statecraft which it had not only ignored in the 1940's but had specifically condemned. Thus the process involves not just the turning from one legitimate technique to another but the legitimizing of a formerly illegitimate alternative. This aspect of the development of soft loan policy should be noted because it is rarely illuminated by government documents, businessmen's speeches, or scholarly analysis. Government officials, whether in Congress or the executive, have an incentive to conceal the legitimizing process lest they be accused of irresponsibility. The adoption of policy alternatives which were formerly considered illegitimate is therefore usually described by government officials as the adoption of an alternative which was not "really" bad before, just misunderstood, and which must be understood in terms of new extenuating circumstances. "No responsible person," Milton S. Eisenhower assures us, "would

[1] U.S., Congress, House, Committee on Foreign Affairs, *Background Material on Mutual Defense and Development Programs: Fiscal Year 1965*, 88th Cong., 2d sess., Committee Print, 1964, p. 24.

favor having an agency of the United States Government make economically unsound loans."[2]

Many businessmen do not want to call attention to the legitimizing of soft loans as a technique of statecraft because they are opposed to the legitimization process. They want to avoid setting a precedent; therefore they describe, and sometimes even approve of, the use of soft loans only in "unusual" or "abnormal" situations and only with a great deal of qualification. A business leader giving approval to establishment of the Development Loan Fund, for example, hardly wants to go on record as favoring "unsound" or "unbusinesslike" activities by the government. Business leaders who are opposed to foreign aid, however, often call attention to the fact that soft loans were once regarded as "unsound" activities. Thus, the concealing of the legitimacy aspects of soft loan policy is not done by all business leaders but by those who have resigned themselves to tolerate soft loans because of what they judge to be extenuating circumstances. Such men want at least to salvage a commitment to "sound businesslike" procedures in "normal" times.

Scholars have seldom noted the process by which soft loans gained respectability. Economists, understandably, have had little interest in this aspect despite the fact that many do understand what has happened.[3] What the economists do not adequately understand is why it has happened the way it did. They complain about public "misunderstanding"[4] of soft loans and treat the problem as one of education rather than politics. They do not consider that this "misunderstanding" might have played a vital role in the process of political legitimation of the soft loan policy alternative. Political scientists have added even less illumination to this aspect of soft loans. In fact, they have not only failed to

[2] *The Wine Is Bitter: The United States and Latin America* (Garden City, N.Y.: Doubleday, 1963), p. 154.

[3] Raymond F. Mikesell, for example, notes that there is something unusual about soft loans. He insists that they "cannot be regarded as true loans." Raymond F. Mikesell (ed.), *U.S. Private and Government Investment Abroad* (Eugene: University of Oregon Press, 1962), p. 297.

[4] Cf. *ibid.*, pp. 345–46. See also Peter B. Kenen, *Giant among Nations* (Chicago: Rand McNally & Co., 1963), pp. 192–93. "Why not be frank?" says Kenen. "Let us return to grants instead of obscuring the distinction between bankable loans and development assistance."

illuminate but have broken lamps, snuffed out candles, and covered windows. They have said little about soft loans, and what they have said has often been misleading or wrong. One undergraduate textbook in American foreign policy, for example, takes its definition of soft loans directly from a government publication in which legislators were trying to conceal the legitimizing process by arguing that soft loans were really not loans of "doubtful validity."[5] In this case, in fact, the government publication presented a more sophisticated analysis of soft loans than did the textbook "explanation" of the report. The first step in understanding the evolution of American soft loan policy is recognition that "at the beginning of the aid period, some 10–15 years ago, the idea of soft loans was considered to be quite heretical."[6]

"Prior to World War II," a veteran American diplomat has observed, "with the exception of wartime loans, certain emergencies, and a modest amount of foreign lending by the Export-Import Bank established in 1934, government-to-government assistance was virtually unknown."[7] Thus government loans, even soft ones, were not unknown in the 1940's, but they had not yet come to be regarded as legitimate except in extreme emergencies. The National Advisory Council on International Monetary and Financial Problems (NAC) explained that the loan to Great Britain in 1946, a governmental soft loan, was not to be regarded as setting a policy precedent: "It is the view of the Council that the British case is unique and will not be a precedent for a loan to any other country."[8]

[5] Cf. Cecil V. Crabb, Jr., *American Foreign Policy in the Nuclear Age* (Evanston, Ill.: Row, Peterson & Co., 1960), p. 415.

[6] H. W. Singer, "International Aid for Economic Development: Problems and Tendencies," *International Development Review*, VI (March, 1964), 17.

[7] Charles E. Bohlen, "Economic Assistance in United States Foreign Policy," *Department of State Bulletin*, March 28, 1960, p. 495.

[8] "Statement of the Foreign Loan Policy of the United States Government by the National Advisory Council on International Monetary and Financial Policies," National Advisory Council Document No. 70-A, February 21, 1946, reprinted in *Report of the National Advisory Council on International Monetary and Financial Problems* submitted to Congress March 8, 1946, p. 17. Henceforth the Council will be referred to as National Advisory Council or NAC. This document will be cited hereafter as "Statement of the Foreign Loan Policy of the United States Government by the NAC," 1946.

EVOLUTION OF SOFT LOAN POLICY:
FRAMEWORK FOR ANALYSIS

Although the United States has used soft loans as techniques of statecraft for promoting various goals, it has adopted them as an important continuing policy alternative only with regard to the professed goal of spurring economic development in under-developed countries.[9] The following analysis will focus on the development of soft loans as a technique of American foreign policy for promoting economic development in underdeveloped areas. This policy development will be described in terms of a set of four questions: (1) Did the United States government want to promote economic development in underdeveloped areas and why? (2) How did the United States government want to promote economic development? (3) Why were some alternatives chosen and others rejected? (4) What was the effectiveness of the method chosen for achieving the goal of promoting economic growth?

The first question, that relating to whether economic development was a goal of American foreign policy, could be endlessly —and fruitlessly—debated. Providing empirical data on this matter is not a primary goal in this study, but since some have questioned the very existence of such a foreign policy goal, brief attention will be given to examining empirical evidence of its existence. For much of the analysis, however, the existence of this policy goal is assumed. This should not be taken to mean that the importance of the goal has been fixed. It is a basic assumption of the following analysis that foreign policy has many goals, of differing degrees of importance, and that the relative importance of a goal affects the choice of techniques to be used in pursuing it.

The second question to be answered is how the United States wanted to pursue the goal of promoting economic development. In other words, what was the American policy with regard to

[9] The term "underdeveloped countries" will be used, unless otherwise indicated, to refer to countries with an annual per capita income of less than $500. The term will be used interchangeably with "developing country," "less developed," and "poor countries." The terms "economic development" and "economic growth" will be used to refer to a sustained increase in annual per capita income, unless another definition is specifically noted.

economic development during a given period of time. This will be a description of which policy alternatives were adopted and which were rejected. The discussion of this question will focus on three alternative ways of promoting economic growth: (*a*) relying on the domestic economy to generate internally enough capital for an increase in the growth rate, (*b*) facilitating the import of external capital through private channels, and (*c*) furnishing external capital through public channels.[10] The American policy on soft loans at a given time can be described as a series of answers to such questions as: Should American capital be transferred to underdeveloped countries? How much should be transferred? On what terms? Through what channels? The question of what policy alternatives were selected is separable from that of why they were selected, which is the third question with which the discussion will deal.

Why did the United States government choose the policies it did and reject other policies? In explaining why policy was what it was, the discussion will be concerned first with the external setting; second, with the internal setting; and third, with the decision makers' perception of this situation and its effect on their selection of a policy alternative. The external setting will include relevant activities in the United Nations, the International Bank for Reconstruction and Development (IBRD), and the international situation in general. The internal setting will include the general domestic situation, the views of the business elite, and the views of Congress.[11] The activities of the executive branch will be described in the section on the decision makers' perception of the situation and the effect of this perception on the selection of a policy.

The fourth and last step in describing the evolution of American soft loan policy is an evaluation of the effectiveness of the policy techniques adopted for achieving the goal of economic growth. Which of the obstacles to economic growth could be attacked

[10] Capital is here defined as those goods and services which a nation abstains from consuming in order to use them to increase the nation's productive capacity.

[11] Note that the Congress is being treated as part of the internal setting rather than as "decision maker." This does not mean, of course, that Congress does not participate in decision making; it merely means that for convenience this "participation" will be described as a part of the internal setting of the executive branch which has primary responsibility for the conduct of foreign affairs.

by the policy chosen, and what were the determinants of the effectiveness with which this attack could be carried out?

The foregoing framework for analysis will be applied to four time periods: 1943–48, 1949–53, 1954–57, and 1958–62.

I. WAS ECONOMIC GROWTH A GOAL OF UNITED STATES POLICY?

In a widely read book on foreign aid Charles Wolf, Jr., notes that "during the 1948–1950 period, concern for the economic development of underdeveloped areas appeared as a final innovation in United States aid."[12] Although this statement is true, it contains an intellectual trap for the unwary. The United States was concerned about the economic development of underdeveloped areas before 1948, but economic aid was not used as a technique for dealing with this problem. From the viewpoint of the student of foreign aid, concern for economic development was an innovation; but to one interested in the evolution of techniques for dealing with economic development, economic aid was the new element appearing during the 1948–50 period.

American interest in the economic growth of poor countries in the 1943–48 period was related to the broader foreign policy goals of peace and prosperity. There was a belief that peace and economic stability were related in some undefined way. In a message to Congress on tariffs and trade President Roosevelt stated: "We know that we cannot succeed in building a peaceful world unless we build an economically healthy world."[13] We can find similar references to the economic foundations of peace in State Department planning documents as early as 1943, in speeches by American representatives at Bretton Woods, and in other policy statements by government officials.[14] In a major statement

[12] *Foreign Aid: Theory and Practice in Southern Asia* (Princeton, N.J.: Princeton University Press, 1960), p. 57.

[13] Text reprinted in *New York Times*, March 27, 1945, p. 36. See also the text of President Roosevelt's message to Congress on the Bretton Woods proposals in which he states that "international political relations will be friendly and constructive . . . only if solutions are found to the difficult economic problems we face today." *New York Times*, February 13, 1945, p. 17.

[14] United States, Department of State, *Postwar Foreign Policy Preparation 1939–1945, General Policy Series*, No. 15, pp. 141, 241, 468, 560–61. The Undersecretary of State emphasized that "there can be no really stable world as long as hunger

of American foreign loan policy the National Advisory Council argued that "economic stability will foster peace. This program of foreign lending is essential to the realization of the main objective of the foreign economic policy of the United States, which is to lay the economic foundations of peace."[15]

Economic development abroad was viewed as a requisite not only for peace but for prosperity as well. Economic growth was related to higher levels of international trade, which in turn were related to higher levels of production and consumption because of the economic advantages of international specialization. The goal of economic growth was also seen as a means by which the United States could insure full employment at home. In retrospect we realize that the problem facing the United States after World War II was not deflation but inflation. The memory of the depression, however, was still fresh, and government officials were understandably concerned about both the problem of long-run full employment and the short-run problem of reconversion of American industry from wartime to peacetime employment. James F. Byrnes, then Director of War Mobilization, called attention to the problem of maintaining full employment during reconversion in a letter to the President and Congress in January, 1945: "We must export goods," Byrnes argued, "if we are to provide jobs for all of our workers."[16] The general policy statement of the Export-Import Bank, issued in 1945, also noted that loans for economic development were justified because "the best trading partners of the United States are countries which have reached the highest state of economic development."[17] Concern

---

exists. Even we, in our heaven-blessed homeland, can never live in permanent security and well-being until that problem has been solved. Thus it fits directly into the long-range interests of the United States and the American people. This is an emergency problem but it is a long-range problem too." "America's Place in World Affairs," *Department of State Bulletin,* January 21, 1945, p. 88. Secretary of the Treasury Henry Morgenthau, Jr., opened the Bretton Woods Conference with a plea for recognition that the depression had destroyed "international faith." Text reprinted in *New York Times,* July 2, 1944, p. 14.

[15] "Statement of the Foreign Loan Policy of the United States Government by the NAC," 1946, p. 21.

[16] Text reprinted in *New York Times,* January 2, 1945, p. 12.

[17] "General Policy Statement of the Export-Import Bank of Washington," *Department of State Bulletin,* September 23, 1945, p. 442. Wolf disputes the validity of the assumption that rich countries make better trading partners for the United States. He does this, however, by using a table which compares American trade with

for foreign economic growth as a means of promoting American exports was also voiced by the NAC in 1946: "Only by the reestablishment of high levels of production and trade the world over can the United States be assured in future years of a sustained level of exports appropriate to the maintenance of high levels of domestic production and employment."[18]

The justification of American concern for economic development of underdeveloped areas in terms of the broader goals of peace and prosperity may have been wise or unwise; this is not the issue here. At this point we are concerned only with the evidence of such a concern.[19] The evidence indicates that the State Department, the President, the NAC, and the Export-Import Bank all agreed with the policy stated by Secretary of the Treasury Henry Morgenthau to the closing session of the United Nations Monetary and Financial Conference at Bretton Woods: "Long-term funds must be made available also to promote sound industry and increase industrial and agricultural production in nations whose economic potentialities have not yet been developed. It is essential to us all that these nations play their full part in the exchange of goods throughout the world."[20] Given the goal of economic development, then, the next question concerns the techniques of statecraft by which the United States pursued the goal in the 1943–48 period.

---

rich countries and poor countries in 1955. Wolf's conclusion that "there is apparently no marked connection between higher income and increased trade with the United States" is misleading and not justified by the table since the table does not compare trade with the same countries in two time periods. Few would argue that rich countries, regardless of geographic location, tariff and quota arrangements, or transportation costs, always make better trading partners; yet this is the proposition that Wolf refutes. The question of whether a given country, other things being equal, will trade more with the United States as its economic growth proceeds remains open. Cf. Wolf, pp. 276–77.

[18] "Statement of the Foreign Loan Policy of the United States Government by the NAC," 1946, p. 17.

[19] Wolf argues that economic gains from trade are unattainable goals of foreign aid; therefore, he concludes, they should not be aid objectives "because, in effect, they *can't* be." This study specifically rejects Wolf's assumption that unattainable goals cannot be foreign policy objectives. It will treat goals as defined by the policy makers as the real objectives. It is quite possible that policy makers will decide to pursue unattainable goals. Cf. Wolf, p. 281.

[20] Speech of July 22, 1944, reprinted in *Department of State Bulletin*, July 30, 1944, p. 112.

II. HOW TO PROMOTE ECONOMIC
GROWTH: TECHNIQUES

In choosing a technique of statecraft the American policy makers were faced with several alternatives which could plausibly be considered useful in stimulating foreign economic growth, among which was the possibility of deliberately refraining from certain activities, such as providing government grants.[21] The policy makers chose several techniques and varied the emphasis given to each.

Reliance on Domestic Effort

No principle of United States policy toward underdeveloped areas has been more consistently embraced than the proposition that the underdeveloped countries themselves are primarily responsible for their own economic development. In his message to Congress on the Bretton Woods proposals, President Roosevelt made it abundantly clear that he considered economic development a domestic matter. "The main job of restoration is not one of relief," he emphasized. "It is one of reconstruction which must be largely done by local people and their governments. They will provide the labor, the local money, and most of the materials. The same is true for all the many plans for the improvement of transportation, agriculture, industry, and housing, that are essential to the development of the economically backward areas of the world."[22]

The American desire to rely on foreign domestic efforts as a means of spurring economic growth was also reflected in its reluctance to grant public loans for economic development. The NAC indicated that domestic efforts must do the job because the American government could meet "only a small proportion" of the development needs of foreign countries.[23]

[21] A peculiar conception of policy as "doing something" has led many to describe a policy of "doing nothing" as a lack of policy. We must distinguish, however, between a deliberate decision to do nothing and a lack of any relevant decision. The latter may be called a lack of policy; the former may not, according to the conception of policy used here.

[22] "Message of the President to the Congress on the Bretton Woods Proposals," *Department of State Bulletin*, February 18, 1945, p. 221.

[23] "Statement of the Foreign Loan Policy of the United States Government by the NAC," 1946, p. 18.

This technique of advising poor countries to rely on their own efforts rather than on the United States was based first on the American argument that external capital was not so important in the development process as the underdeveloped countries seemed to think; and second, on the belief that trade liberalization would reduce even further the need for external capital. International trade is a substitute for international movement of the factors of production; and since capital is one of the factors of production, free trade will reduce the need for moving it from one country to another. Thus, United States policy aimed at convincing poor countries that they should rely on domestic efforts to stimulate growth and at reducing the amount of capital needed to achieve a given rate of development by lifting restrictions on trade.

STIMULATION OF PRIVATE CAPITAL FLOW

Although United States policy from 1943 to 1948 emphasized the need for domestic effort, it also recognized that the capacity to save of countries with low per capita incomes was limited. After all, what can one save if one consumes only enough to slow the rate at which one is starving? All agreed that the transfer of some capital to the underdeveloped areas was desirable, despite a disagreement between the United States and potential recipients of capital concerning how much was needed to achieve a given growth rate. There was also disagreement regarding the channels through which such capital should flow. The United States government chose to direct its efforts toward stimulating the flow of private capital by trade liberalization, by improvement of the "climate of investment," and by rapid reconstruction of European countries, which were likely to be important sources of capital.

TRADE LIBERALIZATION

The reduction of barriers to international trade would permit foreign nations to earn the foreign exchange needed to import capital goods from the United States; thus the transfer of particular items of capital equipment would be effected via regular trade channels.[24] Furthermore, the willingness of American private in-

[24] Note that we should distinguish between a net capital inflow and the movement in international trade of particular items of capital equipment. A net capital inflow is here defined as an excess of imports over exports.

vestors to lend abroad would be enhanced by their perception that underdeveloped countries had a means of earning dollars with which to service external debt. An American investor is more likely to invest money in a foreign sugar plantation, for example, if he thinks that the sugar can be sold in the United States market.

United States efforts toward trade liberalization focused on the establishment of an International Trade Organization (ITO). Although the American proposals for a charter for the ITO did not contain specific arrangements for promoting economic development, it was believed, according to one of the key State Department planners, that the charter would contribute indirectly to economic development by opening markets and thus making it easier to earn the funds required to finance economic development.[25]

A similar emphasis on the close relationship between American trade policy and the transfer of capital from the United States to foreign countries recurs in statements by government officials throughout the 1943–48 period. President Roosevelt emphasized the need for an American trade policy which would allow foreigners to earn the foreign exchange they needed to pay their debts to Americans, and the NAC expressed concern about the effect of American willingness to spend abroad on the ability of foreigners to service large American loans.[26] If foreigners were to finance their imports from the United States by loans from the private capital market, they would need to be able to earn dollars in order to service the debt thus incurred; therefore, the executive branch argued, American trade barriers should be lowered. Trade liberalization was thus viewed as one technique for stimulating private in-

[25] Clair Wilcox, *A Charter for World Trade* (New York: Macmillan, 1949), p. 141. Wilcox was Director of the Office of International Trade Policy in the Department of State during much of the time when the ITO proposals were being prepared. This book provides authoritative background on American foreign economic policy from 1943 to 1948.

[26] President Roosevelt's message to Congress on tariffs and trade noted: "We must recognize, too, that we are now a creditor country and are destined to be so for some time to come. Unless we make it possible for Americans to buy goods and services widely and readily in the markets of the world, it will be impossible for other countries to pay what is owed us." *New York Times*, March 27, 1945, p. 36. See also: "Statement of the Foreign Loan Policy of the United States Government by the NAC," 1946, pp. 19–20; and U.S., Congress, House, *Report of Activities of the National Advisory Council on International Monetary and Financial Problems to March 31, 1947*, 80th Cong., 1st sess., 1947, H. Doc. 365, p. 24.

vestment by making it easier for foreigners to service foreign debt incurred through private channels. This private investment would in turn promote economic development.

IMPROVEMENT OF "INVESTMENT CLIMATE"

According to United States foreign policy makers, one of the main obstacles retarding the flow of private capital to under-developed areas was the absence of a "favorable climate of investment." Such an "explanation" of the problem of underdeveloped countries, however, was merely a truism since a "favorable investment climate" was defined as one that attracted private capital, and an "unfavorable investment climate" was one that did not. The process of "creating a favorable climate of investment" was, by definition, one of meeting the terms of the private investors. Private investors themselves determined what was a "favorable climate" and what was not. Thus the techniques for improving the "investment climate" concentrated on convincing the governments in poor nations that they should acquiesce to the demands of the private investment community that they forswear the right of expropriation, adopt "sound" monetary and fiscal policies, and minimize government competition with private enterprise—among other things. The efforts of the United States government to improve the "climate of investment" in underdeveloped countries consisted of advice on the merits of free private enterprise, explicit refusal to provide alternative means of financing, and the use of diplomatic pressure to "encourage" the creation of the desired "climate."

To representatives of the less developed nations it must seem that the United States never tires of citing the advantages—real and imagined—of an economic system based on private enterprise. The main advantages of private investment cited by American policy makers were: first, private investment is more "flexible," presumably referring to the relative absence of governmental "red tape." Second, private investment is "non-political," presumably referring to a supposed absence of interference in domestic political affairs by private investors. And third, private investment often carries with it technical knowledge and managerial skill.[27]

Some spokesmen for American policy were less restrained than

[27] These advantages are cited by Wilcox, p. 145.

those who emphasized the foregoing advantages. Assistant Secretary of State Spruille Braden, for example, assured Latin Americans that "private enterprise is the best and in most circumstances the only really sound means to develop the known or unknown resources of a new country. . . ." He disapproved the emergence of a "school of thought" which "overlooks or even in a few cases condemns the use of private capital." In giving reasons why Latin Americans should rely on private investment, he pointed out that "the selective processes of society's evolution through the ages have proved that the institution of private property ranks with those of religion and the family as a bulwark of civilization." The Assistant Secretary found it comforting, however, to note that "in a world ridden with stateism, at least the American republics still affirm the self-reliant, virile principles of private enterprise." And in order to quell the fears of Latin Americans with regard to possible "exploitation" by private investors, Braden explained that "business mores everywhere have steadily improved during the last few decades."[28]

If the praising of free enterprise emphasized the *desirability* of private investment as a source of external capital, the explicit refusal to furnish alternative means of financing emphasized the *necessity* of relying on private capital. In 1946 the United States indicated its reluctance to provide alternatives to private investment by informing those seeking capital that the "International Bank will be the principal agency to make foreign loans for reconstruction and development which private capital cannot furnish on reasonable terms."[29] The Export-Import Bank was viewed as a supplementary agency for foreign lending. Thus the United States policy, in effect, informed the potential recipients of capital that they could expect no capital from the United States other than that furnished by private investors, the IBRD, and the Export-Import Bank.

In accord with this policy of "encouraging" reliance on private capital by limiting the alternative sources of capital, the American policy emphasized what the IBRD and the Export-Import

[28] "Private Enterprise in the Development of the Americas," *Department of State Bulletin,* September 22, 1946, pp. 539–42.

[29] "Statement of the Foreign Loan Policy of the United States Government by the NAC," 1946, p. 17.

Bank would *not* do. Secretary of the Treasury Morgenthau expressed the hope that the IBRD would "scrupulously avoid undertaking loans that private investors are willing to make on reasonable terms."[30] And Assistant Secretary of State Dean Acheson added that the World Bank was "not created to supersede private banks."[31] The "General Policy Statement of the Export-Import Bank of Washington" included a special section devoted to outlining what the Bank would not do. Among the forbidden activities was competition with private investment.[32] Thus, the American policy was to induce reliance on private capital, insofar as this could be obtained on "reasonable" terms. What constituted "reasonable" terms would, of course, be decided by administrators of the World Bank and the Export-Import Bank.

The third method by which the United States sought to improve the "climate of investment" in underdeveloped countries was by diplomacy. In the face of what a former negotiator has called "determined opposition," American diplomats fought for the establishment of rules for "fair" treatment of foreign capital at international meetings in London (1946), Geneva (1947), and Havana (1948).[33]

RECONSTRUCTION OF EUROPE

The United States policy was designed to stimulate private investment through trade liberalization, improving the investment climate, and the reconstruction of the economy of Europe. Promoting foreign investment in underdeveloped countries was obviously not the most important objective of the European Recovery Program, but there was a general recognition that a full-scale attack on the long-range problem of poverty in underdeveloped countries

[30] Quoted in *New York Times*, November 24, 1943, p. 9.

[31] "The Place of Bretton Woods in Economic Collective Security," *Department of State Bulletin*, March 25, 1945, p. 473.

[32] *Department of State Bulletin*, September 23, 1945, p. 443.

[33] See Wilcox, pp. 140–52. The meetings were the first meeting of the Preparatory Committee for an International Conference on Trade and Employment appointed by the United Nations Economic and Social Council in London from October 15 to November 26, 1946; the second meeting of the Preparatory Committee at Geneva from April 10 to August 22, 1947; and the United Nations Conference on Trade and Employment at Havana from November 21, 1947, to March 24, 1948.

could not even begin until Europe had been reconstructed. Secretary of State George C. Marshall noted that the war had destroyed long-standing commercial ties, private institutions, banks, insurance companies, and shipping companies, as he was announcing American plans to aid in the reconstruction of Europe.[34] All of these institutions were also required for reviving the flow of private foreign investment. The European economy had been an important source of development capital before the war, and it was hoped that it would be again.

Furnishing of Capital through Public Channels

United States policy for promoting economic growth in less developed areas gave primary emphasis to the techniques of reliance on domestic efforts and stimulation of private investment. The recognition, however, that developing countries would need some capital which private investors would not supply on "reasonable" terms if they were to grow at a rate judged by American policy makers to be desirable led the United States to furnish a limited amount of capital through public channels. American provision of public capital was based on three guiding principles: keep it small; keep it under American control; and minimize the competition with private investment.

which channels?

Public capital from the United States was channeled to underdeveloped countries through one multilateral organization and one American agency, the World Bank and the Export-Import Bank, respectively. The Export-Import Bank was, of course, under complete American control; the World Bank was less so. Through voting arrangements weighted according to the amount of a nation's financial contribution, the United States controlled about one-third of the total IBRD votes, enough to give it a decisive voice in the administration of the Bank's affairs. The United States control of the channels through which public capital was transferred to underdeveloped countries provided a means for influencing the terms on which such capital was offered.

[34] Speech at Harvard University on June 5, 1947, reprinted in *Department of State Bulletin*, June 15, 1947, p. 1159.

ON WHAT TERMS?

Public capital could be supplied as a grant, soft loan, or hard loan. In accordance with the desire to keep publicly supplied capital limited in amount and to minimize competition with private lending, the United States chose hard loans. The Export-Import Bank announced that it would make capital available only for "specific purposes" which served to promote the export and import trade of the United States. Its loans were repayable in dollars at rates of interest high enough "to avoid what might be construed as competition on a rate basis with private sources of credit."[35]

The lending policies of the World Bank will be discussed later; it suffices here to note that it too lent money on hard terms. IBRD interest rates were comparable to those in the commercial market, the difference being that the IBRD would supposedly be prepared to take greater risks than commercial lenders. Repayment was to be in the currency which the Bank had to use to make the loan. Thus, it was possible that the Bank would use sterling to obtain rupees to lend to country X. This would mean that country X incurred an obligation to repay the Bank with sterling. The effect of this arrangement, however, was similar to requiring repayment in the currency lent.[36] The IBRD also avoided making loans for projects for which private capital was available on "reasonable" terms. American policy statements on IBRD operations always referred to the making of economically "sound" loans.[37] And "sound" loans, during the 1943–48 period, were regarded as the antithesis of soft loans; therefore the insistence on "sound" loans was one way of ruling out soft loans.

SUMMARY

In summary, United States policy makers relied primarily on three techniques of statecraft to promote economic development

[35] "General Policy Statement of the Export-Import Bank of Washington," *Department of State Bulletin,* September 23, 1945, pp. 441–46.

[36] The IBRD could, in cases of "acute exchange stringency," accept repayment in local currency on a temporary basis not to exceed three years.

[37] See, for example: "Message of the President to the Congress on the Bretton Woods Proposals," *Department of State Bulletin,* February 18, 1945, p. 221; and William L. Clayton, "The Importance of the Bretton Woods Proposals in the Post-War Economic Policy of the Department of State," *Department of State Bulletin,* March 18, 1945, p. 440.

in poor nations. The first and most important was insistence that economic growth was primarily a domestic matter which could be effected largely by local efforts without large-scale outside help. Second, and next in importance, was the technique of enabling and encouraging underdeveloped countries to get external capital from private sources. This was to be done by trade liberalization, improvement of the "climate of investment," and by reconstruction of the European economies. The third technique, the one least emphasized by American policy, was providing public capital in small amounts through institutions controlled by the United States on terms which would minimize competition with private investment. This survey of the policy alternatives chosen by American policy makers describes *how* the United States decided to promote economic development, but it does not explain *why* certain alternatives were chosen and others rejected.

III. WHY TECHNIQUES WERE CHOSEN OR REJECTED

In explaining why United States policy was what it was, the following analysis will consider the relevant aspects of the international and domestic milieu within which the policy was made, the decision makers' perception of this situation, and the consequent response to it. In examining the domestic and international setting for policy, the discussion will focus only on those aspects which were relevant either to the selection of a policy alternative or to the effectiveness of that policy in achieving its goal.

EXTERNAL SETTING: 1943–48

GENERAL INTERNATIONAL SITUATION

Those aspects of the general international situation from 1943 to 1948 which were most relevant to the evolution of American soft loan policy included the beginning of the "cold war," the emergence of an attitude toward the economic role of government that differed from the attitude prevalent before World War II, and the beginning of what has come to be called the "revolution of rising expectations" in the underdeveloped areas of the world.

"Cold War"

Viewing the international situation in terms of the so-called "cold war" between the United States and the Soviet Union has become so commonplace that we easily forget that such a situation is relatively new—and probably relatively temporary—when viewed in terms of American diplomatic history. The period 1943–48 marked the emergence of the international distribution of power now called "bi-polarism." The war ended with the former European "Great Powers" prostrate; Germany, Japan, France, and Great Britain no longer held the military power of earlier times. Russia too had been badly damaged by the war, but ranked second only to the United States in military power. The beginning of the 1943–48 period found the two superpowers fighting a common enemy, the Axis powers; and at the end of the war it was still far from clear that the world political situation was rapidly assuming a pattern in which the United States and the Soviet Union were face to face without intermediate buffer zones and mediatory forces—a pattern of bi-polarity. The period ended, however, with the blockade of Berlin and the Communist coup in Czechoslovakia in 1948. We may dispute the exact date of the beginning of the "cold war," but it is generally agreed that by the end of 1948 the war had begun. The significance of this development for the evolution of American soft loan policy is that soft loans were later viewed by many as a response to the "cold war" activities of the Soviet Union. American diplomat Charles E. Bohlen has noted the relationship between America's emergence as a superpower and economic assistance programs:

We found ourselves catapulted in the space of some 15 years from a position of relative security, when we could divert our entire energies to our own national development and the advancement of our own society, to a position of responsibility in the world perhaps unequaled in human history. These fundamental changes in the world, and in particular our position in it, underlie the whole question of foreign aid.[38]

Government and Economy

The breakdown of the international financial system brought about by the economic dislocations of the interwar period accom-

[38] "Economic Assistance in United States Foreign Policy," *Department of State Bulletin,* March 28, 1960, p. 496.

panied and was largely responsible for a widespread change in attitudes toward the role of government in a nation's economy. The shock of depression caused many to reconsider their opinions on the economic responsibilities of governments, and to conclude that governments should not stand by helplessly in the face of economic disaster but should "do something." Most of the nations of the world other than the United States emerged from World War II with the firmly established belief that government was responsible not only for maintaining short-run economic stability but for promoting long-run economic growth as well. With regard to the short-run goal of economic stability the United States agreed. "I take it as an axiom," Treasury Secretary Morgenthau told the delegates at Bretton Woods, "that after this war is ended no people—and no government of the people—will again tolerate prolonged and wide-spread unemployment."[39] The question of government planning to promote long-run economic growth was one on which the United States was at odds with most other nations.

The change in attitude toward the role of government was significant for soft loan development in three ways: (1) It affected the internal setting of American policy. (2) It affected the debt-servicing capacity of foreign nations. (3) It affected the attitude of foreign nations toward the American policy of free trade. The internal setting was affected mainly by the reaction of the business community to the new role of governments. A continuing issue in foreign aid discussions from that time forward was the question of whether the United States government should "subsidize socialism" in recipient nations. Foreign investors were also concerned about the effect of managed currencies on the remittance of their earnings. Management of currencies by government-affiliated central banks had become an economic fact of life in almost every country outside the United States. This meant that governments had first priority in the use of foreign exchange, and if there were not enough to go around, the government obligations would come first.

One of the most frequently heard arguments for giving soft loans is the lack of capacity to service foreign debt in underdeveloped nations. The rise of managed currencies affected the

[39] Speech of July 22, 1944, reprinted in *Department of State Bulletin*, July 30, 1944, p. 112.

debt-servicing capacity of these countries first by increasing the importance of politics and second by removing the limit on the amount of debt that could be serviced in local currency. Under managed currencies no government is likely to default because of a shortage of local currency; it can always resort to the printing press to obtain that. It can only be forced to default by reason of a lack of foreign exchange. The growth of government control of currency in general and of foreign exchange in particular has increased the importance of political factors in debt service. In recent years, capacity to service foreign loans has almost always been a matter of the *willingness* and ability of *governments* to make or permit international transfers for payment of service on external obligations.[40] And the willingness of governments to do anything usually involves politics. The debate over soft loans, however, continues to use a vocabulary developed for an era without managed currencies, and therefore it places too much emphasis on "capacity," too little on "willingness."

The new attitudes toward government also dampened the enthusiasm of other countries for the American trade liberalization proposals. The spread of economic depression from one country to another during the 1930's had increased nations' desire to insulate their national economies from the caprice of external events over which they had no control. The dispute over the role of foreign trade in the postwar world has been an issue from that day to this in the debate over foreign assistance.

The Underdeveloped World

Another development in the international situation which was to have an effect on American policy was the first awakening of the underdeveloped world to the wonders of the twentieth century. When India achieved independence, a nation of one-half billion people entered the world scene. Pressure on the already developed countries to help in the development of poorer countries began to grow as the underdeveloped countries pressed their demands for help at international meetings in Mexico City, London, Geneva, Havana, Bogotá, and Bretton Woods. At the Havana Conference in 1948, reports Clair Wilcox, the most violent and protracted con-

[40] This discussion of the importance of managed currencies draws on Mikesell, pp. 378-79.

troversies were those evoked by issues raised in the name of economic development.[41] The period ended with a symbol of things to come in the form of the revival by Latin American countries of their proposal for a regional intergovernmental financial institution to provide capital for development.

UNITED NATIONS

The United Nations was destined eventually to serve as the primary channel through which the underdeveloped countries could exert pressure on the United States to make soft loans. Between 1943 and 1948 the groundwork for later activity was laid. The Economic and Social Council (ECOSOC) set up the Economic and Employment Commission, which held its first two sessions in 1947. This commission in turn set up a Subcommission on Economic Development composed of experts from Brazil, China, Czechoslovakia, India, Mexico, United States, and the Soviet Union—the United States being the only nation likely to become a large capital exporter. From this subcommission was to come the first major proposal for the establishment of a United Nations soft loan agency.

The efforts of the underdeveloped countries in the United Nations revolved around the establishment of two propositions: first, that the development of poor countries is important; and second, that external financial assistance is necessary. Specifically, the underdeveloped countries charged that the United States underestimated the importance of their economic growth vis-à-vis the reconstruction of Europe and vis-à-vis other alternatives involving the allocation of American resources. They indicated their belief that the United States failed to give enough weight to the importance of external capital assistance in economic development in criticism of the International Bank. The Bank, they said, was: (1) too slow in providing capital; (2) too concerned with placing restrictions on its loans; and (3) too little concerned with the problems of the underdeveloped countries. Thus the pressure on the Bank, and by implication on the United States, to provide more capital on easier terms began to grow.[42]

[41] Wilcox, p. 48.

[42] All comments on United Nations activities, unless otherwise indicated, are based on the *Yearbook of the United Nations* for the appropriate year. For one expression of views on IBRD operations see United Nations General Assembly Resolution 198 (III), December 4, 1948.

INTERNATIONAL BANK

The activities of the IBRD are particularly relevant to an understanding of the development of soft loans in American foreign policy. The United States had declared that the IBRD would be the principal international lending agency for making development loans. World Bank policies became, in effect, the policies of the United States by tacit approval. World Bank policies were in accord with United States policy, not only as a result of tacit approval, but also as a result of American influence in the organization based on its voting power, its control of the presidency, and its economic power to undermine Bank activities. The Bank also influenced later soft loan evolution by its effect on the views of the business community, Congress, and the underdeveloped countries with regard to soft loans. In fact, the Bank eventually played an important role in the process of legitimizing soft lending as a technique of statecraft, but during the 1943–48 period it had to concentrate on establishing its own claim to legitimacy. As one semiofficial Bank biographer put it:

Today the World Bank seems as solid an institution as any on earth. In 1946, when it began work, its reputation was much less reassuring. It was the oddest of unknown quantities; emanating a whiff of insubstantial international idealism, and surrounded by all those suggestions of whimsy and unorthodoxy that experienced investors most distrust.[43]

Questions Bretton Woods Left Open

Lack of agreement among participants in international conferences—or indeed any conference with political overtones—is often concealed by ignoring controversial points or by burying them in ambiguous language. Both techniques were used at Bretton Woods. "The biggest question at issue," according to R. F. Harrod, "was never fully discussed, namely, whether the Bank should be a sound conservative institution on normal lines, or depart from orthodox caution in the direction of greater venturesomeness."[44] Thus, the question of whether the Bank should make soft loans was unsettled.

The Articles of Agreement required the Bank to refrain from lending when private capital was "available on reasonable terms."

[43] James Morris, *The Road to Huddersfield* (New York: Pantheon, 1963), p. 50.

[44] *The Life of John Maynard Keynes* (London: Macmillan Co., 1951), p. 580.

Available when? It might be that private capital would be available on "reasonable" terms several years hence even though not available in the immediate future. The time factor is rarely considered by scholars analyzing World Bank operations. Also, what are "reasonable" terms? Opinions may differ; who is to decide? Except in special circumstances, the Bank was supposed to make loans only for specific projects, but no one was quite sure just what a "specific project" was. And even if one did define "specific project," one was still left with the impossible requirement of evaluating its economic potential without reference to political considerations. Besides estimating the likelihood that its loans would be repaid, the Bank was directed by the articles to "act prudently in the interests both of the particular member in whose territories the project is located and of the members as a whole." The admonishment to "act prudently" is hardly a clear guide for action. The possibility of diverging interpretations of the Articles of Agreement increased the importance of administering Bank affairs, and the question of who would run the Bank was therefore salient in early Bank history.

Search for a President

The policies of the International Bank are largely determined by the president and his staff. One observer has described it as "a sort of autocracy" in which everything "circles around" or "leads up to" the president.[45] Since the question of voting had been settled at Bretton Woods, the struggle for control of the Bank after that focused on the selection of a president.

The search for a president was influenced by an early decision that the Bank would try to float its own bonds in private capital markets instead of guaranteeing loans raised by member governments from private investors, as had been originally anticipated at Bretton Woods.[46] Despite its reputation as a $10 billion institution, the IBRD commanded relatively little money at its inception. Of its subscription capital, 80 per cent was merely a government

[45] Morris, pp. 54–55. The importance of the president is also stressed by Raymond F. Mikesell, *United States Economic Policy and International Relations* (New York: McGraw-Hill, 1952), p. 200.

[46] Alec Cairncross, *The International Bank for Reconstruction and Development* ("Essays in International Finance," No. 33 [Princeton, N.J.: Princeton University Press, 1959]), p. 7.

guarantee in case the Bank got into trouble; 18 per cent consisted mostly of currencies which could not be used; and only 2 per cent was gold. Therefore, the Bank decided to try to raise money in private capital markets, and in the 1940's this meant the United States capital market. Since the Bank would be trying to raise money in Wall Street, member governments agreed in 1946 that the president should be able to inspire the confidence of Wall Street bankers.[47]

The first president was Eugene Meyer, owner of the *Washington Post* and a former Federal Reserve Board member. The posts of vice-president and American executive director were held by a former Budget Bureau director and State Department official, respectively. Meyer resigned in December, 1946, amid reports of friction caused by the lack of a clear demarcation of authority between the president and the American executive director, who was in turn responsible to the National Advisory Council. Reports of these organizational difficulties, coupled with Meyer's intimation that political pressure had been put on him in his capacity as president, shook the confidence of Wall Street and decreased the willingness to buy IBRD bonds.[48] The *New York Times* described the Wall Street attitude:

> The principal concern of the investors is that Mr. Meyer's successor, when named, will merit the same high degree of confidence that they accorded him. The importance of an experienced, conservative executive in that post cannot be over-emphasized, they assert, because of the nature of the international lending operation. The World Bank, like the Export-Import Bank, by the terms on which it was established, is limited to making loans for which there is a reasonable prospect of payment. And it may not lend where the funds are otherwise available, to avoid competition with private lending agencies. But how wide is this area to be, the investors ask? Without a thoroughly conservative management, the bank might easily move into loans which are of questionable soundness.[49]

Following the resignation of Meyer there was a series of unsuccessful attempts to fill the post of president. Finally John J. McCloy, a Wall Street lawyer, accepted the post on the condition

[47] *New York Times*, March 24, 1946, p. 1.

[48] *New York Times*, December 15, 1946, Part 3, p. 1.

[49] December 8, 1946, Part 3, p. 1.

that the United States director and the vice-president would be, respectively, Eugene R. Black, vice-president of the Chase National Bank of New York, and Robert L. Garner, vice-president of the Guaranty Trust Company of New York.[50] Thus the complexion of the management was changed from one representing former government employees and administration supporters to one representing the American financial community.[51]

Suggestions that the IBRD is subservient to the United States have been variously denounced as "a complete travesty," a "myth," or as "alleged."[52] While the main concern here is not with the question of subservience of the World Bank to the United States, it is worth noting in passing that the question may be poorly framed. Perhaps we should ask: (1) What is the degree of subservience? (2) To which agencies or interest groups in the United States is it subservient? (3) On what types of issues? There are at least the following reasons for expecting some degree of subservience, to some groups, on some issues: (1) The United States economy is so big relative to the world economy that the IBRD would have an incentive to co-ordinate its efforts with those of the United States even if the United States were not a member. American aid programs, for example, could seriously undermine the effectiveness of any IBRD activity. (2) The United States is a member and is the biggest contributor. This has two consequences: (a) the United States holds one-third of the voting power; and (b) its position as the biggest *potential* contributor affects Bank policies. (3) The Bank depends, although to a diminishing degree, on the American private capital market. (4) The United States has always selected the Bank president, who presumably has "internalized" American values which lead him to look at things in the American frame of reference. Any proof that the Bank is not subservient to American interests must account for these facts; none to date has done so.

---

[50] *New York Times*, March 1, 1947, p. 1. It was also reported that McCloy had secured the agreement of the State and Treasury Departments to the proposition that the Bank should carry out a more limited program of "safer" loans than had been originally expected. *New York Herald Tribune*, February 20, 1947.

[51] Mikesell, *United States Economic Policy*, p. 199.

[52] Cairncross, p. 31; B. E. Matecki, *Establishment of the International Finance Corporation and United States Policy* (New York: Praeger, 1957), p. 162; and Robert E. Asher *et al.*, *The United Nations and Economic and Social Co-operation* (Washington: Brookings Institution, 1957), p. 166.

IBRD Policies

The usual approach to explaining the policies of the World Bank is based on the Articles of Agreement and the formal statements of the Bank since 1945. A less fruitful approach is difficult to imagine since the articles are so vague and ambiguous that they tell us little about the actual shape of Bank activities. Besides being vague, the articles require the Bank to eschew all political considerations in its activities, a provision the Bank's administrators found impossible to implement. Thus the administrators have had an incentive to explain their actions, which involve political considerations, in terms which tend to conceal that involvement. The result of analysis based on the Articles of Agreement and the Bank's formal statements has been a tendency to describe the Bank as similar to a conventional commercial bank. This need not have been the result, as the following analysis will show, since the Bank has been fairly candid on several occasions despite the formal ban on its consideration of politics.

IBRD and commercial banks.—Conventional commercial bankers pursue a goal different from that of the IBRD. The commercial banker is interested in making money, but the administrators of the IBRD have viewed its goal as promoting economic reconstruction and development. Keynes had a dictum that the Bank would not have discharged its duty if it had not dissipated its assets within ten years;[53] and although few at Bretton Woods accepted this dictum, all agreed that the Bank's primary purpose was not to earn profits. Any student of Adam Smith knows that concentration on maximizing profits can be an effective way of promoting economic growth. The commercial banker may well be inadvertently promoting this broader goal. If this were the case—as seen by Bank administrators—there might be little to distinguish the behavior of the IBRD with a primary goal of promoting growth from that of the private bank in pursuit of profit. Those in charge of the IBRD, however, decided that they could best stimulate economic development by behaving in ways quite different from commercial lenders.

The private lender's goal of profit leads him to concentrate on answering two important questions in considering a loan application: Will the borrower be able to repay? Can he be trusted to

[53] Harrod, p. 580.

repay? The commercial lender may be interested in the borrower's past debt-paying record and in how he allocates his resources—*but only as these aid him in answering the foregoing questions.* The IBRD, on the other hand, indicated an interest not only in assuring repayment of its loans but in repayment of other debts of the potential borrower as well. The IBRD also made it clear that if, in its judgment, the policies of the government were tending to favor the public sector of the economy too much, no loans would be available regardless of the ability and willingness to repay a specific loan. From the borrower's point of view it is none of the private lender's business what he does as long as the lender is guaranteed to get his money back. In dealing with the World Bank, however, borrowers have confronted a lender interested in what is "good" for the borrower.[54]

The importance of understanding the differences between IBRD practice and commercial lending practice arises from the difference between bargaining situations and other situations. Bargaining situations are those in which the ability of one participant to gain his ends is dependent to an important degree on the decisions that the other participant will make.[55] In a transaction between a private lender and a borrower, public or private, there is less conflict than in transactions with the IBRD. The private lender accepts as given the political and economic situation of the potential borrower, and together they work out the amount of debt which the potential borrower can safely incur. It is true that opinions may differ on this point, but borrower and lender presumably share a common interest in reaching a correct estimate. The IBRD, on the other hand, in considering a loan application, does not accept as "given" many of the things which a private lender does. It does not, for example, accept the political and economic situation of the potential borrower as given. The degree of conflict involved in the situation is thus considerably greater than in a private lender's negotiations. In private lending terms, it is as if a boy were trying to borrow money to study law. The banker, despite his trust in the boy's ability and willingness to repay the loan, tells him that

[54] The ambiguity of "good" was no problem. The staff at the IBRD would decide what was "good" (sound) and what was "bad" (unsound)—while maintaining a watchful eye on the American financial community.

[55] Thomas C. Schelling, *The Strategy of Conflict* (Cambridge, Mass.: Harvard University Press, 1960), p. 5.

lawyers are bad people and that he should be a farmer. The banker
then adds that he is going to "encourage" the boy to become a
farmer instead of a lawyer by refusing to loan him the money to go
to law school. In such a situation the banker would have refused to
accept as given the boy's desire to study law and would have taken
upon himself the task of changing the boy's desires. Similar examples are rare in private lending practice because bankers are
usually more interested in making money than in reforming their
potential borrowers. Examples of the strategic withholding of
loans, however, in IBRD practice are numerous because the IBRD
is more interested in promoting economic growth than in earning
money. To a potential borrower who estimates his debt-servicing
capacity in terms of a given political and economic situation, the
IBRD is likely to reply, "Change the situation." In reply to underdeveloped countries that complain of a "need" for capital on
lenient terms because of their "inability" to attract private capital
and service orthodox loans, the Bank is likely to advise changing
governmental policies so as to enable them to attract private
capital and service hard loans.

IBRD and politics.—A major proposition of this study is that
much of the confusion in the debate over soft loans stems from a
lack of understanding of the political aspects of IBRD loan operations. The common interpretation is that IBRD loans "were
granted on the conventional banker's criterion of credit-worthiness, defined as the ability to repay loans in hard currencies in
which the money was disbursed."[56] The analysis which follows will
show that this is a misleading way to describe Bank activities and
that even if this were true, it still would not follow that the Bank's
operations were removed "from the sphere of international or
domestic politics."[57]

Assuming for the moment that credit-worthiness were the only
concern of the World Bank, would it be possible to remove the
Bank from politics? It was noted earlier that the advent of managed currencies made willingness of governments to service debt
more important than it had been when the governments did not
control the allocation of foreign exchange. The political factor of

[56] John D. Montgomery, *The Politics of Foreign Aid* (New York: Praeger, 1962),
p. 182.
[57] *Ibid.*, p. 184.

willingness to service debt thus increased in importance while the economic factor of ability decreased in relative terms. Professor Mikesell has observed that a "full evaluation of credit worthiness cannot be made apart from broad considerations relating to a country's economic, social, and political development."[58] Furthermore, he speculates that political factors are the "most fundamental consideration in the determination of credit worthiness."[59] Thus even the private commercial lender, interested only in profit, must weigh political factors. Private investors continually make implicit judgments about politics. Few businessmen, for example, would expand their plant facilities if they thought this would cause the government to expropriate their holdings without compensation; yet few of them are aware that they are making implicit assumptions predicting political behavior when they decide to add a new wing to their plant.

The World Bank has admitted that "creditworthiness is not determined by economic forces alone."[60] The necessity of weighing political factors has put the Bank in an embarrassing situation. The articles say that "only economic considerations shall be relevant to their decisions"; they say nothing about "political objectives" as the Bank implies in explaining its position in the following passage:

Although the Bank is precluded by its charter from making or denying loans to achieve political objectives, it cannot ignore conditions of political instability or uncertainty which may directly affect the economic and financial prospects of the borrower. An examination of the political situation, to the extent that it may bear upon the soundness of the proposed loan, is therefore included in the initial investigation.[61]

Thus the IBRD, as all investors, must consider political factors; but the Bank goes beyond the private bankers in viewing the consideration of politics not only as necessary but desirable as well. It is here that the difference in goals discussed above finds its signifi-

[58] U.S. Private and Government Investment Abroad, p. 325.

[59] Ibid.

[60] International Bank for Reconstruction and Development, The International Bank for Reconstruction and Development: 1946–1953 (Baltimore: Johns Hopkins Press, 1954), p. 43. See also the similar wording in a later edition of this book: International Bank for Reconstruction and Development, Policies and Operations of the World Bank, IFC, and IDA, 1962, p. 32.

[61] Ibid., p. 61.

cance. That the Bank believes it both desirable and necessary to concern itself with political factors becomes obvious when we examine its approach to the problem of economic development. In its *Third Annual Report* the Bank gave its view of the obstacles to economic development in underdeveloped areas. They included: (1) lack of capital; (2) lack of technical and managerial personnel; (3) economic instability; (4) inadequate development planning; (5) low educational levels; and (6) political instability.[62] An ordinary commercial banker would take the lack of capital as his area of concern and ask what amount of money he could safely lend to the country, given the situation as described in the other five parts of the list. The IBRD, however, interested itself not merely in capital but in the over-all problem of economic growth. The Articles of Agreement charge the Bank to "facilitate the investment of capital for productive purposes," "to promote private foreign investment," and to "act prudently in the interests" of its members. Suffice it to say that the opinion of the president of the IBRD, imbued with the outlook of the New York financial community, as to what constitutes "prudent action" may not coincide with that of the prime minister of Ruritania.

Strategic nonlending.—The Bank's approach to the problem of overcoming the obstacles to economic development was quite different from the approach one would expect a conventional bank to adopt. The IBRD, in effect, exists to drum up business for its competition, the private investors. In the face of demands from the underdeveloped countries for the maximum amount of capital on the easiest possible terms in the shortest period of time, the IBRD was replying, in effect, that they really did not need as much capital as they imagined; the capital they did need was private, not public; and the reason they were short of private capital was that their governments were following undesirable policies. The solution, therefore, was for the IBRD to withhold loans in a strategic attempt to encourage (blackmail) the governments into changing their policies.[63]

[62] International Bank for Reconstruction and Development, *Third Annual Report, 1947–1948*, pp. 15–16.

[63] Strategic nonlending is defined as the withholding of loans which the potential lender believes could be repaid at conventional rates of interest in foreign exchange over a conventional time period. The concept implies the existence of reasons for withholding loans other than an estimate of capacity and willingness to service the proposed loan.

Regarding the amount of capital needed in underdeveloped countries the Bank said, "Indeed, in the long run foreign investment may impede rather than accelerate development along sound lines unless domestic conditions furnish a firm economic base for such investment."[64] Much of the recent explanation of the adoption of soft loans describes the effort of the IBRD to transfer capital to poor countries as one limited by the requirement that its loans be repaid in hard currency with interest and by the requirement that the Bank lend only for the foreign exchange costs of specific projects. The situation as depicted by most observers is one in which the goal is to maximize the transfer of capital to poor nations, and the ability of the IBRD to contribute to such a goal is limited. Thus the IBRD activities are described in terms of what the Bank "can" or "cannot" do. Such a description of the situation leading up to the adoption of soft loans is highly misleading. In the 1943–48 period, at least, the Bank took the position that too much capital might actually be undesirable. This creates the possibility that the IBRD might on occasion have withheld loans, not because they would not be repaid in convertible currency, but because the Bank thought the loans might retard development.

The Bank, however, did recognize the lack of capital as an obstacle to development, but it asserted that this obstacle should be overcome by increasing the free flow of private capital.[65] The Articles of Agreement admonish the Bank to "facilitate" investment, not just to invest; and the Bank has taken that admonition seriously. It is thus misleading to describe the IBRD as "first and foremost a lender on long-term."[66] If one understands the principle of strategic withholding of loans, it is more useful to describe the IBRD as first and foremost a "nonlender."

Because so many arguments for soft loans are based on the assumption that the IBRD made all the loans it *could*, given its organizational setup, we must examine the reasons for the Bank's withholding loans in order to evaluate the later arguments for soft loans. We must consider first the hypothesis that the Bank withheld loans in order to enable itself to raise money in private cap-

[64] IBRD, *Third Annual Report*, p. 20.

[65] International Bank for Reconstruction and Development, *Second Annual Report, 1946–1947*, p. 13.

[66] Cairncross, p. 6.

ital markets. This was undoubtedly one limitation, but there are
two reasons for questioning whether such an explanation is sufficient to explain all Bank loans withheld. First, the Bank did not
confine itself to justifying the denial of a loan application in terms
of the effect on its fund-raising capacity.[67] It used in addition such
reasons as the nation's outstanding bad debts, governmental policies favoring government ownership of business, governmental
policies favoring inflation, and other policies posing obstacles to
the development process—in the opinion of the Bank. These justi-
fications brought a shower of abuse for the IBRD from the underdeveloped countries; it would have been easier to justify loan
denial in terms of the need to maintain the confidence of Bank
investors.

A second reason for rejecting the hypothesis that the Bank was
interested only in maintaining the confidence of its creditors is that
a decade after its creation it was still pursuing the same policies.
It had become a respected institution in private investment circles,
and the underdeveloped countries were prompt in paying their
debts to the Bank because of their expectations of future loans
from the Bank. Since underdeveloped countries tended to consider
servicing of IBRD loans as having a prior claim on foreign exchange, the Bank could have made many more loans had it been
willing to stand by and see the borrowers default on private obligations in order to service IBRD loans. The private owners of
IBRD bonds cared only about their dividends, but the Bank was
interested in preventing default on private obligations as an indirect result of its lending.[68] This was an example of the Bank's withholding a loan in order to promote private lending by preventing
default on private obligations.

What other reasons, then, did the IBRD give for withholding
loans? The most important limitation on Bank lending results from
the requirement in the Articles of Agreement that the Bank ab-
stain from lending when private capital is available on terms which
the Bank considers reasonable. The problem here is that private
capital is *always* available on some terms and in the long run. If it

[67] The Bank did, of course, cite this as one justification. IBRD, *Second Annual
Report*, p. 14.

[68] Such a possibility, it will be remembered, arose with the advent of managed
currencies.

is not available on reasonable terms this year, perhaps it will be next year—provided the IBRD refrains from lending. The discussion of the availability of private capital tends to treat governmental policies as constants; the IBRD has not. Transportation is often cited as an example of a project well suited to IBRD loans because private capital is unavailable; such projects are described as "non-self-liquidating." We wonder whether those who so describe the situation have ever driven on the Pennsylvania Turnpike or ridden on a privately built American railroad. Instead of dealing with obfuscations such as "non-self-liquidating" projects and "favorable climates of investment," the IBRD has been relatively candid in giving advice to underdeveloped countries.

The Bank has refused to accept the political and economic situation as given and has asked *why* private capital is not available on reasonable terms. In the Bank's view the reasons are mainly political; that is, they are the result of governmental policies. The IBRD approach, therefore, is to decide whether withholding loans today will cause governments to change their future policies in order to attract private capital on reasonable terms in the future. In describing the "economic investigation" which is part of processing a loan application, one Bank publication notes the Bank's interest in "whether the economic and financial policies of the government are well adapted to the needs of the country or whether some modification of these policies would remove obstacles to the development process or strengthen the country's balance of payments position."[69]

The first step in increasing the free flow of private capital, according to the Bank, is "the improvement of the credit position of many of the countries concerned."[70] The most effective thing the underdeveloped countries could do would be to "clear up their external debt records."[71] "Accordingly, the Bank's normal practice is to inform loan applicants who are in default on foreign obligations that the Bank will be unable to assist them unless and until they take appropriate steps to reach a fair and equitable settlement of their debts."[72]

[69] IBRD, *International Bank: 1946–1953*, p. 61.

[70] IBRD, *Second Annual Report*, p. 13.

[71] *Ibid.*

[72] IBRD, *International Bank: 1946–1953*, p. 54.

Another reason private capital may not be available on reasonable terms, in the opinion of IBRD officials, is that private capital is subject to "inequitable and restrictive legislation."[73] The question of what constitutes "equitable" regulation of business is hardly a purely economic one and is the subject of political debate in nearly every nation in the world including the United States. In the eyes of IBRD officials, withholding a loan from a country with "inequitable" legislation concerning business is a way to avoid subsidizing such a practice, but in the eyes of a potential recipient, the Bank is trying to blackmail him into changing governmental policy.

The International Bank also encourages governments to rely on private capital by frowning on government ownership of enterprise. Some of this frowning has been camouflaged by the concept of management considerations, but this camouflage is easily seen through as the Bank explains that "management considerations are also an important factor in the Bank's reluctance to finance government-owned projects in the field of competitive industry."[74] Among practices which the bank uses "strategic nonlending" to discourage is the "use of scarce foreign exchange resources to effect a shift of ownership of public utilities or other enterprise from foreign private to government hands, if done for political rather than economic reasons."[75] As one IBRD biographer put it: "It can hardly be denied that inextricably mixed up in its attitudes was a conviction that capitalism was the right way, that private enterprise was best, and, as a rule-of-thumb dogma, that the less State interference, the better."[76]

If we are to understand later soft loan debate, we must first acquaint ourselves with the Bank principle which is here labeled "strategic nonlending." A major proposition in this study is that the significance of IBRD activities is based more on what the Bank did *not* do than on what it did do. The IBRD was interested first in influencing the behavior of governments and only secondarily in making loans. The *Second Annual Report* referred to the goal of exerting a "helpful influence" on member governments in order to

[73] IBRD, *Second Annual Report*, p. 14.

[74] IBRD, *International Bank: 1946–1953*, p. 49.

[75] *Ibid.*, pp. 54–55.

[76] Morris, p. 43.

get them to remove trade barriers and adopt sound financial programs.[77] The *Third Annual Report* erased all doubt regarding the objectives of the Bank as seen by its officials:

It seems clear that the real measure of the Bank's effectiveness will be, not so much the number or amount of its loans and guarantees, significant as they may be, but rather its success in influencing attitudes— in promoting a realistic, constructive approach to development problems on the part of its members and in fostering a greater degree of confidence among investors.[78]

Given the primary goal of influencing governmental attitudes, it becomes useful to know what the Bank thought of governments in general. The IBRD view that it is a better judge of what constitutes "sound policy," "equitable legislation," and "development along sound lines" than the government of the nation involved has irked many underdeveloped countries, but the view is consistent with the following statement of the IBRD concept of governments:

It must be remembered that governments, however conscientious, are apt to be subject to political pressure to emphasize short-run objectives which promise immediate advantage rather than policies designed primarily for the long-run development of their countries, particularly where long-range policies entail some sacrifices of immediate benefits or adversely affect important local interests. In this type of situation, the Bank's insistence upon appropriate economic and financial measures to create a favorable environment for development over the long term has not infrequently provided a countervailing influence of some considerable degree.[79]

Imaginary limits on IBRD lending.—The activities of the World Bank are usually described by scholars in terms which ignore the influence of judgments by Bank officials. The officials are treated as puppets with little control over what the Bank does or does not do. Thus, the loans withheld are described as those which "could not" be made because of "limits" on IBRD activities. It has been argued here that many of these limits are self-imposed and that they can be usefully understood in terms of a bargaining situation.

[77] IBRD, *Second Annual Report,* p. 8.

[78] IBRD, *Third Annual Report,* p. 21.

[79] IBRD, *International Bank: 1946–1953,* p. 55.

To put this in specific terms, the Bank statements reflect the belief that the amount of capital requested from the Bank by underdeveloped countries depends to an important degree on the amount the governments of those countries think is likely to be forthcoming. The planning of the over-all development effort will be affected by these estimates of the amount of capital likely to be available from the IBRD and other sources. If a government estimates that no capital is likely to be forthcoming from public sources, such as the IBRD, it may treat foreign private investors differently from the way it would if it thought that there was a high probability of obtaining capital from public sources. In fact, if there were reason to believe that large amounts of public capital might be made available, the governments of potential recipient nations might have an incentive to treat private foreign investment especially harshly in order that they could later show a greater "need" for public capital.

Many of the Bank's efforts to limit itself have reflected the desire to clarify for the governments of potential borrowers the criteria of Bank lending. Similar tactics have been discussed by students of game theory. The essence of these tactics, according to T. C. Schelling, is some "voluntary but irreversible sacrifice of freedom of choice."[80] They rest on the paradox that the power to constrain an adversary may depend on the power to bind oneself. The IBRD was clearly trying to constrain potential borrowers with regard to their treatment of private foreign investors, their treatment of the private sector of their economy in general, their fiscal and monetary policies, and the relative emphasis in development programs on agriculture and foreign trade. In pursuing these goals it relied primarily on the technique of binding itself by declaring that it would not lend to governments pursuing undesirable policies.[81] Failure to recognize the significance of the IBRD attempts to bind itself has led many to overlook its most important technique for attaining its goals. One author, for example, lists the guaranteeing of private loans and the financing of "basic projects" as the means by which the IBRD sought to stimulate private in-

[80] Schelling, p. 22.

[81] It is unfortunate that blackmail has acquired undesirable moral connotations, since it is a useful concept for social analysis. Understanding the use of threats, as in blackmail, is essential to the study of foreign aid. No moral condemnation is intended in the use of the term in this study. On this point see Schelling, p. 13.

vestment.[82] There is no mention of the most important technique used by the Bank to stimulate private investment—the refusal to lend for purposes which, in the judgment of the Bank, could be financed by private capital.[83]

Failure to recognize the existence of self-imposed limits on Bank activities has resulted largely from the belief that the withholding of IBRD loans could be explained in terms of a number of limits imposed by the Articles of Agreement. The three requirements most often cited as limits on Bank lending are the ban on competition with private investors, the limiting of loans to specific projects, and confining financing to foreign exchange costs of projects.[84]

It was pointed out earlier in the discussion that the prohibition of competition with private capital does not constitute an effective limit of Bank operations because it is left to Bank officials to determine whether private capital is available on "reasonable" terms. Also, since no time factor is noted in the Articles of Agreement, the Bank can choose any time factor it desires. It can, in other words, decide whether to base its judgment of a loan on the amount of private capital likely to be available next week, next year, or next decade. The ban on competition with private capital would, of course, be impossible to take literally since all IBRD loans compete with private capital in the long run and on terms which someone would regard as "reasonable." The limitations on Bank lending related to competition with private capital are self-imposed and result from the interpretation by Bank officials of the ambiguous language in the Articles of Agreement.

Few aspects of IBRD operations have been so misunderstood as the "specific project" provision. The project approach is supposed to limit total IBRD lending because of the limited number of de-

[82] Delbert A. Snider, *Introduction to International Economics* (Homewood, Ill.: Irwin, 1954), p. 435.

[83] The effectiveness of binding oneself in bargaining depends on one's ability to make the adversary believe that one is irreversibly bound. The IBRD was hampered by its inability to make its threat to withhold loans credible in the eyes of underdeveloped nations. The effectiveness of this policy will be discussed later. For a discussion of the threat in bargaining situations see Schelling, pp. 35–43.

[84] Cairncross (p. 16) cites specific projects and foreign exchange costs as two conditions governing the Bank's lending policy and limiting its loans which arise directly out of its charter. Snider (p. 428) emphasizes the ban on competition with private capital.

velopment projects which can be financed by "hard loans."[85] By constant references to two types of projects, the "bankable" and "nonbankable," this type of argument implies that projects are intrinsically one or the other. They are not. A nation might be able to finance a totally worthless project—such as digging holes and filling them again—by means of a loan from the World Bank calling for repayment at commercial interest rates in foreign exchange if it were earning foreign exchange from some other project in the economy. On the other hand, a government might default on a loan used in developing a "bankable" project, such as development of a petroleum field, because a corrupt government official stole all the foreign exchange from the treasury before the loan payment could be made.

National economies do not present themselves to IBRD officials neatly carved into easily identifiable specific projects, each with a tag designating it either "bankable" or "nonbankable." The World Bank officials can exercise judgment in deciding what constitutes a project. Is a project, for example, a railroad tie, track, switch engine, train, set of operators, a whole railroad system, or a transportation system? The capacity of a nation to service foreign debt and thus to determine whether a project is "bankable" or not depends on its over-all foreign exchange earnings, not on foreign exchange generated by a particular project. Given a particular country at a given time, with governmental policies, resources, consumption and production patterns, and foreign exchange earning capacity as given, one could carve the economy into a set of projects. He could then say that the total estimated foreign exchange earnings would permit the country to finance 10 per cent of all the projects in the economy through IBRD loans. Or he might divide the country so that 20 per cent of each of one-half the total projects could be financed by the IBRD. Ultimately, of course, one could designate only those projects which could be financed entirely by "hard loans." The point is that these can be any projects or parts of projects as long as the total foreign exchange earnings of the nation enable it to service its external debt.

It is useful to distinguish between the proposition that the

---

[85] See the comments by Harlan Cleveland in his introduction to Robert G. A. Jackson, *The Case for an International Development Authority* (Syracuse, N.Y.: Syracuse University Press, 1959), p. 7.

project approach need not limit IBRD lending and the proposition that it does not. It has been argued thus far that project lending need not be a limit because of the ambiguity of the term "project" and because the "bankability" of a project is not determined by the nature of the project but by the over-all foreign exchange position of the country. Yet typical descriptions of the IBRD are the following: "The necessity for the IBRD to be guided predominantly by sound business standards means . . . that there is not now any international organization which could finance non-self-liquidating projects in the underdeveloped countries."[86] "It is impossible . . . to raise money for various forms of social investment which the Bank rules out as unproductive; housing, schools, health services, and so on."[87] Such propositions notwithstanding, it is quite possible for the IBRD to finance such "non-self-liquidating" projects as schools, health services, and housing. To illustrate this possibility, suppose that the Venezuelan government plans to build irrigation projects and improve habors. It is possible for the IBRD to loan money for a "specific project" such as harbor improvement. If it does this, the effect is to make available to the Venezuelan government additional resources which it had intended to spend on harbor improvement but which now can be transferred to financing health services and housing. The net effect of the IBRD loan in this case would be to permit the building of health services and housing; yet in the bookkeeping sense the loan was tied to a specific harbor improvement project. The only sensible way to measure the immediate economic impact of an IBRD loan is to ask in what way the economy is different from what it would have been in the absence of the loan. If harbor improvements would be undertaken even in the absence of an IBRD loan, but health services and housing would not, then the impact of the IBRD loan would be to finance health services. It is thus conceivable that the IBRD could finance health services and housing around the globe merely by tying its loans to "specific projects," such as harbor improvement, which would be financed in the absence of IBRD loans. On paper, however, the Bank would have financed no hous-

---

[86] William Y. Elliott *et al.*, *The Political Economy of American Foreign Policy* (New York: Henry Holt, 1955), p. 343.

[87] Cairncross, p. 18.

ing or health services.[88] Thus we must conclude that the "specific project" requirement need not limit IBRD loans, since the IBRD could always find some project to which to tie its loan in a book-keeping sense if it wanted to make funds available to a nation.

The fact that the specific project provision need not limit World Bank activities does not mean that it does not. If Bank officials perceive it as a limit, it may actually be one, although a self-imposed one. IBRD officials, however, have made it clear that they do not perceive the specific project provision as a limit, which is not to say, of course, that they have viewed it as useless. In the first place, Bank officials quickly discovered that there was no such thing as an intrinsically "bankable" or "sound" specific project, that one could not evaluate a specific project except in terms of a country's over-all foreign exchange position, which in turn depended upon a variety of governmental policies. The *Third Annual Report* complained:

. . . There is lacking in many countries any well-formulated concept of the over-all lines along which sound development is most likely to make progress. In the absence of such a general pattern of development, it is difficult to estimate the relative importance and urgency of different undertakings, their ability to function economically, and the need for power, transportation and other basic facilities to support them.[89]

During the early years of the Bank, underdeveloped countries often criticized it for confining itself to specific projects and ignoring their problems viewed from the point of view of the nation as a whole. This criticism nettled the officials of the IBRD so much that they took pains to explicitly refute this charge, claiming that the Bank does exactly the opposite of what it is accused of doing.[90] The limit on Bank loans to underdeveloped countries in the period between 1946 and about 1953 arose not from the specific project provision but from the refusal of Bank officials to consider loan

[88] Although the economic insignificance of the project approach should be obvious to any economist, few of them have discussed it. The best discussion is in Thomas C. Schelling, *International Economics* (Boston: Allyn & Bacon, 1958), pp. 439–56.

[89] IBRD, *Third Annual Report*, p. 16.

[90] "In the early days of Bank operations, there was considerable criticism of the specific project approach, but the criticism was almost always based on the assumption that the Bank examines the merits of particular projects in isolation, without reference to their relation to the over-all development needs of the borrowing country. In fact the Bank does precisely the opposite." IBRD, *International Bank: 1946–1953*, p. 44.

applications for isolated projects, which was in turn based on the officials' recognition of the impossibility of evaluating the economic consequences of a project without reference to a country's over-all situation and plans.

Criticism of the IBRD by underdeveloped countries has prompted Bank officials to reply that the problem is not what the IBRD *cannot do,* but what the governments of poor countries *will not do.* Each group tries to shift the blame to the other. One result of this attempt by the Bank to emphasize the responsibility of governments in underdeveloped countries for their plight has been a relatively candid statement by Bank officials of their view of the extent to which the specific project provision limits their activities. "The *only* requirement which it imposes," according to the Bank, "is that, before a loan is granted, there shall be a clear agreement both on the types of goods and services for which the proceeds of the loan are to be expended and on the uses to which those goods and services are to be put."[91] Yet, even this statement of the degree to which Bank activities are limited by the specific project provision cannot be taken at face value. Although it is true that Bank officials desire advance agreement on the use of loan proceeds, tying the loan to a specific project neither requires nor ensures that the impact of the loan will be the financing of the project to which the loan is administratively tied. Are IBRD officials aware that by financing "sound" projects in the "right" industries they may be freeing resources for financing "unsound" projects in the "wrong" industries?[92]

The Bank recognizes, of course, that by financing one particular investment project, it may be releasing for some other investment activity resources already available to the borrower. This is a principal reason why the Bank seeks to consult with its member countries not only concerning the merits of projects for which loans are requested but concerning the country's projected investment expenditures as a whole.[93]

[91] *Ibid.,* p. 44. Italics mine.

[92] "If the country is financing unsound projects in the wrong industries with its own resources, and is doing so because we have taken care of sound projects in the right industries, the net effect of our program is to make possible the unsound projects and the wrong industries." Thomas C. Schelling, "American Aid and Economic Development: Some Critical Issues," *International Stability and Progress* (New York: American Assembly, 1957), p. 160.

[93] IBRD, *International Bank, 1946–1953,* p. 50.

The Bank's insistence on advance agreement on the use of loan proceeds is not "required" by the specific projects provision at all, but arises from its interest in knowing what it is financing. In laying out its basic operating principles in 1947, the Bank emphasized control over the use of funds by its insistence on avoiding long-term commitments, arrangements for observers to visit the recipient country, and continual consultation between the IBRD and the recipient.[94] If the specific project provision need not and does not limit total IBRD lending, why do Bank officials cling to it? First, the Articles of Agreement demand lip service. Second, the specific project approach provides a useful façade behind which the IBRD can and does advise on governmental policies affecting all parts of the economy. If someone objects to IBRD advice on governmental fiscal policy, Bank officials can always justify it in terms of the possible ramifications of fiscal policy on the project they are financing—no matter how remote such ramifications might be. And third, the specific project approach provides a useful mechanism for joint consultation with the government in the recipient country and for channeling a continuing flow of information from the country to the IBRD. Whereas governments might be sensitive about Bank demands for information on the state of the economy if the Bank loans were for general purposes, they are apparently less so when the demands are justified in terms of the Bank's interest in a specific project. The significance, in sum, of the specific project provision is tactical, not economic.[95]

The requirement that the Bank confine itself, except in special circumstances, to financing the foreign exchange costs of specific projects is similar to the project requirement in its limiting effects. There are none that Bank officials could not avoid if they so desired.

The three "limits" on IBRD activities commonly cited by students of foreign aid—the ban on competition with private capital, the specific project provision, and the foreign exchange costs provision—are all either nonexistent or self-imposed in accordance with the Bank practice of strategic nonlending.

[94] IBRD, *Second Annual Report*, pp. 15–18.

[95] Cf. Schelling, *International Economics*, p. 456.

IBRD: Summary

During the period 1943–48 the IBRD concentrated on three main goals: (a) reconstruction of Europe, (b) organizing itself and selecting a president, and (c) working out a set of operating principles which included the concept of strategic nonlending. Strategic nonlending was a means by which the IBRD sought to bind itself with regard to certain types of loans. The IBRD threatened to withhold loans in order to "encourage" governments to pass legislation more favorable to private foreign investors, control inflation, to pay private external debts, to avoid government-owned enterprises, to improve the "climate of investment" in other ways, and to plan development programs in order to provide a basis for the IBRD to judge the net effect of a proposed loan.

The IBRD was thus withholding potentially orthodox loans. Loans which could be described as soft or in some sense unorthodox were out of the question. The effectiveness of strategic nonlending depended on making the IBRD lending criteria as clear and unambiguous as possible. It was feared that soft loans would have the opposite effect. Eugene Black warned in 1948 against camouflaging grants as loans and called for a clear-cut distinction between loans and grants.[96]

As far as the development of soft loan policy is concerned, it is important to note that the Bank was acquiring legitimacy in the eyes of Congress and the American business elite because of its conservative management and policies. Also, the foundation of the continuing debate with the underdeveloped countries over the question of external capital was laid during this period. The preceding lengthy discussion has described the basis of the IBRD approach to economic development; future sections will emphasize modifications in that approach. Thorough discussion of the IBRD is worthwhile not only because of the later importance of that institution in legitimizing soft loans but because during the 1943–48 period United States foreign policy accepted the IBRD as the primary agency for making development loans.

[96] *New York Times,* September 17, 1948, p. 37.

INTERNAL SETTING: 1943–48

DOMESTIC SITUATION IN GENERAL

The American domestic situation between 1943 and 1948 was dominated by the desire for a rapid return to "normalcy" and the desire to avoid the "mistakes" of the interwar period.

Return to Normalcy

Although the desire for a return of "normalcy" was widespread, there was disagreement with regard to what was to constitute "normalcy." We recognize remnants of the New Deal debate in the public discussion of the economic role of the government in the postwar world. After the United States had announced its plans for postwar economic organization, the *New York Times* complained:

> The Administration has been piling one post-war plan upon another, and nearly all of its plans have one feature in common. Nearly all assume that the world can be saved only by increased governmental intervention, by increased governmental management of economic affairs, by increased governmental power.[97]

Instead of governmental organization, the *Times* advocated an early announcement by the United States government of its intention to balance its budget after the war and "inducement" of foreign governments to stop meddling in economics by demanding "internal reforms" in return for American aid. Better still, according to the *Times*, leave it to the private investors to "discipline" wayward foreign governments:

> So far as possible, the loans would be made by American private investors, who, through their representatives, would be in a much better position diplomatically to insist on sound policies within the borrowing nation than our own Government would be.[98]

The planning for the postwar economic organizations was thus carried on in an atmosphere in which the question of the economic role of governments in general was still unsettled. Today the responsibility of government in maintaining full employment tends to be taken for granted; it is easy to forget that legislation committing the government to this goal was not passed until 1946.

[97] December 4, 1943, p. 12.   [98] July 1, 1944, p. 14.

It was no coincidence that full employment was one of the first areas in which the government's responsibility expanded. The experience of the 1930's had led to a widespread belief that the United States economy had a "natural" tendency toward recession; consequently the maintenance of employment levels was expected to be the major American economic problem after World War II. In retrospect, of course, we can see that the real problem in the American economy after World War II was not deflation but inflation.

The significance of the controversy over the role of government in the economy for the development of soft loan policy lay in the fact that soft governmental loans could not become legitimate until relatively orthodox "hard" loans by governments had come to be so regarded. At this time there was some question as to whether lending money was a proper function of any government any time. Also the fear of postwar unemployment affected American foreign economic policy by encouraging government planners to give special attention to the ability of foreign nations to buy in the American market and thus support American employment levels.

"Mistakes" of Interwar Period

Among the informed public there was a widespread desire to avoid repeating the experience of foreign default on loans, which had caused so much irritation on both sides of the Atlantic during the interwar period. In the first place, it was argued, it was a mistake to lend the money; and secondly, the United States should not have raised its tariffs so high that foreigners could not earn the foreign exchange to pay their debts. Lend-lease aid was consequently put on a nonrepayable basis with an eye to avoiding default on loans after World War II.

American private investors had also lent huge sums to foreign nations during the 1920's, especially the period from 1924 to 1928. This large influx of capital so disorganized the public finances of many borrowing countries that they defaulted not only on these loans but on many previous loans made on a more cautious basis.[99] The belief that the inflated scale of borrowing in the

[99] Arthur Salter, *Foreign Investment* ("Essays in International Finance," No. 12 [Princeton, N.J.: Princeton University Press, 1951]), p. 17.

1920's had undermined all foreign investment made many wary of proposals for foreign lending by any but the most conservative criteria. "Whatever *loans* are made . . . should be made strictly on a business basis," warned the *New York Times*.[100]

Coupled with the painful memory of the defaults was a sense of joint responsibility which viewed Americans as partly to blame for the defaults because their eagerness for profit had led them to make "unsound" loans and because they had kept their tariff levels high. The defaults had caused many to be aware of the relationship between American commercial policy and the debt servicing capacity of foreign nations. Thus the American domestic situation was marked by a mistrust of "hard" loans and a predilection for freer international trade.[101]

Another aspect of the American desire to avoid repeating previous mistakes was the belief that the disruption of international capital markets had led to the general economic problems of the 1930's, which, in turn, had hastened the economic collapse of Germany and the rise of Hitler. As was noted above, American policy reflected this idea of the economic causes of war, and in this respect the informed public was in general agreement. Such a belief, moreover, is not unusual in the light of the public debate in the previous decade of economic causes of war in terms of everything from Marxism to the "munitions makers' conspiracy."[102]

In sum, the domestic situation was not propitious to suggestions that the American government engage in unorthodox foreign lending. Besides some opposition to government financial operations in general, there were beliefs that "unsound" loans could undermine all foreign investment and even cause wars.

BUSINESS ELITE

The advice of businessmen to government officials considering a loan application is similar to that given by *Punch* to "persons about to be married": "Don't!" Business objections to foreign aid in the 1943–48 period, as in later periods, revolved around one central concern, which was to keep the sphere of public activity

---

[100] December 3, 1944, Part 4, p. 8.

[101] For a description of the American climate of opinion in 1943 see *New York Times*, December 5, 1943, Part 4, p. 6.

[102] The year 1935, for example, marked the publishing of Eugene Staley, *War and the Private Investor* (Garden City, N.Y.: Doubleday, 1935).

limited. Insofar as governmental policies affected the economy, business wanted them to favor the private sector. The president of the Chase National Bank of New York probably struck a responsive chord in the hearts of many businessmen when he called for scrapping the IBRD and International Monetary Fund (IMF) in 1944. He counseled instead reliance on "sound" internal policies, private investment, and removal of trade barriers.[103] The business view of the problem of economic development was similar to that of the IBRD in placing primary emphasis on the unwillingness or incompetence of governments to do what was needed to attract private capital. Given their view of the role of governments it is not surprising that they wanted the government to: (*a*) avoid public lending, (*b*) protect private loans already made, and (*c*) enable foreigners to repay past and future loans by lowering trade barriers.

Avoid Public Lending

It helps to understand foreign economic policy if we distinguish between neglecting to lend and deliberate avoidance of such lending.[104] The difference is that between oversight and blackmail. The latter involves threatening not to provide alternative sources of capital, although in this case the threat takes a negative form. The interest of businessmen in deliberate avoidance of public loans arises from their recognition that the treatment foreign governments give to private investors depends not so much on the actual degree to which public capital provides an alternative means of financing but on the *expectations* of these governments regarding the probability of obtaining public capital. Behavior by foreign governments which businessmen regard as harassment could result from the expectation that public capital will be forthcoming—even though such an expectation might be unjustified.

Businessmen were also interested in the actual as opposed to the expected rate of public lending because of the rise of managed currencies. Governments that control their foreign exchange reserves can decide, in the face of a shortage, to give some external debts priority. Private investors feared that public loan obligations

---

[103] *New York Times,* September 16, 1944, p. 28.

[104] This, of course, is the same distinction made in discussing strategic nonlending and the IBRD.

would take precedence over private ones; therefore, they were interested in minimizing public lending.

American bankers were not only unhappy with managed currencies abroad, they also feared that the system would spread to the United States. A number of bankers were reported to be opposed to the IBRD on the grounds that it might necessitate the establishment of a central bank in the United States similar to those maintained abroad.[105] Thus, it was feared that public loans would increase the domestic role of government.

Protect Private Investment

The traditional business concept of the role of government calls for the government not to invest but to promote private investment. In 1944 one observer noted the general acceptance in financial circles of the proposition that "the only true security for a foreign loan is the attitude of our State Department. If the State Department declines to use muscle when foreign debtors default, the loan will not be repaid. The British," he added, "generally have been willing to use muscle. . . ."[106] The businessman's view of "encouraging" foreign governments to improve the "climate" of investment included not only deliberate avoidance of public loans but also a positive incentive in terms of "muscle."[107] In the 1943–48 period many businessmen had not yet given up a nostalgic yearning for the days when the government went in and took over the customs service of a country in default.

Free Trade

Business in general favored trade liberalization in this period, although we should add that Congress is usually more sensitive to what business in particular, rather than in general, thinks about

[105] *New York Times,* June 10, 1944, p. 8.

[106] *New York Times,* November 5, 1944, Part 3, p. 6.

[107] R. D. Kellog, a specialist in international banking, also criticized the State Department for not taking a stronger stand on debt service by foreign countries. "American investors cannot be asked to place their money in foreign countries," he said, "if the State Department is going to sit complacently by while debtor nations blandly assure it that, since foreign exchange is not adequate for all purposes, debt service and profits on equity investments must be the first to suffer." This situation, he warned, "means the death knell of international finance in the old sense of the word, and, of course, it means retarding the development of all the newer areas of the world." *New York Times,* November 19, 1944, Part 3, pp. 6–7.

tariffs. Spokesmen for industries vitally interested in a specific tariff are more likely to hold a congressman's attention than those giving mild approval to the general principle of lower trade barriers. Still, a number of business leaders voiced support for trade liberalization, pointing especially to the need for enabling foreigners to service external debt.[108] Some even went so far as to claim that private investors should not be allowed to invest abroad unless American trade barriers were lowered.[109] The gist of statements by many business leaders in the 1943–48 period was that foreign aid by governments would not be required if the United States liberalized trade. We should note, in preparation for the later development of soft loan policy, that such a position involved a big "if."

Business and the IBRD

The announcement in 1943 of plans for establishing an international bank aroused little enthusiasm in the business community. For one thing, any plan connected with the name Keynes was suspected of economic heresy.[110] Whatever the objections were to the proposed bank, however, they did not compare with those raised against the proposed International Monetary Fund; consequently the bank proposal received little discussion prior to the Bretton Woods Conference. Shortly before the opening of the conference, the United States Chamber of Commerce published a study questioning the wisdom of a multilateral as opposed to a bilateral approach, expressing concern about the possible impact on private lending, and suggesting the lack of a need for an international bank.[111]

Despite the fact that the Bretton Woods proposals made promotion of private investment a major goal of the IBRD, the business community remained cool toward the plan. The National

108 The American delegation to the International Business Conference, a private organization, discouraged foreign businessmen from counting on loans from the United States and advised instead that they rely on free trade—after the United States lowered its trade barriers. The position of the American delegation was "trade not aid." *New York Times,* November 15, 1944, Part 3, p. 31. See also *New York Times,* October 1, 1946, p. 31.

109 *New York Times,* November 5, 1944, Part 3, p. 9.

110 See, for example, *New York Times,* July 4, 1944, p. 15; November 17, 1943, p. 4; and December 2, 1943, p. 35.

111 *New York Times,* June 25, 1944, p. 10.

Foreign Trade Convention, for example, withheld approval in the fall of 1944.[112] In 1945, however, several business groups, led by the Committee for Economic Development, approved the Bretton Woods proposals; more accurately, they acquiesced to the proposals.[113] And by 1947 American businessmen were firmly ensconced in key administrative posts of the IBRD.

In the reaction of the business community to the Bretton Woods proposals we can see the beginning of a characteristic response to foreign aid proposals—initial opposition, followed by grudging approval, coupled with a desire to have businessmen occupy important administrative positions. All of this was aimed at ensuring "sound" practices; and, whatever else "sound" practice might have included, it definitely ruled out unorthodox lending.

CONGRESS

Three aspects of the role of the legislative branch in foreign economic policy will be examined: (a) the changing role of Congress, (b) Congress and trade liberalization, and (c) Congress and foreign aid.

A New Role for Congress

Probably no change in the American foreign policy making process in the last thirty years has been more significant than the increased importance of Congress, which resulted from the increasingly frequent use of foreign policy techniques based on economic instruments of statecraft. Looking back on the period before World War II, Charles E. Bohlen mused, "It was extremely difficult in those days to generate any interest in Congress, particularly in the House of Representatives, in our foreign relations. This has radically changed. Now Congress is called upon annually to appropriate vast sums of money" for the implementation of our foreign policy.[114] Nothing is more helpful to the student of foreign aid than an early realization of the importance of legislative control of the purse strings in foreign policy making.

112 *New York Times*, October 15, 1944, Part 3, p. 6.

113 *New York Times*, March 20, 1945, p. 1; March 24, 1945, p. 13; February 5, 1945, p. 21. The American Bankers Association and the U.S. Chamber of Commerce continued to withhold approval of the IMF.

114 "Economic Assistance in United States Foreign Policy," *Department of State Bulletin*, March 28, 1960, p. 499.

Congress and Trade Liberalization

It was noted above that trade liberalization was a primary goal of American foreign policy during this period. Other nations, although not fond of the idea of free trade, were willing to go along with the Americans on this point in order to gain access to the huge United States market. They withheld approval of the Charter for the International Trade Organization, however, pending approval by Congress. They remembered that once before the United States had led the way toward world organization and backed out at the last moment.

The main vehicle for expression of Congressional views on trade liberalization was the Reciprocal Trade Agreements Act of 1934. This act was extended periodically from 1937 to 1945, without significant amendment. In 1945 the act was extended for three years, and the President's tariff-cutting authority was broadened so that he could reduce tariffs to 50 per cent of the rates prevailing on January 1, 1945. The year 1945 marked the legislative high point of the trade liberalization program. From 1945 until 1962 amendments were restrictive rather than expansive of the President's power. In 1948, for the first time in over fifteen years, a Republican Congress was in charge of reviewing the program. The Republicans showed their dislike for the program by limiting its extension to one year and by inserting a "peril point" amendment which required the Tariff Commission to survey all commodities on which the President proposed to negotiate agreements and to specify rates of duty below which, in the commission's judgment, tariffs could not be lowered without injuring American industry.

Even in 1945—the legislative apogee of free trade—protectionist voices rumbled in the background with ominous implications for the future of ITO. Although the Colmer Committee (the House Special Committee on Postwar Economic Policy and Planning of the 78th and 79th Congresses) had supported the removal of trade barriers, the House Ways and Means Committee was less enthusiastic.[115] The favorable report on the extension of the Re-

115 Cf. U.S., Congress, House, Special Committee on Post-War Economic Policy and Planning, *The Post-War Foreign Economic Policy of the United States*, 79th Cong., 1st sess., 1945, Report No. 541. Cited hereafter as House Special Committee, *The Post-War Foreign Economic Policy of the United States*, 1945.

ciprocal Trade Agreements Act was accompanied by a minority report signed by ten congressmen, which accused the State Department of wanting to "put the American worker, the American farmer, and the American businessman on the international auction block."[116] "Obviously," the minority report argued, "we cannot hope to provide jobs in this country, and at the same time maintain our domestic price and wage levels, restore industry and agriculture to a normal peacetime basis, or even maintain our representative system of government, if our shores are to become a dumping ground for the surplus products of the world."[117] The minority also called attention to the opposition to the act voiced by spokesmen for the cotton textile, wool manufacturing, metal manufacturing, chemical, glassware, sugar, watch, and other industries.[118]

In opposing the act the minority used an argument which, because of its later significance, it is well to note. They argued that reduction of trade barriers was unjustified because "the steady reduction of rates under the trade-agreements program has given the United States one of the lowest tariff levels of all the countries of the world."[119] This argument was used repeatedly in later years despite its specious nature. Comparing tariff levels tells us nothing whatsoever about the relative degree to which these levels restrict trade.

Evidence of latent protectionist sentiment in Congress was not confined to statements of formal opposition to the Trade Agreements Act. The majority report of the Ways and Means Committee noted with approval the efforts of the executive branch to protect the interests of American producers in implementing the program. They also looked favorably on the tacit agreement of the executive branch to insert "escape clauses" into all future agreements.[120]

[116] U.S., Congress, House, Committee on Ways and Means, *Foreign Trade Agreements,* 79th Cong., 1st sess., 1945, Report No. 594, Part 2, p. 4.

[117] *Ibid.,* p. 3.

[118] *Ibid.,* p. 9.

[119] *Ibid.,* p. 2.

[120] *Ibid.,* Part 1, pp. 8–9. The tacit agreement with Congress regarding the escape clause began in 1942. The provision gives assurance that if "as a result of unforeseen developments and of the concession granted" on a product, the product is "being imported in such increased quantities and under such conditions as to cause or threaten serious injury to domestic producers of like or similar products," this government or the other government shall be free to withdraw the concession.

Thus, even in the 1943–48 period the executive was reluctant to administer its existing legislative authority vigorously lest protectionist sentiment in Congress be aroused. It is not surprising that other nations were skeptical about the ability of the executive branch to get Congressional approval for the ITO. We who study the role of Congress in American foreign aid policy should note well that in the 1943–48 period Congress had little sympathy for the executive branch's proposed alternative to foreign aid—lowering trade barriers.

Congress and Foreign Aid

The United States Constitution was designed to ensure a certain amount of executive-legislative institutional rivalry. It succeeded. The development of foreign aid policy should be viewed not only in terms of this general Congressional hostility toward the executive but also in terms of the special sensitivity of Congress regarding economic policy. It is not surprising that bipartisan support for foreign policy tended to break down with regard to foreign economic policy during this period.

If there was one point that Congress made clear between 1943 and 1948, it was that it disliked foreign aid. This became obvious during consideration of the Bretton Woods proposals, the British loan, and the Marshall Plan. The plan for a World Bank had just been announced when Senator Robert A. Taft began the attack by denouncing the bank plan as "part of the general New Deal program to create new methods of deficit spending."[121] Shortly before the Bretton Woods Conference, a letter signed by Walter H. Judd, Clare Boothe Luce, Christian Herter, John Vorys, J. Wadsworth, and others warned: "As yet we have to find a single member of the Republican party [in Congress] . . . who approves of what he conceives to be Secretary Morgenthau's proposal."[122] The negotiators at Bretton Woods in 1944 were well aware of Congressional reluctance to surrender control over the purse strings. "The Bank," according to R. F. Harrod, "had been dressed, with an eye to Congress, to look as orthodox as possible."[123]

In the Congressional debate on the loan to Great Britain the

121 *New York Times*, October 12, 1943, p. 39.
122 *New York Times*, June 23, 1944, p. 18.
123 Harrod, p. 578.

arguments included objections to financing socialism, failure to obtain adequate concessions from the British, and setting a precedent for foreign loans that would impose an "intolerable burden" on the American taxpayer.[124] But the common thread in the Congressional debate was that Congress found foreign aid a generally distasteful business. The lack of Congressional enthusiasm for the loan to Britain prompted the French to hasten to get their loan application in before the Congress abandoned foreign loans altogether. "The highest officials here," an observer in France reported, "nurture no illusions about the United States attitude toward foreign loans as it has been manifested in Congress. . . ."[125]

Another sign of Congressional dislike of aid programs was the insistence that part of the Marshall Plan funds be on a loan basis instead of a grant basis as the executive had requested. It is possible, of course, to favor loans because they seem more "businesslike," because they strengthen the "moral fiber" of the borrower, or for other reasons; but the question that most interested Congress was what the total cost would be. Representative John Vorys later stated that the loan requirement had been a technique for cutting the total net cost of the program. "I was responsible," he said, "for having $1 billion of the Marshall Plan money, the first year, in the form of loans or guarantees. We were either going to do that or have the amount cut by some such amount."[126]

In summary, between 1943 and 1948 certain Congressional attitudes became increasingly evident: a dislike for appropriating money to aid foreigners, a greater aversion to grants than to loans if money had to be appropriated, and a lack of enthusiasm for lowering trade barriers.

PERCEPTION OF THE SITUATION AND SELECTION OF AN ALTERNATIVE

The decision making process can be conceived as choosing one alternative from among others or as a process of elimination of alternatives. Although it amounts to the same thing, focus on the

---

[124] William Adams Brown, Jr., and Redvers Opie, *American Foreign Assistance* (Washington: Brookings Institution, 1953), pp. 104–5.

[125] *New York Times*, February 24, 1946, p. 22.

[126] U.S., Congress, House, Committee on Foreign Affairs, *Hearings, Mutual Security Act of 1957*, 85th Cong., 1st sess., 1957, p. 339.

elimination of alternatives calls attention to aspects of decision making which are often overlooked. Since this study is primarily concerned with the evolution of soft loan policy, the question of why soft lending was rejected as a policy alternative will be of central importance. It will be argued that soft lending as a technique for promoting the economic development of underdeveloped areas was rejected during the 1943–48 period as unnecessary, undesirable, and impolitic.

SOFT LOANS: UNNECESSARY

During the early postwar period the United States policy never questioned the desirability of the development of poor countries. "The issue," as Clair Wilcox noted, "was not whether it should be promoted, but how."[127] Such a description of the issue, however, tends to conceal the difference of opinion between the United States and the less developed countries with regard to how much development, how fast. For the United States, economic growth in these areas was not a high priority goal. In the first place, it was overshadowed by the importance attached by American policy makers to the reconstruction of Europe.

Secondly, the nature of the cold war was only beginning to become apparent to the policy makers during this period. George Kennan's famous "Mr. X" article laying out the policy of containment did not appear until 1947.[128] There was, thus, little connection between developing poor countries and cold war activities as far as American policy makers were concerned. The sense of urgency with regard to the problem of economic development which we detect in later years was absent during this period.

The American choice of techniques other than soft loans depended also on the policy makers' concept of the process of economic growth. In their view economic development was primarily a matter of freeing trade, improving the "climate" for private investment, and letting growth occur. Indeed, it is difficult to imagine their holding a different view since the problem of rapid transformation from underdeveloped to modern society had not been studied much. The economic history of Europe and the United States indicated that economic development took a cen-

[127] Wilcox, p. 142.

[128] X, "Sources of Soviet Conduct," *Foreign Affairs*, XXV (July, 1947), 566–82.

tury or so even under favorable conditions. And economists could contribute little to the policy makers' understanding of economic growth since they were only beginning to give it serious attention themselves. With the exception of the work of Karl Marx and J. A. Schumpeter, economics had tended to have a static bias, and economists, therefore, could offer scant advice on how to bring about rapid changes in basic economic structures.[129]

Given the low priority of economic development of underdeveloped areas relative to other foreign policy goals and given the above concept of the growth process, American policy makers decided that soft loans would be unnecessary because trade liberalization, supplemented by increased flow of private capital, could do the job. And if these measures were not sufficient, the underdeveloped countries could look to the IBRD and the Export-Import Bank for additional capital.

SOFT LOANS: UNDESIRABLE

Soft lending as a technique for promoting economic development was regarded by American policy makers not only as unnecessary but undesirable as well. Soft loans were public loans, and public loans were considered less desirable than private ones because private loans tended to strengthen the free enterprise system.

Policy makers also feared that unorthodox public loans might undermine capital markets, as had happened with private loans after World War I. William McChesney Martin, then president of the Export-Import Bank, noted the importance of the "principle of repayment" and warned that it was particularly important that there be no "confusion" about grants and the Export-Import Bank loans.[130] The United States wanted other nations to take external financial obligations seriously, and it was feared that a blurring of the distinction between loans and grants might encourage "irresponsibility" in this respect.

In presenting the plans for the European Recovery Program the

---

[129] "Although many useful ideas on the economics of underdevelopment can be found in the works of the great economists of the past, as a serious subject of study it began to emerge only during the 'forties of the present century." A. N. Agarwala and S. P. Singh (eds.), *The Economics of Underdevelopment* (New York: Oxford University Press, 1958), p. 3.

[130] *New York Times,* November 30, 1948, p. 41.

State Department argued against soft loans not only on economic but political grounds as well:

The question of grants as against loans should be realistically approached. It must be recognized, for example, that where the past and present situation of a country or its future prospects give little chance of repayment it would be both misleading and unwise to furnish aid on a loan basis. To furnish assistance by way of loans when there is substantial doubt that the recipient country will be able to repay the loan and with the idea that at the proper time the obligation to repay may be modified or forgiven, would only be the source of difficulties and perhaps bitterness in the future.[131]

SOFT LOANS: IMPOLITIC

Besides the executive branch view that soft loans were unnecessary and undesirable as a means of financing economic development, there was good reason to reject them as imprudent in terms of domestic politics. The executive branch had a difficult enough time getting money from Congress for the British loan, the Marshall Plan, and the Greek-Turkish aid program.[132] Getting Congress to appropriate money for soft loans to underdeveloped nations was out of the question. Congress even turned down a request in 1948 for expanding the lending authority of the Export-Import Bank to make conventional loans. Still, we should note that legislative hostility applied to foreign aid in general and applied to soft loans only as opposed to conventional loans or no loans at all. In the Marshall Plan debate, Congress indicated that soft loans were at least better than grants.

The business community, for reasons noted in the discussion of the business elite, was opposed to public lending in general but especially to unorthodox lending. That the executive branch was sensitive to business views on international loans is illustrated by Wilcox's admission that the American proposal on international investment at the Geneva conference in 1947 was "in response to suggestions made by such bodies as the National Foreign Trade Council and the National Association of Manufacturers."[133] The

---

[131] U.S., Congress, Senate, Committee on Foreign Relations, *Outline of European Recovery Program: Draft Legislation and Background Information*, submitted by the Department of State, 80th Cong., 1st sess., Committee Print, 1947, p. 45.

[132] Note that 80 per cent of the American quota for the IBRD was in the form of a guarantee and caused no drain on the Treasury.

[133] Wilcox, p. 146.

business community's fears with regard to "unsound" public financial operations were also quelled by the knowledge that men with
business backgrounds were in charge of the IBRD, Export-Import
Bank, and the administration of the European Recovery Program
(ERP) in 1948.[134]

IV. EFFECTIVENESS OF POLICY: 1943–48

TRADE LIBERALIZATION

The relatively sharp decrease in the average level of American
tariffs during this period is likely to be misleading (Fig. 2). Since
American tariffs were so high in the 1930's, they could be de-

[134] John F. McCloy was president of the IBRD; Paul Hoffman was in charge of
the ERP; and William McChesney Martin headed the Export-Import Bank.

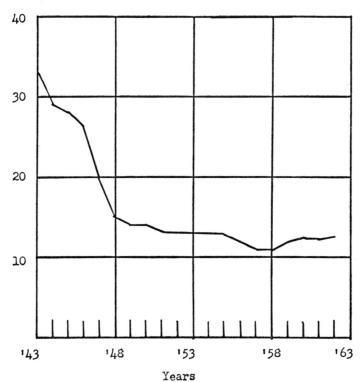

Fig. 2.—Average United States tariff rates as per cent of value, 1943–62. Source:
U.S., Bureau of the Census, *Statistical Abstract of the United States,* 1957 and 1964.

creased with regard to many products without a corresponding fall in the degree to which trade was being restricted. For example, if a 10 per cent tariff suffices to keep out all imports of product X, it does little good to reduce the tariff on product X from 40 to 20 per cent. The effectiveness of trade liberalization in promoting economic development depended on the degree to which the restrictiveness—not the average level—of American tariffs was curtailed.[135]

We can hardly overemphasize the importance of trade liberalization as viewed by most of the nations of the world. An observer at Bretton Woods in 1944 noted:

. . . Commercial policy . . . is held to be the clue to the whole show, for there is practically no one here who has the slightest confidence in the efficacy of any of the machinery in process of building in the absence of an American trade policy that lowers tariff barriers and makes it possible for the world's greatest creditor nation to perform her proper function of buyer.[136]

Vigorous reduction of American restrictions on trade might have stimulated growth in three important ways: (1) The increased ability to earn foreign exchange would have made it easier for underdeveloped nations to import those goods which were especially costly to produce at home, thus taking advantage of international specialization. (2) The increased ability to earn foreign exchange would have strengthened their capacity to service foreign debt. (3) The expected increase in debt-servicing capacity would have increased the readiness of private foreign investors to lend to the underdeveloped countries.[137]

In retrospect we see that the policy of advocating freer trade lacked effectiveness because it did not result in enough actual lowering of trade barriers. Thanks largely to the United States Congress, the ITO was to be stillborn, and the President's authority and inclination to lower tariffs were reduced.

[135] On this point see Commission on Foreign Economic Policy, *Staff Papers* (Washington: U.S. Government Printing Office, 1954), pp. 277–80, 293–97.

[136] *New York Times*, July 16, 1944, Part 4, p. 7.

[137] This statement, of course, involves the assumption that other things remain equal.

PRIVATE INVESTMENT

United States policy aimed not only at freeing trade, but also at stimulating private foreign investment. This policy also proved relatively ineffective, not because private investment failed to promote growth, but because private investment did not increase much.[138] Why did private capital not flow in greater quantities than it did in the 1943–48 period?

It is helpful to divide the obstacles to private foreign investment into those which were beyond the control of underdeveloped countries and those which were not.[139] The fundamental determinant of the flow of private investment to underdeveloped countries is the expectation of the potential investor regarding the profit he is likely to derive from the undertaking. We will be hampered in understanding American policy during this period if we think in terms of projects which are "naturally" unprofitable—or "non-self-liquidating."[140] Many supposedly unprofitable projects can be made highly profitable by a change in governmental policy. Public utilities, for example, can be highly remunerative if allowed to exploit a monopoly position. And it was an objective of American policy during this period, in its bilateral contacts as well as through the IBRD, to bring about a change in governmental policy in underdeveloped countries in order that the profitability of certain projects might be increased. Governments can make a project profitable and thereby improve the "investment climate" by paying a subsidy, granting tax relief, stifling competition, or by other means.

[138] It is sometimes argued that private investment does not promote economic growth because it tends to concentrate in extractive industries. Those using this argument usually work from an implicit definition of economic growth as industrialization. It might be hard to convince Venezuelans that petroleum investments, which are responsible for 90 per cent of Venezuela's foreign exchange earnings, do not help their economic development.

[139] For a useful discussion of obstacles to private investment in underdeveloped countries see J. N. Behrman, "Promotion of Private Overseas Investment," ed. Mikesell, *U.S. Private and Government Investment Abroad*, pp. 165–90.

[140] A typical analysis runs as follows: "And this is perhaps the basic reason that private funds are so small: because public funds are so small. Businessmen cannot be expected to invest in hospitals, ports, schools, and roads. The returns from such projects are insufficient; and even if there were any profits, it would take too long to reap them." John W. Spanier, *American Foreign Policy since World War II* (rev. ed.; New York: Praeger, 1962), p. 186. Contrary to the implication of such analysis, roads are unprofitable mainly because of governmental attitudes toward toll roads.

Three obstacles merit particular attention. The first, and most important, is the threat of governmental regulation or even expropriation. To the extent that this threat was lessened, business expectations would be affected favorably. The second is the threat of inflation, and the obvious remedy is for governments to take anti-inflationary measures. The third, convertibility or the repatriation of earnings, may be a problem. Governments could improve their "climate of investment" by giving private foreign investors a prior claim on foreign exchange earnings.

Given, then, that governments could have affected the expectations of potential private investors, we may ask why they did not do more than they did in this period. First, there is reason to believe that the American attempt to blackmail the underdeveloped nations into relying on private capital was unsuccessful because the threat to avoid providing public capital lacked credibility. It lacked credibility for the following reasons: (1) The 1943–48 period was characterized by change and reorganization in many spheres of life, and it was difficult to convince the underdeveloped nations that the American position was fixed. (2) The United Nations provided the governments of underdeveloped nations with a new forum in which to call for a new deal. They wanted at least to try this new tool before resigning themselves to reliance on private investment. (3) United States policy did provide precedents for giving both soft loans and grants to Great Britain and the Marshall Plan countries; there was thus reason to believe that the United States could be induced to reconsider its threat. Notice that the belief that American policy might be changed not only weakened the incentive to treat private investors more favorably but also provided a disincentive to do so. One can demonstrate a greater "need" for public capital if he can point to the lack of private investment in his nation; therefore he has an incentive to discourage private capital.[141]

Besides their incredulity regarding the American threat, the

[141] This is probably what Robert Strausz-Hupé had in mind when he told a Congressional committee: "There can be little doubt that the emphasis in our economic policy upon outright grants and low-interest Government loans has been a major factor in creating an unfavorable climate for private investment in the underdeveloped areas of the world." U.S., Congress, Senate, Special Committee To Study the Foreign Aid Program, *Hearings, The Foreign Aid Program*, 85th Cong., 1st sess., 1957, p. 592.

governments of the underdeveloped nations had another, more important, reason for not changing their policies toward foreign investment. This period witnessed the beginning of a rising tide of nationalism in many underdeveloped nations, which involved ideological considerations militating against improving the treatment of foreign private investors. The first consideration was a growing national pride which sometimes bordered on xenophobia. In Latin America there was a long-standing resentment of the "Colossus of the North," and in other parts of the underdeveloped world resentment of former colonial masters was widespread. In the eyes of many poor countries the foreign private investor was a symbol of colonial "exploitation." In estimating the reluctance of underdeveloped nations to welcome private foreign capital it matters little whether the resentment was justified or not. It was the strength, not the justice, of the resentment that made governments wary of the foreign private investor.

A second aspect of the growing national feeling in poor countries was the view of government and the economy. Pressures for government to take responsibility for economic growth were growing. Opie and Brown observed that many of the underdeveloped countries had "turned to government planning, control of investment, and ownership of basic industries in one form or another, in disregard of the effect on the attraction of foreign capital."[142] This tendency also discouraged governments from adopting more friendly attitudes toward private investors.

A third aspect of the rising wave of nationalism was the desire for "modernization." Modernization meant primarily industrialization to underdeveloped nations; and while private investment in banana plantations or oil might be useful in promoting economic growth defined in terms of income per capita, it was not what they wanted.[143] The colonialist past of many encouraged the belief that agriculture was somehow degrading and that heavy industry was upgrading. Thus, the fact that private investors had little interest in heavy industry weakened the incentive for underdeveloped nations to treat them better.

In sum, the nationalist sentiment in underdeveloped countries opposed foreigners, private investors, and investment in non-

---

[142] Brown and Opie, p. 388.   [143] See Wilcox, pp. 140–52.

industrial areas of the economy. Because the American threat to avoid public lending lacked credibility and because of growing nationalism, governments in underdeveloped countries did not make many radical changes in their treatment of private foreign investors.

Besides those obstacles to foreign investment which governments in underdeveloped nations could control, there were others which were beyond their control.[144] These included: (1) The unsettled world situation and the threat of war caused potential investors to be uncertain. (2) To some extent the political instability in the underdeveloped countries themselves was beyond the control of the governments involved. This also increased uncertainty in investors' minds. (3) The restrictive United States trade barriers tended to reduce expectations of profit from investing in foreign industries which might export to the United States. (4) Discriminatory United States taxation of American foreign investors and lack of clarity in American anti-trust laws also discouraged the potential private investor.[145]

RELIANCE ON DOMESTIC EFFORT

American policy was supposed to stimulate domestic efforts. The ineffectiveness of this policy was partly explained by the nature of the class structure in most underdeveloped countries. The local people who could invest had little incentive to do so. They viewed the rising nationalist feelings as a threat to their position. The American policy was not designed to affect the situation as described in 1943 by Frank W. Fetter:

> In a number of industrially backward countries the principal obstacle to domestic investment is not the absence of local funds that might be invested but a scale of social values, combined with political instability, which causes the wealthy groups within the country to spend their incomes on foreign travel or on foreign and domestic luxuries. In more than one Latin-American country that is reputedly "short of capital," the sums that have been spent in Paris in the last half century by

[144] They could, of course, compensate for those beyond their control by paying subsidies, for example.

[145] On these problems see Ralph I. Straus, *Expanding Private Investment for Free World Economic Growth*, a special report prepared at the request of the Department of State, April, 1959.

wealthy natives would have endowed the country with a modern transportation system and a well-equipped industrial plant.[146]

In short, the rich feudal aristocracy in many underdeveloped nations cared little about the "revolution of rising expectations." The maharajas' lot has not improved, for example, since the British left India.

SUMMARY

In sum, the American policy of trade liberalization, promotion of private investment, and reliance on domestic efforts was not very effective. Trade was not liberalized much; private investment was not particularly stimulated; and domestic efforts were weak. There was even an additional factor working against the success of the United States policy for promoting economic growth defined in terms of income per capita. In the underdeveloped areas the rate of population growth was beginning to increase. This phenomenon later became known as the "population explosion"; but the dimensions of the problem were largely unforeseen in the 1943–48 period. The problem of increasing income per capita, in other words, was getting tougher every day. There was even the danger of slipping backward.

[146] Frank Whitson Fetter, "The Need for Postwar Foreign Lending," *Papers and Proceedings of the Fifty-fifth Annual Meeting of the American Economic Association,* 1943, p. 343.

III Point Four: Reconsideration
1949–53

I. WAS ECONOMIC GROWTH A GOAL
OF UNITED STATES POLICY?

In 1950 Secretary of State Dean Acheson told a Congressional committee that they had before them a bill which established "economic development of underdeveloped areas for the first time as a national policy."[1] Evidence was presented in discussing the period 1943–48 which would suggest that the Secretary was exaggerating the degree to which the Act for International Development represented a new concern for economic growth. The important thing to note, however, is that the period 1949–53 contained this clear statement of economic development in poor nations as a goal of American foreign policy. Since President Truman's inaugural address in January, 1949, no presidential inaugural address has omitted reference to this foreign policy goal. President Truman's fourth point in a program for peace set the keynote for much of this period:

We must embark on a bold new program for making the benefits of our scientific advances and industrial progress available for the improvement and growth of underdeveloped areas.

More than half the people of the world are living in conditions approaching misery. Their food is inadequate. They are victims of disease. Their economic life is primitive and stagnant. Their poverty is a handicap and a threat both to them and to more prosperous areas. . . .

I believe that we should make available to peace-loving peoples the

[1] U.S., Congress, Senate, Committee on Foreign Relations, *Hearings, Act for International Development*, 81st Cong., 2d sess., 1950, p. 5. Cited hereafter as Senate Committee on Foreign Relations, *Act for International Development Hearings*, 1950.

benefits of our store of technical knowledge in order to help them realize their aspirations for a better life. And, in cooperation with other
nations, we should foster capital investment in areas needing development. . . .

The old imperialism—exploitation for foreign profit—has no place in
our plans. What we envisage is a program of development based on
the concepts of democratic fair-dealing.

All countries, including our own, will greatly benefit from a constructive program for the better use of the world's human natural resources. Experience shows that our commerce with other countries
expands as they progress industrially and economically.

Greater production is the key to prosperity and peace.[2]

The broader foreign policy goals in terms of which promotion of
economic development was justified resembled those of the immediate postwar period—prosperity and peace.

PEACE AND ECONOMIC DEVELOPMENT

During the 1949–53 period American policy statements reflected
concern for the national security aspects of economic development
in terms of vague concepts of the economic causes of war, less
vague concepts of the relationship between communism and poverty, and relatively concrete concepts of the relationship between
underdeveloped areas and strategic raw materials for use in rearmament. The idea that economic factors are important in pre-
serving peace was a legacy of the preceding decade; and although
vague, it did not necessarily reflect naïveté. It may well have been
a manifestation of awareness that the nations of the world were
becoming increasingly interdependent, coupled with a humble
admission that the specific implications of such a state of affairs
were difficult to predict. In a world of rapid change, where one
nation's actions seem to impinge increasingly on those of other
nations, what can one say with assurance? "We can be sure,"
Acheson warned, "that the masses of people will no longer be
satisfied with half a loaf."[3] A similar negative assertion was
voiced by President Truman in addressing the United Nations
on October 24, 1949: "We cannot achieve permanent peace and

[2] President Truman's Inaugural Address, January 20, 1949.

[3] "Economic Policy and the ITO Charter," *Department of State Bulletin,* May
15, 1949, p. 624.

prosperity in the world until the standard of living in under-developed areas is raised."[4] Thus, even before the advent of the Korean War, United States policy viewed economic development as related to broad national security considerations. The Act for International Development, Acheson informed Congress, is a security measure. "And, as a security measure, it is an essential arm of our foreign policy, for our military and economic security is vitally dependent on the economic security of other peoples."[5]

During the period 1949–53 a new reason for United States concern for economic development emerged. American policy makers realized that the containment policy applied not only to Europe but to the underdeveloped lands as well, and they became concerned with the relationships among democracy, communism, and economic development. In cautious and qualified terms the policy makers speculated that "while material well-being is no guaranty that democracy will flourish, a healthy and prosperous people is a far more fertile field for the development of democracy than one which is undernourished and unproductive. That is why we are and must be preoccupied with the long-term problem of economic development."[6] We cannot be sure, the policy makers argued, that economic development will result in democracy, but we can be sure that "failure on our part to act in ways that will expand trade and help fulfill the pent-up aspirations of the under-developed areas can assure the loss of large regions important to the security of the United States."[7]

The underdeveloped areas were important to American security also as potential sources of supply for strategic raw materials. The Korean War brought this point forcefully to the attention of the policy makers.

PROSPERITY AND ECONOMIC DEVELOPMENT

The concept of economic growth as related to American eco-nomic well-being was also a legacy from the early postwar period.

---

[4] Quoted in Richard P. Stebbins, *The United States in World Affairs, 1949* (New York: Harper & Bros., 1950), p. 101.

[5] Senate Committee on Foreign Relations, *Act for International Development Hearings*, 1950, p. 5.

[6] Dean Acheson, "Waging Peace in the Americas," *Department of State Bulletin*, September 26, 1949, p. 464.

[7] Robert E. Asher, "The Economics of U.S. Foreign Policy," *Department of State Bulletin*, July 6, 1953, p. 8.

In announcing his Point Four program the President had noted that the United States stood to gain from increased trade with developing nations. There was less attention during this period, however, to the need for exports as a prop for general employment levels. The postwar inflation had quieted the nagging fear of depression that had permeated earlier discussions of economic foreign policy. There was more emphasis during this period on the economic benefits of rising levels of world trade.

In 1952 the policy makers were reminded of the long-term economic importance of the underdeveloped areas to American prosperity by the President's Materials Policy Commission (Paley Commission). This commission examined the "adequacy of materials, chiefly industrial materials, to meet the needs of the free world in the years ahead."[8] The commission emphasized the speed with which the industrial nations were gobbling raw materials and pointed out that "even with all that the United States resource base, and its technology, can supply, . . . there will remain an increasing demand for materials."[9] "The areas to which the United States must principally look for expansion of its mineral imports," the commission observed, "are Canada, Latin America and Africa, the Near East, and South and Southeast Asia."[10] And in order to clarify the implications of the study, the commission explicitly stated its "belief that if we fail to work for a rise in the standard of living in the rest of the world, we thereby hamper and impede the further rise of our own."[11]

On the grounds of both national security and economic considerations, the policy makers in this period believed economic development in less developed areas to be desirable. The question of its importance relative to other policy goals will be discussed later. The next consideration relates to choosing policy techniques during the 1949–53 period.

II. HOW TO PROMOTE ECONOMIC
GROWTH: TECHNIQUES

The relative importance of the various techniques of statecraft during the 1949–53 period resembled policy choices in the

---

[8] President's Materials Policy Commission, *Resources for Freedom* (5 vols.; Washington: U.S. Government Printing Office, 1952), I, 1.

[9] *Ibid.*, p. 59.   [10] *Ibid.*, p. 60.   [11] *Ibid.*, p. 3.

previous period, reliance on local efforts ranking first, promotion of private investment second, and furnishing of public capital third.

RELIANCE ON DOMESTIC EFFORT

United States policy continued to stress the importance of domestic efforts in the development of poor countries. In discussions of economic development in various United Nations organs, the United States had little trouble securing the agreement of all to this general principle. The disagreements revolved around the specific questions of how much capital was needed and who should provide it. The United States position was that "most of the capital needed for economic development must come from the underdeveloped areas themselves."[12]

STIMULATION OF PRIVATE CAPITAL FLOW

TRADE LIBERALIZATION

The executive branch continued to press for lowering of American trade barriers, but the prospect of success steadily diminished during the 1949-53 period. With regard to the relationship between the ITO and economic development, the Secretary of State observed that he knew of "no other road to the development of the kind of world trading system in which the world's productive energies can be transformed into the highest levels of material well-being."[13] Yet, in 1950, efforts by the administration to push the ITO through Congress were abandoned as futile.

In 1953, however, the incoming Republican administration gave new emphasis to liberalizing trade as a technique for pro-

[12] Statement by Dean Acheson, Senate Committee on Foreign Relations, *Act for International Development Hearings*, 1950, p. 5. In 1949 Acting Secretary of State James Webb stated: "Most development projects involve a large element of local resources and labor which cannot be effectively introduced from outside. Furthermore, it would not seem wise from the standpoint either of the borrower or of the lender to encourage the formation of too heavy an external debt by these countries. It is hoped that technical assistance can be given where needed to help them channel domestic savings into productive enterprises." U.S., Congress, House, Committee on Foreign Affairs, *Hearings, International Technical Cooperation Act of 1949*, 81st Cong., 1st sess., 1949, pp. 7-8. Cited hereafter as House Committee on Foreign Affairs, *"Point IV" Hearings*, 1949.

[13] Dean Acheson, "Economic Policy and the ITO Charter," *Department of State Bulletin*, May 15, 1949, p. 627.

moting economic development.[14] "Trade not aid" was a slogan which explicitly designated trade liberalization as an alternative to foreign aid in promoting economic growth abroad. Thus, although efforts to free trade by the Truman administration early in the 1949–53 period were stymied, the period ended with renewed stress on the importance of trade liberalization as a policy technique.

IMPROVEMENT OF "INVESTMENT CLIMATE"

The importance of improving the foreign "investment climate" was a point on which both the Truman and Eisenhower administrations could agree. Throughout the period spokesmen for the Democratic administration emphasized the need for foreign governments to treat private foreign capital in a friendlier manner, and in his first "State of the Union" message the Republican President committed his administration to "doing whatever our Government can properly do to encourage the flow of private American investment abroad. This involves," he added, "as a serious and explicit purpose of our foreign policy, the encouragement of a hospitable climate for such investment in foreign nations."[15] The means by which the United States sought to improve the "investment climate" included, as they had in the 1943–48 period, advice, denial of alternative means of financing, and diplomacy.

Advice

Within a week after President Truman's inaugural address, Secretary of State Acheson, in commenting on the Point Four proposal, complained about the failure in many places to "understand that unless the conditions are created by which investors may fairly put their money into that country, then there is a great impediment to development."[16] The policy makers attacked

[14] "Indeed, a common remark in Washington in the years of the first Eisenhower administration and even before he took office was that freeing of international trade was one issue on which the President had a deep and strong personal conviction." Raymond A. Bauer, Ithiel de Sola Pool, and Lewis Anthony Dexter, *American Business and Public Policy* (New York: Atherton, 1963), p. 29. See also Sherman Adams, *Firsthand Report* (New York: Harper & Bros., 1961), pp. 381–95.

[15] "The State of the Union Message of President Eisenhower to Congress," *Department of State Bulletin*, February 9, 1953, p. 208.

[16] *New York Times*, January 27, 1949, p. 4.

this lack of "understanding" by advising the underdeveloped nations that the dearth of private investment in their nations was their own fault. "In a sense," advised a State Department official, "the real decision must be made by these countries themselves, since only they can decide whether they want our capital to participate in their development. If they want it, they must, in turn, create the 'climate' necessary to attract it."[17] And in case foreign governments had not quite understood the admonitions of the previous administration, Milton S. Eisenhower, in a report which was adopted as official policy, gave some detailed advice on how to improve the "investment climate":

Measures which can be taken by foreign governments to attract private capital are too well known to require extensive discussion: They include *adequate* opportunities for *fair* profit, *reasonable* provisions for transfer of earnings and amortization, *equitable* labor and management laws and regulations, and *freedom* from fear of discriminatory treatment, expropriation with *inadequate* compensation, or *unfair* Government intervention. Inflation and financial instability also play a part in many countries in discouraging or repelling private investment. A genuine belief in the value to the community of private competitive enterprise and private profit is perhaps the most fundamental requirement.[18]

American policy makers advised not only on the need for attracting foreign capital, but also on the relative merits of private as opposed to public enterprise. "This country," Acheson reminded the Latin Americans, "has been built by private initiative, and it remains a land of private initiative. The preponderance of our economic strength depends today as in the past upon the technical and financial resources and, even more, upon the abilities and morale of private citizens. I venture to say that the same thing is true of the other American nations."[19]

American policy statements also contained, as they had in the

[17] George C. McGhee, "United States Economic Relations with South Asia," *Department of State Bulletin*, February 27, 1950, p. 343.

[18] Milton S. Eisenhower, "United States–Latin American Relations: Report to the President," *Department of State Bulletin*, November 23, 1953, p. 711. Italics mine. The matter of defining the italicized words was entirely up to the potential private investor. The flow of private investment depended on his subjective attitudes, not on the objective existence of fair, reasonable, and adequate conditions.

[19] *Department of State Bulletin*, September 26, 1949, p. 465.

past, references to the fact that private foreign investment brought with it valuable technical knowledge and management experience which did not accompany public capital.[20] Thus, United States policy advised the underdeveloped nations with regard to ways to attract private capital, the desirability of a private enterprise system, and the advantages of private as opposed to public foreign capital.

Refusal To Provide Alternative

Besides giving advice, the United States policy was designed to illustrate to the underdeveloped countries the necessity for attracting private capital. Throughout this period the United States staunchly refused to consider the various schemes for increasing the flow of public capital which were proposed in the United Nations and in its own national councils. American policy limited provisions of public capital to the Export-Import Bank, the International Bank for Reconstruction and Development, and some technical assistance. And these were to be operated in such a way as to minimize the degree to which they competed with private capital. "In providing assistance for economic development," Acheson observed, "it would be contrary to our traditions to place our government's public funds in direct and wasteful competition with private funds. Therefore, it will be our policy, in general, not to extend loans of public funds for projects for which private capital is available."[21] This threat to withhold public capital in order to induce other governments to rely on attracting private capital was repeated by the Eisenhower administration in 1953.[22] It should be noted, however, that the refusal to provide alternative sources of capital was not so extensive as that in the 1943–48 period, since Congress did begin a technical assistance program in 1950 with an appropriation of about $30 million.[23]

---

[20] See, for example, Willard L. Thorp, "India's Participation in Economic Development Programs," *Department of State Bulletin,* February 25, 1952, p. 295.

[21] *Department of State Bulletin,* September 26, 1949, p. 465.

[22] See statements by the Secretary of State and the Secretary of the Treasury. U.S., Congress, Senate, Committee on Foreign Relations, *Hearings, Mutual Security Act of 1953,* 83d Cong., 1st sess., 1953, pp. 24, 100, and 170. Cited hereafter as Senate Committee on Foreign Relations, *Mutual Security Hearings,* 1953.

[23] Part of the confusing folklore of foreign aid is the distinction between "technical assistance" and "capital assistance." If a nation with an even balance of exports

Diplomacy

In the "multilateral diplomacy" of the international forums, such as the United Nations, the United States continued trying to get other nations to improve their "investment climates." During the 1949–53 period the United States attempted to negotiate treaties with foreign countries containing an investment clause covering such topics as the right of American capital to enter freely into business, nondiscriminatory treatment for established investors, freedom from restriction regarding ownership, assurances of convertibility of earnings and capital, and provision for prompt and adequate compensation in the event of expropriation.[24] These treaties aimed at creating an "atmosphere favorable to increased private investment abroad."[25] The United States methods of "encouraging" other nations to improve their "investment climates" thus included advice, refusal to provide alternatives, and negotiation of commercial treaties.

INVESTMENT GUARANTY

Besides trade liberalization and efforts to get other nations to improve their treatment of private capital, American policy during this period added another technique for stimulating the flow of private investment, the investment guaranty. This approach marked a retreat from previous insistence that the underdeveloped countries themselves must be wholly responsible for attracting capital. Under the investment guaranty program the United States government assumed responsibility for certain "nonbusiness" risks of private foreign investors, such as convertibility and expropriation. This approach, applicable to the Marshall Plan countries

---

and imports decided to import more "technical know-how," it would have an excess of imports over exports and would—according to most definitions—experience a net capital inflow. If the money to pay for the additional "technical know-how" were furnished by private lenders, the transaction would probably be described as a private capital movement. But if the money were furnished by the United Nations, it would probably be described by students of foreign policy as "technical assistance."

24 Marina von Neumann Whitman, *The United States Investment Guaranty Program and Private Foreign Investment* ("Princeton Studies in International Finance," No. 9 [Princeton, N.J.: Princeton University Press, 1959]), p. 13.

25 Dean Acheson, *Department of State Bulletin*, September 26, 1949, p. 465.

since 1948, was applied to the underdeveloped areas beginning in 1951.[26]

FURNISHING CAPITAL THROUGH PUBLIC CHANNELS

As in the 1943–48 period, the American policy makers did not rule out the technique of furnishing capital to underdeveloped areas via public channels, although this technique continued to be subordinated to promoting the private transfer of capital. The basic principles of American policy on the provision of public capital remained the same: keep the amount small; keep it under American control; and minimize the degree of competition with private investors.

WHICH CHANNELS?

Although the United States did contribute to the United Nations technical assistance program during this period, it placed major emphasis on the World Bank as a channel for transferring capital and on the bilateral channels furnished by the Export-Import Bank and the Mutual Security Program.[27] The American opposition to multilateral channels other than the IBRD was emphasized in the United Nations debate on the establishment of a multilateral fund for economic development. "The Government of the United States," the American representative stated, "has consistently and strongly opposed the establishment of international machinery for making grants and long-term, low-interest

[26] For a discussion of the development of the United States investment guaranty program see Whitman, pp. 20–45.

[27] A statement submitted to Congress in 1951 on the "Determination of Loan and Grant Assistance to Southeast Asia and Other Underdeveloped Areas" read in part: "It is . . . the policy of the Administration that the lending operations for development of the underdeveloped areas should be undertaken by the established lending institutions, namely, the Export-Import Bank and the International Bank." U.S., Congress, Senate, Committee on Foreign Relations and Committee on Armed Services, *Hearings, Mutual Security Act of 1951*, 82d Cong., 1st sess., 1951, p. 605. Hereafter cited as Senate Committee on Foreign Relations and Committee on Armed Services, *Mutual Security Act Hearings*, 1951. For other statements on the primacy of these two institutions see the following: House Committee on Foreign Affairs, *"Point IV" Hearings*, 1949, p. 8; Senate Committee on Foreign Relations, *Act for International Development Hearings*, 1950, pp. 5–6; and U.S., Congress, House, *Report of Activities of the National Advisory Council on International Monetary and Financial Problems*, 82d Cong., 1st sess., 1951, H. Doc. 239, p. 9. Hereafter cited as NAC, *NAC Report, 1951.*

loans."[28] And in the unlikely event that his audience had failed to understand, he added, ". . . I trust I have made it unmistakably clear that it is the proposed *machinery* to which we are opposed."[29]

ON WHAT TERMS?

American policy called for the bulk of public capital to be in the form of conventional loans, repayable in dollars at interest rates set with an eye on the private capital market and maturation periods of from five to thirty years. A statement submitted to Congress in 1951 noted the policy of the administration "with respect to the countries of southeast Asia, as well as with respect to all underdeveloped areas, to place assistance on a loan basis insofar as there is reasonable prospect of repayment and the programs are of such a character as may reasonably be financed on a loan basis."[30] The United States emphasis on the IBRD and Export-Import Bank ensured not only a substantial degree of American control but also that loans would be on conventional terms for purposes which, in the judgment of the businessmen who administered them, did not compete with private investment. Both of these institutions, as was noted in previous discussion, pursued goals other than maximizing the amount of their lending operations. In other words, both restricted loans on grounds other than the absence of capacity and willingness to repay. In 1953 the operations of the Export-Import Bank were even more restricted in response to Treasury Secretary George Humphrey's desire that these be limited to short-term financing of American trade.

Although orthodox lending was the primary form of public capital transfer advocated by American policy makers, the advent of Point Four was an admission that hard loans were not enough. United States technical assistance funds were distributed largely on a grant basis, but the size of the program was limited. "By its very nature," the Secretary of State observed, "this is not and

[28] Statement by Isador Lubin made before United Nations Economic and Social Council on June 23, 1952, reprinted in *Department of State Bulletin*, July 14, 1952, p. 73.

[29] *Ibid.*

[30] Senate Committee on Foreign Relations and Committee on Armed Services, *Mutual Security Act Hearings*, 1951, p. 605.

never will be a big-money enterprise."[31] Also, requiring that grants be used for technical assistance was a means of exercising control over the use of the funds and thereby minimizing competition with private investors. The funds were spent for projects which were unlikely to have been financed by the recipients in the absence of technical assistance, thus avoiding to some extent the substitutability problem.[32]

In 1951 technical assistance programs were assimilated by the Mutual Security Program, and the prospects for additional grant aid for economic development brightened—or darkened, depending on one's viewpoint. The National Advisory Council, however, cautioned that only "extraordinary economic assistance" would be on a grant basis.[33] And hopes that grant aid for economic development would be greatly increased were further undermined when W. Averell Harriman, director of the program, indicated that less than 10 per cent of Mutual Security funds was going into technical and economic assistance for the Near East, Asia, Africa, and Latin America.[34] The transfer of public capital on a grant basis was thus a new technique by which the United States sought to stimulate economic development, but it was of minor importance compared to the conventional loan technique. The United States representative remarked in the United Nations debate that grant assistance for economic development had been available and probably would continue to be so, but he never-

[31] Senate Committee on Foreign Relations, *Act for International Development Hearings*, 1950, p. 13.

[32] Note that the question of whether the projects undertaken by technical assistance, such as malaria control, would have attracted private capital is irrelevant to a determination of the degree to which technical assistance resulted in increased competition with private investors if the technical assistance projects would have been financed by the local government in the absence of such aid. The relevant question in such a case relates to the use made by the government of the resources freed.

[33] NAC, *NAC Report*, 1951, p. 9.

[34] U.S., Congress, House, Committee on Foreign Affairs, *Hearings, Mutual Security Act Extension*, 82d Cong., 2d sess., 1952, p. 6. Cited hereafter as House Committee on Foreign Affairs, *Mutual Security Hearings*, 1952. One observer was prompted to comment that "the Mutual Security Act displayed what seemed a remarkable indifference to the so-called underdeveloped countries of Asia, Africa, and the Western Hemisphere." Richard P. Stebbins, *The United States in World Affairs, 1951* (New York: Harper & Bros., 1952), p. 238.

theless argued that the underdeveloped countries should rely mainly on the IBRD and the Export-Import Bank.[35]

The United States policy makers chose to promote economic development by hard loans and grants, but they rejected soft lending as a technique. To the extent that policy makers thought it desirable to stimulate economic development in a nation at a rate faster than that allowed by conventional loans, they wanted to use grants instead of soft loans:

> The position has been taken by the executive branch that where the financial situation of the aid-recipient countries warrants, aid ought to be made available on a loan basis but that these loans ought to be sound and repayable; not questionable or "fuzzy" loans. If sound and payable loans cannot be made in terms of the over-all position and prospects of the country, then aid ought to be on a grant and not on a pseudo- or quasi-loan basis.[36]

PUBLIC CAPITAL: PORTENTS

Throughout the 1949–53 period United States policy required loans for economic development to be repaid in dollars. In 1953, however, Congress inserted in the Mutual Security Act of 1951, as amended, a requirement that no less than $100 million of the funds be used to finance the export of surplus agricultural commodities. This provision, section 550, authorized the sale of such commodities for local currency which was in turn to be used to promote the purposes of the Mutual Security Program. Insofar as the transaction involved the transfer of resources to foreign countries in return for inconvertible currencies, this "sale" was similar to a soft loan.

SUMMARY

Although the broad outlines of American policy for promoting economic development between 1949 and 1953 resembled those of the previous five years, there were significant changes. Reliance on local efforts remained the primary technique, but there were indications of its diminishing importance. The policy makers, through technical assistance, investment treaties, and investment

[35] United Nations A/C.2/SR. 147, November 20, 1951, pp. 14–16.

[36] Senate Committee on Foreign Relations and Committee on Armed Services, *Mutual Security Act Hearings*, 1951, p. 613.

guaranties, were groping for new techniques by which to aid local efforts. Speeches by both Truman and Eisenhower advocated using money saved from disarmament to speed economic development, thus acknowledging the desirability—if not the possibility —of less reliance on local effort.[37]

Stimulating private foreign investment continued to be important. Trade liberalization as a means of spurring private investment decreased in importance, while increased attention was focused on improving the "investment climate" by treaties and other means and on efforts to compensate for poor "investment climates" through investment guaranties.

Transfer of capital through public channels increased in importance, but was still a minor technique compared to reliance on domestic efforts and promotion of private capital. To the degree that public capital was transferred, American policy emphasized the technique of orthodox loans from the IBRD and to a lesser extent the Export-Import Bank. In accordance with this emphasis on hard loans, the lending authority of the Export-Import Bank was increased by $1 billion during this period.

The policy makers introduced grants as an additional technique for providing public capital for economic development. This is significant as an indication that United States policy on the transfer of public capital was being reconsidered. Soft loans, however, remained taboo.

III. WHY TECHNIQUES WERE CHOSEN OR REJECTED

EXTERNAL SETTING: 1949–53

GENERAL INTERNATIONAL SITUATION

Five aspects of the international situation in general deserve attention: (a) European reconstruction, (b) the Korean War, (c) the fall of Nationalist China, (d) the death of Stalin, and (e) the emergence of the "dollar gap."

During 1947 it became apparent that the economic reconstruction of Europe was going to take longer than had initially been ex-

[37] Text of speech by President Truman reprinted in *New York Times*, October 25, 1950, p. 18; and text of President Eisenhower's speech reprinted in *New York Times*, April 17, 1953, p. 4.

pected. The slow recovery of Europe meant that during the 1949–53 period no significant amount of aid for economic development could be expected from any source other than the United States. Also, the drain on American resources in aiding Europe resulted in a decreased willingness and capacity to aid underdeveloped areas.

The onset of the Korean War in June, 1950, and the consequent preoccupation with rearmament also tended to reduce the American willingness and capacity to transfer public capital to underdeveloped areas. The increased demand for raw materials which accompanied rearmament efforts strengthened the foreign exchange earning capacity of underdeveloped nations, and the United States hastened to point out that this should reduce the amount of external capital needed to attain a given level of growth.[38] Although the immediate effect of the Korean flare-up was to intensify rearmament efforts, a longer-term significance derived from the fact that it made policy makers more aware of the degree of United States dependence on less developed areas for strategic raw materials.

In 1949, the Nationalist Chinese forces were routed by the Communists. The significance of this for the development of American foreign aid policy is that it provided the setting in which the policy makers began to perceive a rivalry between totalitarian and democratic methods of economic development. India and Communist China were to become the leading exponents of these two methods in the eyes of American policy makers. Some countries, President Truman informed Congress, can attract private capital to finance most of their outlays for economic development, but in others, where private capital cannot "meet the need, this Government must provide substantial quantities of supplies and equipment to assure real progress on vital programs of development. That is the direction we are taking in India today," he added, "and in other places where the need is particularly urgent."[39]

[38] United Nations A/C.2/SR. 147, November 20, 1951, p. 15. This favorable change in the terms of trade for the less developed nations proved to be only temporary, however.

[39] "Message of the President to the Congress," transmitted March 6, 1952, reprinted in Department of State Bulletin, March 17, 1952, p. 407.

The death of Stalin in March, 1953, marked a turning point in the development of Russian foreign policy. The significance of this event did not become apparent until a later period; suffice it to note that American policy was influenced by the American view of Soviet capabilities and intentions with regard to less developed nations. The U.S.S.R. took a renewed interest in these areas after the death of Stalin.

Another aspect of the international situation relevant to the evolution of American policy toward underdeveloped countries was the "dollar gap." Many foreign nations, including European nations, wanted more dollars than they were earning in trade.[40] There was a world-wide belief that the United States trade barriers should be lower in order to permit foreigners to earn more dollars. Of course it would have been possible to eliminate the "dollar gap" by deflationary policies in other countries, but, as was noted in the previous chapter, the new attitudes toward the government's role in maintaining full employment made this a politically unpopular alternative in most nations. The significance of the "dollar gap" controversy was that it called attention to the relationship between American commercial policy and the transfer of capital abroad. An "Open Letter to Americans" from a Belgian economist was reported to have been "much pondered in Washington" in 1952: "You now hold two-thirds to four-fifths of the world's gold supply, to say nothing of silver. Each year you sell more than you buy to the tune of about seven or eight billion dollars." One of two things, he warned, must happen: "Either you concentrate on yourselves and, after you absorb all this world once had in the way of exchangeable wealth, you live on it like misers, or you integrate with the rest of the world [and] throw open your doors to European, Asian and African goods. If you refuse to buy because you fear competition—you the richest country in the world; then you'll have to give."[41] In other words, if the United States wished to transfer capital abroad, and if it refused to lower trade barriers, it would have to reconsider the

---

[40] We must beware of descriptions of the "dollar gap" which define it in terms of the "inability" to earn enough dollars to meet the "need." On this point see F. Machlup, "Three Concepts of the Balance of Payments and the So-Called Dollar Shortage," *Economic Journal*, LX (March, 1950), 46–68.

[41] Quoted in *New York Times*, October 12, 1952, p. 28.

forms of capital transfer in the light of the limited capacity and willingness of other nations to make the sacrifices necessary to service orthodox loans.

UNITED NATIONS

Between 1949 and 1953 the less developed nations devoted their efforts to convincing the United States that it should contribute to a "Marshall Plan" for the underdeveloped countries. During this period they concentrated on the establishment of an international public agency which would distribute grants and soft loans to underdeveloped countries. "Since 1950," Robert Asher observed, "the major economic battles at the Economic and Social Council and the General Assembly have been fought on this issue."[42]

The previous chapter noted the establishment in 1947 of the Subcommission on Economic Development. This commission, according to chairman V. K. R. V. Rao, gave the problem of financing economic development its first intensive study at its third session in 1949.[43] In its report the subcommission noted the "importance of avoiding burdensome conditions in the period of maturity and interest rates on loans" to underdeveloped countries.[44] It added that on a "realistic assessment it cannot be assumed that the Bank [IBRD] could, in the foreseeable future, be able to make a significant contribution to the massive investments required for economic development involved over a long period" and that even if the Bank could lend more, the terms of Bank loans would "limit the effectiveness of this financing to underdeveloped countries."[45] The subcommission appended to its report

[42] Robert E. Asher *et al.*, *The United Nations and Economic and Social Co-operation* (Washington: Brookings Institution, 1957), p. 480.

[43] V. K. R. V. Rao, "An International Development Authority," *India Quarterly*, VIII (July–September, 1952), 237.

[44] United Nations, Secretariat, Department of Economic Affairs, *Methods of Financing Economic Development in Underdeveloped Countries* (United Nations Publication Sales No.: 1949. II. B. 4), pp. 122–23. Cited hereafter as U.N., *Methods of Financing Economic Development,* 1949. This document contains the relevant parts of the reports by the subcommission, the Economic and Employment Commission, and the IBRD.

[45] *Ibid.*, p. 127. The American member of the subcommission dissented from part of the report, recommending that the less developed countries rely on private capital and the IBRD. *Ibid.*, p. 123. The wariness of the representatives of under-

a proposal by Rao for the establishment of a United Nations Economic Development Administration (UNEDA), which would finance "projects of economic development in under-developed countries which are not financially productive in a banking sense."[46] Such financing was normally to take the form of loans with "liberal" terms of repayment and "nominal" interest.[47] The Economic and Employment Commission, in which the United States and other industrial nations carried more influence than in the subcommission, lacked enthusiasm for the Rao proposal. "The result," according to Rao, "was not only a refusal to consider the proposal to set up a new international agency like UNEDA but also a recommendation by the majority of the Economic and Employment Commission that the Sub-Commission on Economic Development be abolished."[48]

In February, 1950, the ECOSOC requested the subcommission to submit additional information for consideration at the next ECOSOC meeting in the summer of 1950. In its fourth and last session the subcommission returned to the problem of financing economic development. "Warned by the reception that had greeted its previous proposals, especially the proposal of its Chairman, the subcommission went about the job of suggesting the creation of a new international authority with much greater circumspection."[49] This time the subcommission report emphasized the importance of domestic effort and the role of private capital, but it pointed out that:

. . . there is a large field of economic development *requiring* foreign financing that is not *capable* of being serviced through the existing sources of foreign finance. Indeed, any substantial acceleration even of admittedly sound projects of economic development will depend in considerable measure upon the extent to which the prerequisite base of "social and economic overhead capital" is created and broadened in the under-developed countries. It is therefore important that under-developed countries have available to them, as an aid in building up their base of "social and economic overhead capital," facilities for

---

developed countries regarding the political influence of private enterprise was hardly reduced by their observation that the American member, E. G. Collado, was employed by Standard Oil of New Jersey.

46 *Ibid.*, p. 129.   48 Rao, *India Quarterly*, VIII, 248.

47 *Ibid.*, p. 130.   49 *Ibid.*, p. 252.

foreign financing that will impose only a nominal burden of annual payments. This *requires* foreign loans of longer maturities and at lower interest rates than are available from existing sources.[50]

The subcommission refrained from recommending establishment of the UNEDA because they realized that the United States, the only prospective source for substantial contributions, opposed the proposal.[51]

In 1950 the underdeveloped nations continued to call attention to the existence of "non-self-liquidating projects" and to the "need" for special financial arrangements for such projects. In August the ECOSOC noted that "economic development requires the execution not only of self-liquidating projects but also of projects in such fields as transport, power, communications, public health, educational institutions and housing, which, while not always fully self-liquidating, are justified by reason of their indirect effect on national productivity and national income"; and it recommended that institutions providing international loans "make any such loans at rates of interest and on terms of amortization designed to place the smallest feasible burden on the exchange availabilities of the underdeveloped countries, consistent with the maintenance of these institutions as self-supporting entities."[52] A similarly worded resolution was passed in November by the United Nations General Assembly.[53] Neither resolution men-

[50] United Nations E/CN. 1/80: E/CN. 1/Sub. 3/29, May 19, 1950, p. 23. Italics mine. The tendency to discuss the issue in terms of "capabilities" and "requirements" is typical of the soft loan debate.

[51] "They did not make a positive recommendation for the creation of a new international agency on the lines suggested by me like UNEDA, because they realized that the major financial incidence of such an agency would fall on the United States, at any rate for the time being, and they felt that the initiative for such an agency should therefore come from the official spokesman of that country rather than from a mixed body of experts the majority of whom came from countries which would be beneficiaries rather than contributors to such an agency." Rao, *India Quarterly*, VIII, 254.

[52] ECOSOC Resolution 294 (XI), August 12, 1950.

[53] United Nations General Assembly Resolution 400 (V), November 20, 1950, read in part: The General Assembly, ". . . taking account of the fact that some basic development projects are not capable of being adequately serviced through existing sources of foreign finance although they contribute directly or indirectly to the increase of national productivity and national income, . . . recommends that the Economic and Social Council, in giving further study to the problem of the financing of economic development, consider practical methods, conditions and policies for achieving the adequate expansion and steadier flow of foreign capital, both private

tioned why, if such projects increased national income, governments should not tax this increase in order to finance the project —an omission which became typical of the public debate on soft lending.

The pressure emanating from the United Nations for expanding economic aid to poor nations increased with the publication of a unanimous report by a committee of experts in May, 1951, *Measures for the Economic Development of Underdeveloped Countries*.[54] The argument in this report was as follows: The underdeveloped nations have less capital than they need in order to attain a "satisfactory" rate of growth; the IBRD was set up to remedy this situation, but "in view of the need of the underdeveloped countries for capital, the Bank cannot be said to be meeting the challenge of the circumstances."[55] The Bank should set as a target for itself the attainment of an annual rate of lending of not less than $1 billion per year to the underdeveloped countries. This report did not argue, as did most other analyses, that the IBRD was lending as much as it could. It recognized that strategic withholding of loans was an aspect of Bank operations and that the limits on IBRD lending were imposed not by the Articles of Agreement but by a "narrow interpretation" of those articles which "*seemed* to confine it to lending sums of foreign exchange needed to purchase equipment and materials for specific projects."[56] By recommending that the Bank seek to lend a minimum of $1 billion annually, the report was, in effect, advocating abandonment of the Bank's policy of strategic nonlending. The report concluded that even if the IBRD were to expand its lending, it could not supply enough capital; therefore, the report recommended establishment of an International Development Authority (IDA) to disburse grants for economic development. The alternative of having the proposed IDA make

---

and public, and pay special attention to the financing of non-self-liquidating projects which are basic to economic development."

[54] United Nations, Secretariat, Department of Economic Affairs, *Measures for the Economic Development of Underdeveloped Countries* (United Nations Sales Publication No.: 1951. II. B. 2). Cited hereafter as U.N., *Measures for Economic Development*, 1951.

[55] *Ibid.*, p. 82.

[56] *Ibid.*, p. 83. Italics mine.

soft loans was rejected on the grounds that the same effect could be achieved by combining a grant with an IBRD loan.[57]

After this report was published, its proposals were discussed at the sixth session of the Economic, Employment and Development Commission and the thirteenth session of the ECOSOC, with considerable controversy arising over the proposed IDA.[58] In the ensuing sixth session of the General Assembly in the fall of 1951, the controversy boiled up again; and this time the high-income countries, despite their united stand, were unable to prevent passage of a resolution calling for establishment of a special fund to make grants and "low-interest, long-term loans" for "non-self-liquidating projects" in underdeveloped countries.[59]

In June, 1952, the fourteenth session of ECOSOC, after hearing the same arguments put forth many times in the previous two years, requested the Secretary-General to appoint a committee of experts to prepare a plan for a special fund to make grants and soft loans.[60] Recognizing that 1952 was election year for the United States, the ECOSOC asked for the report by March, 1953, a delay which would allow the Americans time to overcome their quadrennial political paralysis.

The committee reported in March, 1953, with a plan especially interesting in three respects: (1) Control was to be shared equally by potential creditors and potential debtors of the fund.[61] (2) Loans by the fund were to "impose no undue burden on the

---

[57] *Ibid.*, p. 86.

[58] The United States position was predictable from the previous discussion of American policy. The United States objected to the following points: (*a*) over-emphasis on the role of governments as opposed to private sector in fostering economic growth, (*b*) insufficient attention to the responsibility of governments in recipient countries for creating a "favorable climate of investment," and (*c*) too much emphasis on grants and not enough on loans from the IBRD. United Nations E/CN. 1/SR. 111, May 17, 1951, pp. 8–13.

[59] United Nations General Assembly Resolution 520 A (VI), January 12, 1952. Favoring the resolution were India, Chile, Egypt, Cuba, Mexico, and other under-developed nations. Voting against it were Australia, Belgium, Canada, Denmark, France, Greece, Luxembourg, Netherlands, the United Kingdom, the United States, and a few others. Since the Communist nations abstained, not one industrialized nation voted for the measure.

[60] ECOSOC Resolution 416 A (XIV), June 23, 1952.

[61] United Nations, *Report on a Special United Nations Fund for Economic Development* (United Nations Publication Sales No.: 1953. II. B. 1).

assisted government."[62] The assisted government could at any time request relaxation of all terms of the loan, including rates of interest, amortization period, grace period, and so on.[63] The plan also included provision for repayment of loans in inconvertible currency, a proposal which differed from the reports on the UNEDA and the IDA.[64] The terms would thus be lenient, indefinite, and amenable to repayment in soft currency. (3) Contributions to the fund could be made in currency which was convertible only to the extent that the contributing nation agreed to such conversion.[65]

In the fall of 1953 the General Assembly debated the report on the Special United Nations Fund for Economic Development (SUNFED). The United States insisted that it was not "prepared to make any contribution to a new international development fund, and did not believe that any further steps could usefully be taken at that time looking to the establishment of such a fund."[66] The supporters of the SUNFED kept the proposal alive by the appointment of Raymond Scheyven, president of the ECOSOC, to survey governmental views on the SUNFED and report to the next session.[67]

The argument for soft loans to underdeveloped countries in the United Nations can be broken into three basic components. First, there is the proposition that large quantities of foreign capital are necessary for economic growth. This was disputed by the United States on the grounds that the "absorptive capacity" of these countries was limited and that preoccupation with heavy industry inflated estimates of capital needs. You do not need foreign capital as much as you think you do, the United States was saying, in effect. Most development projects, observed an acting Secretary of State, involve large elements of local resources and labor which cannot be effectively introduced from outside.[68] President Truman added that "it is possible to make tremendous improvements in

[62] *Ibid.*, p. 55.

[63] *Ibid.*, pp. 55–56.

[64] *Ibid.*, p. 33.

[65] *Ibid.*, p. 13.

[66] United Nations A/C. 2/SR. 259, October 14, 1953, p. 72.

[67] United Nations General Assembly Resolution 724 B (VIII), December 7, 1953.

[68] House Committee on Foreign Affairs, *"Point IV" Hearings*, 1949, pp. 7–8.

underdeveloped areas by very simple and inexpensive means."[69] With regard to the fixation of heavy industry, Dean Acheson complained in 1949: "There is an idea that if every country can only have a steel mill, then all is well."[70] The 1949 report of the Subcommission on Economic Development had argued that development required industrialization which included, "within the framework of available resources and markets," the development of heavy industries such as metallurgy, machine tools, and chemicals.[71] We must admit that it would be difficult to explain the high standard of living in Nebraska, New Zealand, Australia, or Iowa on the basis of such a view of the economic growth process.[72] By 1953 the vigor of United States objections to "excessive" claims for foreign capital had diminished, and the American position rested mainly on grounds of impracticality of its giving additional aid under the circumstances.

The second major proposition in the United Nations debate was that the needed capital was unavailable. Private capital, the World Bank, and the Export-Import Bank, it was argued, were "incapable" of financing "non-self-liquidating" projects. This proposition involved the seldom stated assumption of governmental policies as fixed. It was precisely these governmental policies, relating to the treatment of private capital, that the United States and the IBRD were trying to change. As one observer put it in a similar context, "whether there is a chronic dollar shortage may be doubted. What is not in doubt is that the issue cannot be discussed or understood without reference to monetary and fiscal policy and to exchange rates, prices, and costs."[73] We look in vain, however, for recogni-

[69] "Point Four: An Investment in Peace," *Department of State Bulletin*, July 17, 1950, p. 93.

[70] *New York Times*, January 27, 1949, p. 4. One study claims that the United States eschewed the official use of the terms "industrialized" and "unindustrialized" in an effort to avoid associating economic development with industrialization. Gardner Patterson and Jack N. Behrman, *Survey of United States International Finance 1950* (Princeton, N.J.: Princeton University Press, 1951), p. 102.

[71] U.N., *Methods of Financing Economic Development*, 1949, p. 114.

[72] Cf. Jacob Viner, *International Trade and Economic Development* (Glencoe, Ill.: Free Press, 1952), pp. 61–63.

[73] P. T. Bauer, review of Benjamin Higgins' *Economic Development: Problems, Principles, and Policies*, in *Economic Development and Cultural Change*, X (October, 1961), 99.

tion of this fact in United Nations debate—either by experts or by governmental representatives. The real issue behind the façade of "non-self-liquidating" projects was hardly mentioned. This issue concerned the role of private enterprise in the developing nations. We can understand why diplomats avoided direct reference to this sensitive issue; it is less easy to explain the failure of scholars to distinguish between the real issue and the pseudo-issue.

The third basic element of the argument for soft loans as it evolved in the United Nations was the proposition that because capital "could" not be supplied for "non-self-liquidating" projects, soft loans were in order. The question of the conditions under which soft loans were preferable to grants received scant attention.

It is not clear whether the underdeveloped countries were genuinely convinced that loans on special terms were widely needed, whether they preferred such loans to grants, whether some, whose eligibility for grants might be dubious, wanted to ensure their entree to the agency, or whether the less developed nations simply assumed that the United States would be more receptive to a combination loan-grant agency than to a straight grant agency.[74]

In summary, between 1949 and 1953 the underdeveloped nations strove for United States agreement on the establishment of a United Nations agency to distribute grants and soft loans for economic growth. The three major proposals put forth during this period, UNEDA, IDA, and SUNFED, all conflicted with the basic principles of United States policy regarding the size, control, and relation to private investment of public capital movements. All involved an increase in American public funds for economic aid. This conflicted with the American desire to keep the cost down. All involved a degree of American control over the use of the funds which was less than that involved in bilateral and IBRD activities. This conflicted with the American principle of maximizing the degree of control. All involved forms of financing—grants, soft loans, or both—which were more likely to compete with private investment than hard loans. There was also a fear that grants and soft loans, as proposed, would undermine the international lending

[74] Asher *et al.*, p. 485.

process. This conflicted with the United States rule of minimizing the degree of interference with private capital movements.

INTERNATIONAL BANK

Despite a constant barrage of criticism from the underdeveloped countries the World Bank held to its basic policy, discussed in the previous chapter, of stimulating economic growth through encouragement of private investment. The assumption of the IBRD presidency by Eugene Black in May, 1949, ensured that Bank activities would remain under the guidance of a man holding the respect of the American financial community. As it turned out, Black was to serve in this capacity throughout the ensuing decade. Since the Bank's policies were similar to those of the previous period, only two aspects will be discussed here, the Bank's position on soft loans and the development of a new role for the Bank.

IBRD and Soft Loans

As was pointed out above, the arguments for soft loans assumed that large amounts of foreign capital were required by the underdeveloped nations in order to reach a given rate of economic development. The IBRD officials believed that governments in these countries were likely to exaggerate the importance of foreign capital and to underestimate the importance of establishing an atmosphere of legal and political security for private investment.[75] The Bank's policy was based on the premise that, "whatever the short-run interests of a particular government may be, in the long run it is a disservice to any country to enable it either to overborrow or to borrow for ill-conceived or poorly-planned projects."[76] And, of course, since projects could only be evaluated in terms of the over-all political and economic situation in the country, the

[75] ". . . Any government, however good, is apt to be forced by political necessity to put more emphasis on short-run objectives which promise immediate advantage than on the long-run development of the country, particularly since that normally entails some sacrifice of immediate benefits and may adversely affect important local interests. Certainly no amount of external aid, technical or financial, can replace the essential will and determination on the part of the government of the country concerned to adopt the often difficult and politically unpopular economic and financial measures necessary to create a favorable environment for development." International Bank for Reconstruction and Development, *Fourth Annual Report, 1948–1949*, p. 8.

[76] *Ibid.*, p. 13.

Bank was saying, in effect, that capital should be withheld from nations pursuing policies judged unwise by Bank officials.

Underdeveloped nations would need less capital if they were not so preoccupied with industrialization, according to the Bank. In commenting on the 1949 report of the Subcommission on Economic Development, the Bank observed that "the shortest road to a higher real income is often investment in agriculture."[77] "Excessive emphasis on industry for industry's sake, above all, heavy industry, may leave an underdeveloped country with the symbol of development rather than the substance," warned the Bank.[78]

Another example of deflation of the estimates of foreign capital "needs" by the IBRD is the case of public utilities—often cited as "non-self-liquidating" projects. The Bank's advice called not for special financing but for political action to make utilities "self-liquidating." It is regrettable, Eugene Black remarked, "that, at some times in some countries, the rates charged to the consumer for power are fixed by the authorities more with reference to the political factors of the times than with proper regard to the economic necessities of particular situations."[79] What was needed, argued the Bank, was not more money but less emphasis by governments on regulation of public utilities and heavy industry and more emphasis on creating a "favorable climate" for private investment. To those decrying the scarcity of development capital the IBRD replied that the "principal limitation upon the Bank financing in the development field has not been lack of money but lack of well-planned projects ready for immediate execution."[80] "Eventually more sound projects may be presented to the Bank than it can finance, but that time is not yet in sight," the IBRD pointed out.[81]

Although Bank officials disagreed with less developed countries on the amount of foreign capital needed, they admitted that in some cases it would be desirable to accelerate growth at a rate

[77] U.N., *Methods of Financing Economic Development,* 1949, p. 139.

[78] *Ibid.,* pp. 139–40.

[79] International Bank for Reconstruction and Development, Eighth Annual Meeting of the Board of Governors, *Summary Proceedings,* 1953, p. 9.

[80] IBRD, *Fourth Annual Report,* p. 9.

[81] U.N., *Methods of Financing Economic Development,* 1949, p. 141.

faster than that likely to occur with orthodox lending. "There are," the Bank conceded, "many projects basic to development—primarily in the fields of education, health, road construction, irrigation and reclamation and the like—which are unsuited to private investment and are yet beyond the present economic capacity of many countries to undertake either from local resources or with funds borrowed from abroad."[82] In an obvious reference to Rao's UNEDA proposal the *Fourth Annual Report* noted that the desire of underdeveloped countries to develop faster than their own resources and existing international resources would permit had led to suggestions that loans be made, either by the Bank or by some new agency created for the purpose, at nominal interest rates and repayable over very long periods of time. In opposing these suggestions the Bank urged that if economic development were to be expedited by financing in addition to orthodox loans, "such assistance should be rendered as outright grants rather than in some form of 'fuzzy' loans which would tend to cast discredit upon the integrity of normal international investments."[83] In 1951 Black denounced soft loans on the grounds that (1) they were based on inflated estimates of the amount of capital needed for development; (2) they tended to undermine respect for financial obligations; (3) they were likely to cause international friction; (4) they might retard economic growth by diverting attention away from the need to husband resources.[84] After recording his "emphatic disagreement" with soft loan suggestions, he indicated that proposals for outright grant assistance had merits, but he discounted the likelihood that any significant amount of grant capital would be forthcoming given world conditions.[85] One thing was clear; the Bank preferred grants to soft loans.

[82] IBRD, *Fourth Annual Report*, p. 14. Note that the use of the term "unsuited" reflects a value judgment instead of the economic calculation implied by "non-self-liquidating."

[83] *Ibid.*

[84] International Bank for Reconstruction and Development, Sixth Annual Meeting of the Board of Governors, *Summary Proceedings*, 1951, p. 6.

[85] *Ibid.* Black also disparaged soft lending in a statement before the Second Committee of the United Nations General Assembly, United Nations A/C. 2/SR. 163, December 10, 1951, pp. 113–15.

New Role for IBRD

During the 1949–53 period the IBRD began to carve a new role for itself. Although it had long been the practice of the Bank to lecture debtors and potential debtors and to "discipline" them by withholding loans, the Bank had paid relatively little attention to creditors and potential creditors. Between 1949 and 1953 the Bank enlarged its role as independent critic of international affairs. It began trying to "educate" rich nations, such as the United States, with regard to the importance of the poor countries and the relationship between commercial policy and foreign lending. It should be noted, however, that IBRD criticism of American policy was usually in general accord with executive branch views of what policy should be.

In 1949, shortly after becoming president, Black indicated his displeasure with American commercial policy. "Despite a rather remarkable shift in the attitude of the United States in recent years," he noted, "some of its policies are still basically inconsistent with its position as the great creditor nation of the world."[86] He went on to criticize American import barriers, especially tariffs. In 1953 Black renewed his attack on United States commercial policy, pointing out that liberalization of United States imports was an essential condition for the elimination of the dollar shortage and the expansion of international investment.[87]

. . . the United States, because of its towering position, has no doubt special responsibilities in this field and must play a leading part in every effort to improve world economic conditions.

The United States can hardly reconcile her position as the giant of the world economy with the fear of foreign competition, which is implied, and is indeed expressed, in the maintenance of high trade barriers and other restrictions against foreign goods. The consequence of these restrictions is to deprive foreign countries of the opportunity of earning dollars with which to purchase American goods and to service American capital.[88]

Black also began directing attention to the importance of economic development of poor countries in general. "Perhaps the most

[86] International Bank for Reconstruction and Development, Fourth Annual Meeting of the Board of Governors, *Proceedings*, 1949, p. 11.

[87] IBRD, *Summary Proceedings*, 1953, p. 10.　　　　　[88] *Ibid.*

powerful single force shaping the course of history in our time," he said in his annual address to the Board of Governors, "is the awakening consciousness of the under-privileged masses of the people that the conditions of poverty, ill-health and ignorance in which they live are not preordained and their deep conviction that they have a right to the opportunity to earn a better living for themselves and a better future for their children."[89] He also voiced his opinion that it was the existence of widespread poverty and misery which had stimulated the spread of the "virus" then threatening the peace of the world.[90] In a variety of ways Black kept emphasizing that economic development was important to all nations— developed and underdeveloped alike.[91]

INTERNAL SETTING: 1949–53

DOMESTIC SITUATION IN GENERAL

The 1949–53 period will long be remembered in American history as the "McCarthy era." During this period the American people experienced near hysterical neo-isolationism. Domestic "Red" hunting dominated the news. The implications of this for foreign policy were far-reaching, but two aspects were particularly relevant to foreign aid. In the first place, the preoccupation with domestic problems tended to draw attention away from the rest of the world. And second, the general undermining of respect for the State Department made it even more difficult to get money from Congress for foreign aid.

Another domestic problem which was to affect later foreign aid policy was the domestic agricultural problem. The problem has often been described in terms of too much food, but a more accurate description would be too many farmers. In a world fraught with starving people it would be ridiculous to say that there was a food surplus. The social problem arose from the fact that the income from food production in the United States did not permit American farmers to live on a scale comparable to citizens in other occupations. In order to boost farm incomes the government

[89] International Bank for Reconstruction and Development, Fifth Annual Meeting of the Board of Governors, Summary Proceedings, 1950, p. 9.

[90] Ibid.

[91] See for example IBRD, Summary Proceedings, 1951, pp. 7–9.

agreed to buy certain products which could not be sold on the open market above a given price. The significance of all this for foreign aid is that between February, 1952, and February, 1956, the stocks of the Commodity Credit Corporation (CCC), those in inventory as well as those pledged against outstanding loans and purchase agreements, increased almost fivefold, from less than $2 billion to $9.1 billion.[92] Most of this buildup took place during 1952 and 1953, when annual increases of 70 and 100 per cent were registered.[93] Thus, 1953 ended with giant stocks of surplus agricultural commodities in government storage. This was an important factor in the subsequent passage of the Agricultural Trade Development and Assistance Act of 1954 (PL 480).

BUSINESS ELITE

The attitudes of the American business elite toward techniques of statecraft for spurring economic development remained remarkably stable during this period—considering the rapidity with which the world situation was changing. They emphasized, as in the 1943–48 period, public lending, private investment, and trade.

Public Lending

Whatever the applicability of game theory concepts is to international relations in general, it is useful in conceptualizing the attitude of the business community. Gabriel Almond has observed that the American businessman has a good bargaining sense.[94] And his bargaining instincts are nowhere better illustrated than in his approach to foreign economic policy. In discussing the use of "threats" in bargaining, T. C. Schelling has noted that the "commitment is a device to leave the last clear chance to decide the outcome with the other party, in a manner that he fully appreciates; it is to relinquish further iniative, having rigged the incentives so that the other party must choose in one's favor."[95]

[92] Bruce F. Johnston, "Farm Surpluses and Foreign Policy," *World Politics,* X (October, 1957), 3.

[93] *Ibid.*

[94] Gabriel A. Almond, *The American People and Foreign Policy* (rev. ed.; New York: Praeger, 1960), p. xxix.

[95] Thomas C. Schelling, *The Strategy of Conflict* (Cambridge, Mass.: Harvard University Press, 1960), p. 37.

Statements by American business spokesmen have nearly always called upon the United States government to commit itself, in a manner which governments in underdeveloped countries fully appreciate, to a policy of minimizing transfer of capital through public channels. To describe the opposition of the business community to public capital transfers as based on a fear that they "*might* compete with private investment abroad"[96] is to miss the point. Public capital *inevitably* competes—on some terms and in the long run. The question, from the businessman's viewpoint, is not whether public capital will compete but how. To what extent, in other words, will it decrease the private investor's bargaining power vis-à-vis foreign governments during a given time period? And this bargaining power depends to some extent on the foreign governments' expectations regarding alternative sources of capital. In 1952 the National Foreign Trade Convention called upon the United States government to make it clear, by word and action, that American public funds would not be forthcoming for projects which, "under proper conditions, could be financed by private capital."[97] The real issue is determining what set of circumstances constitutes "proper conditions," not whether the public capital "might" compete.

Thus, Rao's proposal for the UNEDA to make soft loans was denounced by *Fortune Magazine* as the "high point of Point Four nonsense."[98] *Fortune* added:

Word has been spreading throughout the underdeveloped world that private capital, while still as international by nature as in John Bright's day, responds best to kindness and cannot be coerced. This happy trend faces one danger: the U.S. could stop it in its tracks by dangling the rosy alternative of "little Marshall plans" or loans to backward governments.[99]

Throughout the 1949–53 period business statements exhorted the United States government to increase the credibility of its threat

[96] Robert E. Elder and Forrest D. Murden, *Economic Co-operation: Special United Nations Fund for Economic Development* (New York: Woodrow Wilson Foundation, 1954), p. 13. Italics mine.

[97] "Final Declaration of the Thirty-Ninth National Foreign Trade Convention," *Report of the Thirty-Ninth National Foreign Trade Convention* (New York: National Foreign Trade Council, 1952), p. xiv.

[98] "Point IV," *Fortune Magazine,* February, 1950, p. 95.   [99] *Ibid.*

to avoid providing an alternative to reliance on foreign private capital. Perhaps the clearest single statement of business reasoning on this issue was provided in 1951 by the Thirty-Eighth National Foreign Trade Convention:

> It cannot be expected that economic environments conducive to the investment of American private capital will be established in these foreign lands so long as the governments concerned have reason to believe—as they do have reason to believe—that they will continue to be the beneficiaries of the hand-outs our own Government has given them for so long. They have every right to assume, on the evidence afforded, that this profligate practice will continue to be the order of the day. It is clear why this is so: our own Government, conscious of the fact that economic development abroad is highly desirable, has proceeded on the unfortunate assumption that private enterprise is unwilling or unable to undertake the task, and that, in consequence, the free provision of Government funds for the purposes in view is the only course open. This attitude has been seized upon by foreign governments as justification for their refusal to do the things they would otherwise find it necessary to do in order to attract the private capital they need. The dilemma is one which cannot be resolved until our Government brings itself to announce, as a fundamental element of our foreign economic policy, that we look upon industrial development abroad as the particular function of private enterprise, and that, until the receptive and cooperative attitudes called for are shown, no United States Government funds will be made available for *any* purpose except those of the most exigent military or humanitarian nature.[100]

Although business opinions varied on such measures as the Marshall Plan, Point Four, and the proposed International Finance Corporation, the American business elite was united in its opposition to large-scale public capital movements on a continuing basis for promoting economic development.

[100] "A Statement on Foreign Economic Policy" appended to the "Final Declaration of the Thirty-Eighth National Foreign Trade Convention," *Report of the Thirty-Eighth National Foreign Trade Convention* (New York: National Foreign Trade Council, 1952), p. xxxii. For similar statements by business leaders see the following: *New York Times*, April 26, 1949, p. 37; August 5, 1951, Part 3, p. 1; January 19, 1952, p. 22; House Committee on Foreign Affairs, *"Point IV" Hearings,* 1949, pp. 153–62; "Final Declaration of the Fortieth National Foreign Trade Convention," *Report of the Fortieth National Foreign Trade Convention* (New York: National Foreign Trade Council, 1954), pp. xxiv and xxvii (Note: Fortieth National Foreign Trade Convention was held in 1953).

Private Investment

Although references to military intervention as a means of protecting private investment were rare during this period, there was little doubt that business wanted the American government to do more than just refrain from providing public capital. In March 1949 the State Department held a conference with business representatives in an attempt to learn their views. The businessmen made it clear that they regarded investment guaranties by the United States government as the wrong way to approach the problem. As they saw it, foreign governments were responsible for poor "investment climates," and therefore foreign governments should be induced to change their behavior.[101] In 1950 the National Association of Manufacturers (NAM) denounced the investment guaranty proposal on the grounds that it "would tend to remove the incentive for foreign nations to correct errors of financial and economic policy."[102] It is, of course, unlikely that the NAM and the less developed nations would agree on the definition of "error" in this context.

The National Foreign Trade Convention in 1951 noted the reluctance of foreign governments to "meet the conditions requisite to the flow" of private capital and condemned the apparent lack of a "determined disposition on the part of the United States Government to correct this intolerable situation."[103] It demanded that the "tremendous diplomatic, political and economic facilities at the disposal of the United States Government" be used to improve "investment climates" abroad.[104]

Trade

Business leaders in general continued to prefer trade to aid during this period. The United States Chamber of Commerce and the National Foreign Trade Convention again endorsed trade liberalization. Although the National Association of Manufacturers was hesitant about trade liberalizing, the dominant business attitude

---

[101] On this point see William Adams Brown, Jr. and Redvers Opie, *American Foreign Assistance* (Washington: Brookings Institution, 1953), pp. 391–92.

[102] *New York Times,* June 15, 1950, p. 49.

[103] *Report of the Thirty-Eighth National Foreign Trade Convention,* pp. xxxi–xxxii.

[104] *Ibid.,* pp. xxxii–xxxiv.

was favorable.[105] This was further indicated by the strong free trade bias of the Eisenhower administration—the businessman's administration.

CONGRESS

Congress continued to display a degree of discomfort in its post-war role in foreign economic policy. Although individual congressmen provided notable exceptions, the general reaction of Congress was negative regarding both foreign aid and trade liberalization.

Congress and Trade Liberalization

President Truman made the "peril point" clause a campaign issue in 1948, and the Democratic Eighty-first Congress dropped it when it renewed the Reciprocal Trade Agreements Act for two years in 1949. In 1951 the act was again extended for two years, but the peril point provision was put back, and the escape clause was included in the act itself for the first time. In 1953 President Eisenhower decided to await a report from his Commission on Foreign Economic Policy (Randall Commission); therefore he asked only for a one-year extension. Thus the 1949–53 period ended with Congress having successfully fended off executive branch efforts to win approval for the International Trade Organization and extensive reduction of trade barriers under the Reciprocal Trade Agreements program.

Between 1949 and 1953 the executive branch tried to get Congress to treat foreign aid and trade liberalization as alternatives for one another, but Congress persisted in treating them as unrelated matters.[106] Despite explicit statements by Dean Acheson pointing out that foreign aid could be reduced if friendly foreign nations could earn their dollars by selling their products in the United States, the legislative branch kept confronting the administration with those fallacious and hackneyed arguments for protection which every sophomore learns to refute.[107] The outlook for

[105] On this point see Almond, pp. 163–68.

[106] See for example, *New York Times*, December 2, 1949, p. 1.

[107] For Acheson's statement see *New York Times*, May 22, 1952, p. 4. For an illustration of the difficulty of communicating with Congress on trade and aid see the attempt by Senator J. W. Fulbright and Secretary of the Treasury Humphrey to discuss the matter with Senator Bourke Hickenlooper: Senate Committee on Foreign Relations, *Mutual Security Hearings*, 1953, pp. 172–76.

President Eisenhower's "trade not aid" program in 1953 was far from promising.

Congress and Foreign Aid

Congressional dislike of appropriating money for the executive branch to distribute to foreigners was reflected in its attitudes on the cost and control of the various aid programs.

When Secretary of State Acheson testified before Congress on the proposed Act for International Development, the legislators continually asked him to reassure them that the program would not cost much.[108] Senator Connally, Chairman of the Senate Foreign Relations Committee, reflected the prevailing legislative attitude in announcing that: "We've got sooner or later to cut this economic program. We can't go on supporting countries all over the world with handouts just because we like them—or any other reason."[109] During the 1951 Mutual Security hearings Connally observed, "This is the 'gimme' crowd that is up here today, on this whole program."[110] The executive branch required no special sensitivity to discern that new proposals for high-cost foreign aid programs would be unwelcome in Congress.

Congress also signified its desire to reduce the cost of foreign aid programs by its advocacy of loans instead of grants. In 1948 and 1949, despite administration protests, Congress required that a portion of Marshall Plan aid be in loan form. In 1951 a similar proviso, despite similar executive branch objections, was inserted in the Mutual Security Act of 1951. Both the Senate and House reports on the Mutual Security Act of 1951 indicated that Congress preferred loans to grants if public capital had to be transferred.[111] In 1952, however, Congress acquiesced to administration requests that the requirement that 10 per cent of Mutual Security funds be loans be repealed. The Congressional desire to confine

108 Committee on Foreign Relations, *Act for International Development Hearings*, 1950, pp. 15–16, 23.

109 *New York Times*, August 26, 1951, p. 1.

110 Senate Committee on Foreign Relations and Committee on Armed Services, *Mutual Security Act Hearings*, 1951, p. 669.

111 U.S., Congress, House, Committee on Foreign Affairs, *Mutual Security Act of 1951*, 82d Cong., 1st sess., 1951, Report No. 872, pp. 60 and 66; U.S., Congress, Senate, Committee on Foreign Relations and Committee on Armed Services, *The Mutual Security Act of 1951*, 82d Cong., 1st sess., 1951, Report No. 703, p. 40.

foreign aid to loans, while preventing the adoption of a tariff policy which would facilitate the servicing of these loans, was illustrated by the following statement of Representative John M. Vorys, leader of the drive to substitute loans for grants:

> I cannot find out that anybody on behalf of the United States is thinking about the problem that what we need is long-term loans so that during the course of the years we get paid back, not in a lot of industrial imports that we do not want that compete with our products and destroy our own industrial system, but in materials in which we are short.[112]

The attitude of the legislative branch, in short, remained hostile to trade and aid, especially grant aid.

PERCEPTION OF THE SITUATION AND SELECTION OF AN ALTERNATIVE

Although the policy makers continued to reject soft lending as a technique of statecraft, there were signs that they were reconsidering the alternative approaches to economic development.

SOFT LOANS: UNNECESSARY?

The American policy makers faced two questions on the necessity of soft loans. First, was stimulating the economic growth of less developed areas necessary for the accomplishment of broader foreign policy goals? And second, were soft loans necessary in order to promote growth at a rate judged to be satisfactory? American preoccupation with the Korean War and the rearmament of Europe decreased the relative importance of economic development as a goal of United States policy. To the extent that economic growth in underdeveloped areas was judged less important than other goals, the necessity for adopting special ways of spurring that growth was decreased as far as the policy makers were concerned.

There are, however, a number of reasons for believing that the decision makers' perceptions of the need for soft loans were changing with regard to both the importance of economic development and the use of soft loans in promoting that development.

---

[112] House Committee on Foreign Affairs, *Mutual Security Hearings,* 1952, p. 596.

Proposals on Economic Development

One reason for suspecting a revision of executive branch views on economic growth is that they were exposed to several proposals on economic development from domestic sources. Between 1949 and 1953 suggestions that economic aid to underdeveloped countries be increased came from such diverse sources as Senator Brien McMahon, Henry A. Wallace, James P. Warburg, Walter Reuther, and Representative Jacob Javits.[113] These proposals suggested transferring public capital to underdeveloped countries at a rate of from $5 billion to $13 billion annually. This transfer was to involve grants and long-term, low-interest loans.

In addition to these suggestions from outside the executive branch, proposals were generated within the executive. In 1950 President Truman asked Gordon Gray to prepare a report on foreign economic policy. The *Report to the President on Foreign Economic Policies* (Gray Report) was made public in November, 1950.[114] This report declared that the "economic stagnation, political unrest, and extreme poverty of most underdeveloped countries represent a growing threat to the rest of the free world."[115] Given this situation, the report continued, "the need for economic development and progress in these areas becomes daily more pressing, not only for their own welfare, but for the security and the well-being of all the free nations."[116] Although the Gray Report considered private investment desirable, it warned that "under present conditions a heavy reliance on public lending must be recognized as essential for an aggressive development program."[117] This public lending was to be done primarily through the IBRD, with the Export-Import Bank as an important supplement. We should note that the process of reasoning supporting the report's case for reliance on orthodox loans involved the assumption that debt servicing would be facilitated by reduction in American trade bar-

[113] For details on these proposals see *New York Times*, February 3, 1950, p. 2; April 15, 1950; April 30, 1950, p. 5; July 19, 1950, p. 21; September 20, 1950, p. 47; June 15, 1951.

[114] *Report to the President on Foreign Economic Policies* (Washington: U.S. Government Printing Office, 1950).

[115] *Ibid.*, pp. 8–9.   [116] *Ibid.*, p. 12.   [117] *Ibid.*, p. 13.

riers.[118] Despite this assumption, the report estimated a need for as much as $500 million per year in the form of grant aid for economic development—compared to the then current figure of $150 million.[119] Thus, a report prepared for the President argued as early as 1950 that the United States should more than double its grant aid, even if trade barriers were lowered and even if the United States joined the ITO. The report implied, without stating, that failure to liberalize trade would make reliance on conventional loans less feasible and would increase the need for grants.

Less than six months after the appearance of the Gray Report another report on economic development was published by the International Development Advisory Board under the chairmanship of Nelson Rockefeller—*Partners in Progress*.[120] This report stated the belief that "strengthening the economies of the underdeveloped regions and an improvement of their living levels must be considered a vital part of our own defense mobilization."[121] The Rockefeller Report recommended the establishment of an International Development Authority with initial funds of $500 million to be administered under a management contract with the International Bank. This organization was to make grants for projects "of basic importance to the development of underdeveloped countries that cannot be financed entirely on a loan basis."[122]

Although the Gray Report and the Rockefeller Report both suggested increased grants for economic development, neither advocated soft loans. The Republicans had barely arrived in Washington when executive branch advisors presented them with a report favoring soft loans.[123] The report noted that although it had been possible in the past to rely on private capital to finance such undertakings as railroads and power plants, "the temper and characteristics of the present period seem to make public financing of these enterprises necessary."[124] As this report conceived the situation:

[118] *Ibid.*, pp. 63–64, 76.   [119] *Ibid.*, p. 14.

[120] *Partners in Progress*, A Report to the President by the International Development Advisory Board, March, 1951.

[121] *Ibid.*, p. 1.   [122] *Ibid.*, pp. 72–73.

[123] *Economic Strength for the Free World*, A Report to the Director for Mutual Security by the Advisory Committee on Underdeveloped Areas, May, 1953.

[124] *Ibid.*, p. 29.

. . . the most serious limitation in the existing machinery for public investment is its lack of flexibility. The U.S. government and international agencies, financed largely by the United States, can make either outright grants or bankable dollar loans repayable in dollars. They cannot, however, provide funds for essential development projects on terms which lie between these two greatly disparate forms of financial assistance. In domestic private finance, many effective and ingenious financial instruments have been devised to cover the middle ground between straight bonds and ordinary equities, but in international public finance there is apparently no stop between pure gifts and strict loans. This middle ground needs to be explored. . . .[125]

The report went on to suggest "new and different financing instruments," including loans repayable over fifty or sixty years, loans without servicing requirements during an initial grace period, and dollar loans repayable in inconvertible currency.[126]

The Gray Report, the Rockefeller Report, and the report of the Advisory Committee on Underdeveloped Areas shared three characteristics which were especially relevant to later American policy: (1) All emphasized the importance of promoting economic development as a goal of foreign policy. (2) All advocated furnishing more public capital in forms other than orthodox loans. (3) All recommended working closely with the IBRD. Also, it should be noted that by the end of 1953 the executive branch had generated reports containing the basic ideas included later in the Development Loan Fund and the International Development Association.

External Pressures

The American policy makers were also exposed to proposals for expanding economic aid in the United Nations. These were discussed above; it suffices here to note that the UNEDA and SUNFED proposals involved soft loans but the IDA proposed in the United Nations involved grants. There is evidence that the policy makers felt that the underdeveloped countries were pressuring them to expand aid. In interviewing a former member of American delegations to the ECOSOC, Matecki found that the delegate believed that pressure for funds "was exerted upon us constantly at

[125] *Ibid.*, p. 30.

[126] *Ibid.*, p. 31.

all times."[127] Matecki indicated that other interviews elicited similar responses from State Department officials.

Policy makers' perceptions of the situation were also affected by the increased awareness of the "cold war" and the relevance of the underdeveloped areas to it. A concept of the "cold war" as a competition between two ways of life, with the uncommitted nations as targets, emerged during this period. We find executive branch statements referring to underdeveloped nations in cold war terms with increasing regularity. Thus perceptions of the competition with Russia and of the demands of underdeveloped countries were such as to encourage a reappraisal of the adequacy of American policy for promoting economic development.

Internal Prospects

It is probable that the policy makers' perceptions of the internal situation also pointed to the need for reconsideration of soft loans as a policy technique. Soft lending had been judged unnecessary in the 1943–48 period on the grounds that trade liberalization would enable underdeveloped countries to service enough conventional loans to assure a rate of development judged by American policy makers as adequate. Not only were they in the process of revising their estimates of an "adequate" rate of growth, during the 1949–53 period, but also they were coming to realize that Congressional attitudes considerably dimmed the prospects for lowering trade barriers. To the extent that aid in addition to hard loans had been judged necessary by the executive branch, they had favored grants, not soft loans. But it was becoming increasingly obvious that Congress disliked grants.

In sum, the United States policy makers were faced with this question: How does one transfer public capital abroad if commercial policy makes difficult, or even prohibits, servicing of conventional loans—without resorting to grants? Executive branch views of Congressional attitudes, United Nations pressure, and the nature of the "cold war" all increased the prospects for reconsideration of soft loans. The proposals generated by executive branch reports indicated that such a reappraisal was in fact going on.

---

[127] B. E. Matecki, *Establishment of the International Finance Corporation and United States Policy* (New York: Praeger, 1957), pp. 141–42.

Although the 1949–53 period was characterized by indications that the executive branch thought an increase in economic aid was desirable, the year 1953 was not so characterized. Both the Secretary of State and the Secretary of the Treasury testified in 1953 that they thought a reduction of economic aid was in order.[128] Never, since 1953, has the Secretary of State again taken this position.

SOFT LOANS: UNDESIRABLE

In spite of their differing estimates of the need for increasing the flow of public capital to underdeveloped areas, the Republican and Democratic administrations agreed that grants were preferable to soft loans in the event that special financing was necessary. The Truman administration opposed soft loans because of possible effects on the international capital market and international tensions generally. They feared that a heavy burden of external debt might lead to: (a) an increase in exchange and trade restrictions which would be inimical to private trade, (b) discrediting the entire lending process, and (c) default and consequent increase in tension.[129]

Similar arguments against soft loans were used by Harold Stassen, the new Director for Mutual Security, in 1953:

I would say this: In this program we are not recommending any item for a grant which we felt could properly be handled as a loan.

There is an area for loan operations and that should be on a basis of sound economics for the repayment of the loan. We feel that if it must, in fact, be a grant, it is better to face up to it as a grant a right [sic] away than to treat it as a loan and have it as a festering continuing problem between two countries when you know they cannot well repay it. You simply worsen the relationships by calling it a loan when it really has to be a grant.[130]

[128] Senate Committee on Foreign Relations, *Mutual Security Hearings*, 1953, pp. 100 and 170.

[129] See Senate Committee on Foreign Relations and Committee on Armed Services, *Mutual Security Act Hearings*, 1951, pp. 605 and 613; and House Committee on Foreign Affairs, *Mutual Security Hearings*, 1952, p. 597.

[130] Senate Committee on Foreign Relations, *Mutual Security Hearings*, 1953, p. 76.

SOFT LOANS: IMPOLITIC

In terms of domestic politics, expansion of economic aid in the form of grants or soft loans remained unpopular. The business community frowned on such proposals as the IDA, the SUNFED, and the UNEDA, put forth during this period. Business opposed public loans and grants of all kinds for reasons discussed previously.

Congress also lacked enthusiasm for economic aid programs calling for increased appropriations. The expansion of the lending authority of the Export-Import Bank in 1951 was facilitated by the fact that it required no appropriation, since this bank borrows most of its funds directly from the Treasury. The effort of one congressman to reassure himself on this point typified legislative attitudes: "There is no danger of this money coming out of direct taxation, this billion dollars, is there?"[131] The legislators left little doubt in anyone's mind that to the extent that public capital for economic development was to come from Congressional appropriations, Congress would prefer loans to grants.

IV. EFFECTIVENESS OF POLICY: 1949–53

RELIANCE ON DOMESTIC EFFORT

The efficacy of relying on domestic efforts was limited, as it was during the 1943–48 period, by the nature of the class structure in underdeveloped areas. The rich, who could invest, did not identify with the nationalistic sentiments in most countries; and they were unlikely to risk their money in response to patriotic exhortation. The poor could barely stay alive by consuming all their income and could hardly be expected to save much for investment.

PRIVATE INVESTMENT

The effectiveness of American policy for stimulating growth in underdeveloped areas during the 1949–53 period depended to a great extent upon the reduction of American trade barriers. Not only did the United States stay out of the ITO, but the executive branch had to fight in order to prevent tightening of trade restric-

[131] U.S., Congress, House, Committee on Banking and Currency, *Hearings, Increase of Lending Authority—Export-Import Bank*, 82d Cong., 1st sess., 1951, p. 16.

tions. The effect in underdeveloped nations of the trade liberalization which took place at Annecy (1949) and Torquay (1950–51) was curtailed by the exception of many agricultural commodities from the negotiating lists. It was, of course, agricultural commodities that many less developed nations wanted to sell in the American market.

There was also evidence that American trade barriers were impeding the flow of private capital to less developed countries. A survey by the Commerce Department in the early 1950's showed that American businessmen regarded trade barriers in the United States as one of the most important obstacles to private foreign investment.[132]

Thus, the restrictiveness of American trade barriers tended to undermine the efficacy of other United States techniques for promoting economic growth. To the extent that American trade barriers made it more difficult for the underdeveloped nations to earn foreign exchange than it otherwise would have been, they increased the need for outside help in financing a given level of imports, they discouraged foreign private investors, and they complicated the problem of servicing conventional foreign loans.

American attempts to get other governments to improve the "investment climates" in their countries also had limited effectiveness. The American threat not to provide more public capital lacked credibility because of the underdeveloped countries' perceptions that (1) the United States was becoming more interested in them as a result of the "cold war"; (2) the general international situation continued to be one characterized by flux; and (3) United States policy was apparently being reappraised, as indicated by appearance of the Gray and Rockefeller reports and by American experimentation with such new techniques as technical assistance and investment guaranties.

The usefulness of treaties to ensure favorable treatment of private investment was limited because the treaties tended to reflect a pre-existent harmony of viewpoints, with the resulting paradox that where treaty assurances were meaningful they would

---

[132] U.S., Bureau of Foreign Commerce, *Factors Limiting U.S. Investment Abroad (Part 2): Business Views on the U.S. Government's Role* (Washington: U.S. Government Printing Office, 1954), pp. 5, 11–13.

probably not have been necessary and where they were needed they either could not be negotiated or, if they were, often resulted in a document which satisfied neither side and, if anything, only increased the aura of resentment and mistrust so fatal to effective business relationships.[133]

The adoption of investment guaranties reduced the incentives for the underdeveloped nations to improve their "investment climates." By insuring private investors against risks of expropriation and inconvertibility, the United States was, in effect, compensating for the lack of a favorable "investment climate," thus undermining attempts to induce foreign governments to avoid expropriation and exchange restrictions.[134]

The efficacy of American efforts to bring about a change in foreign governments' attitudes toward private capital was curtailed in this period, as in the previous one, by the growing nationalism of underdeveloped nations. Three aspects of this nationalism—emphasis on heavy industry, government planning of the economy, and anti-colonialism—continued to reduce the probability that foreign governments would improve their treatment of private foreign investors. Since each of these aspects was discussed with regard to the 1943–48 period, the discussion is omitted here.

PUBLIC CAPITAL

According to United States policy, the main form of public capital provided to underdeveloped countries during this period was the orthodox loan. Such "hard" lending is more incompatible with high tariff policy than either soft loans or grants. As Sir Arthur Salter concluded, after studying the British experience with foreign lending, "A great creditor country, if it is to retain that position, is bound to buy more than it sells; a high level of exports will only be possible if imports are still higher."[135] The efficacy of reliance on conventional loans thus depended upon whether American commercial policy was such as to enable foreign debtors to earn

[133] Whitman, p. 15.

[134] This conflict between investment guaranties and improvement of "investment climates" is overlooked by Whitman in evaluating the effectiveness of guaranties. Cf. Whitman, pp. 76–77.

[135] Arthur Salter, *Foreign Investment* ("Essays in International Finance," No. 12 [Princeton, N.J.: Princeton University Press, 1951]), p. 53.

foreign exchange to service such loans—without resorting to measures drastic enough to undermine the domestic political support of the governments involved, e.g., extensive deflation.

This problem can be broken into two parts. In the first place, assuming a given degree of political willingness to service foreign debt, a high tariff policy by the United States inhibits the ability to earn foreign exchange to service debt. Secondly, foreign governments were not so willing to institute Draconian economic measures in order to pay external debts as they were before World War I. The spread of the concept of the welfare state made foreign governments even less willing to resort to domestic deprivation in order to pay debts. Thus, partly because of new attitudes toward the role of governments and partly because of its own commercial policy, the United States policy of relying on conventional public loans was limited in effectiveness.

POPULATION GROWTH

Added to the above-mentioned factors limiting the effectiveness of American efforts to spur economic growth was the ever increasing problem of population growth in underdeveloped areas. As technical assistance programs decreased the death rate in these countries, the rate of population growth tended to shoot up. There was even the gloomy prospect that technical assistance efforts would result in increasing the number of people dying of starvation rather than malaria. To the extent that population growth slowed the process of economic growth, technical assistance programs may have resulted merely in increasing the number of miserable people in the world and in delaying the improvement of the conditions of millions of human beings. Students of economic development have been reluctant to admit that humanitarian policies may conflict with rapid achievement of economic development. They have tended to argue, rather, that improved health will lead to greater productivity. The increased "productivity," however, may be more in terms of offspring than gross national product. It cannot be assumed, without investigation, that humanitarian policies are compatible with the promotion of economic growth. This is not the best of all possible worlds—as Malthus reminded us long ago.

IV   The Soft Loan Experiment
1954-57

I. WAS ECONOMIC GROWTH A GOAL
OF UNITED STATES POLICY?

The concern of American foreign policy makers for the economic development of underdeveloped areas was reflected in numerous public statements between 1954 and 1957. In 1954 Secretary of State John Foster Dulles, in a nationwide address, emphasized the need to find a way to make American capital available for economic development abroad.[1] When President Eisenhower announced plans to replace the Foreign Operations Administration with the International Cooperation Administration in 1955, he noted his desire to dispel the idea that concern for foreign economic development was merely a temporary goal. He wanted the new organization to reflect public recognition of the principle that "the security and welfare of the United States are directly related to the economic and social advancement of all people who share our concern for the freedom, dignity, and well-being of the individual."[2] The 1954-57 period ended with an administration request for the establishment of the Development Loan Fund, which was to be used for promoting long-term economic development in less developed areas. This fund was designed to lend credence to what the President called "a clear statement of our intention, in our own national interest, to help the people of less developed countries in their efforts to develop their economies."[3]

[1] Text of speech reprinted in *New York Times*, November 30, 1954, p. 4.

[2] *New York Times*, April 17, 1955, p. 2.

[3] "Mutual Security Program for 1958 Presented to Congress, Message of President Eisenhower," *Department of State Bulletin*, June 10, 1957, p. 923.

President Eisenhower had noted that both American welfare and security were related to foreign economic development. Although the promotion of economic development was still being justified partially in terms of the effect on American employment levels, the general level of trade, and access to raw materials, there was relatively less emphasis put on this aspect and relatively more put on the relation between economic development abroad and national security considerations.[4]

Economic growth in underdeveloped areas was viewed as related to American security in two main ways. First, there was the concept of the relationship between economic development and democracy. If we may pick out the thread of rather unsophisticated arguments on this point, the logic could be described thus: The United States will be more secure if other countries do not have Communist governments; a given country is less likely to turn to communism if there are alternative ways of achieving economic development than it is if no alternative exists; therefore the United States should promote economic development in order to decrease the probability that the country will adopt communism. In 1957 President Eisenhower summarized this position:

> I know of no precise relation between economic well-being and responsible political development. Yet continued poverty and despair are conditions that will foredoom moderate political life in these countries. If the best that these free governments can offer their peoples is endless hopelessness and grinding poverty, then these governments will surely fall. Certain it is that our peace, our political freedom, and our prosperity would not long survive the sweep of Communist despotism over these new nations.[5]

The second way in which economic growth was viewed as related to national security concerned the ability of underdeveloped nations to resist demands made on them by Communist nations.

[4] For examples of justifying economic development in terms of American prosperity see text of Eisenhower's message to Congress on foreign economic policy, *New York Times*, March 31, 1954, p. 18.

[5] "Mutual Security Program for 1958 Presented to Congress, Message of President Eisenhower," *Department of State Bulletin*, June 10, 1957, pp. 925–26. Cf. also text of Eisenhower's message to Congress on foreign economic policy: ". . . Economic growth in under-developed areas is necessary to lessen international instability growing out of the vulnerability of such areas to Communist penetration and subversion." *New York Times*, January 11, 1955, p. 16.

The logic of this position ran as follows: The less competition the Soviet Union has in providing economic aid to underdeveloped countries, the more "strings" it can attach to each transaction; therefore the United States should provide an alternative source of aid for economic development in order to weaken the bargaining position of the Soviet Union vis-à-vis the underdeveloped countries. Secretary of State Dulles suspected that Soviet economic aid programs were "offered as a Trojan horse to penetrate, and then take over, independent countries."[6] Dulles' desire to neutralize the political effectiveness of Soviet economic aid programs was reflected in a statement to a news conference in 1956: "We are in a contest in the field of economic development of underdeveloped countries which is bitterly competitive. Defeat in this contest could be as disastrous as defeat in an armaments race."[7] In sum, with regard to national security the United States was interested in promoting economic growth in order to enable the governments of underdeveloped nations to resist first, internal demands for adoption of a Communist type of system, and second, external demands by governments of Communist nations.

II. HOW TO PROMOTE ECONOMIC GROWTH: TECHNIQUES

During the 1954–57 period the importance of furnishing capital via public channels increased in importance relative to the techniques of relying on domestic efforts and stimulating the flow of private capital. The latter two, however, remained important as techniques for promoting economic development of less developed areas.

RELIANCE ON DOMESTIC EFFORT

As in previous periods, the United States continued to insist that economic growth was primarily a local matter and that American economic aid could not "be more than a marginal addition to any

[6] Quoted in *New York Times,* December 21, 1955, p. 14.

[7] *New York Times,* January 12, 1956, p. 10. Cf. also text of Dulles' speech on "U.S. and Soviet Foreign Economic Aid Strategy," *New York Times,* February 27, 1956, p. 6.

country's development efforts."[8] American deeds in this respect spoke louder than words. The United States steadfastly opposed the creation of an inter-American bank or a Special United Nations Fund for Economic Development during this period, and the public debate tended to focus on three alternatives: (a) abolition of economic aid, (b) aid amounting to one-half of 1 per cent of the GNP, and (c) aid amounting to 1 per cent of the GNP. A few "wild-eyed radicals," like Walter Reuther, advocated using 2 per cent of the GNP for economic aid, but even this plan would hardly have been large enough to relieve the underdeveloped countries of primary responsibility for their economic growth.[9]

STIMULATION OF PRIVATE CAPITAL FLOW

Promotion of economic growth by stimulating international private capital movements was once again a major technique of American statecraft. The executive branch tried to increase the flow of private capital by trade liberalization, improvement of foreign "investment climates," investment guaranties, and tax incentives.

TRADE LIBERALIZATION

In 1954 President Eisenhower summarized his proposed foreign economic policy in terms of four major parts:

Aid—which we wish to curtail
Investment—which we wish to encourage
Convertibility—which we wish to facilitate, and
Trade—which we wish to expand.[10]

He emphasized that these goals were interdependent, that each required the other. "I consider it essential that we achieve each of these objectives, which we must clearly understand are closely interlocked: as we curtail our aid, we must help to close the dollar gap by expanding our foreign investment and trade," President

[8] Statement by John Foster Dulles, U.S., Congress, Senate, Special Committee to Study the Foreign Aid Program, *Hearings, The Foreign Aid Program,* 85th Cong., 1st sess., 1957, p. 398. Cited hereafter as Senate Special Committee to Study the Foreign Aid Program, *Hearings,* 1957.

[9] For Reuther proposal see *New York Times,* March 25, 1956, p. 30.

[10] *New York Times,* March 31, 1954, p. 18.

Eisenhower said in his message to Congress.[11] The President's message to Congress on foreign economic policy in 1955 resembled that of the previous year. He again pointed out that expanding private foreign investment and curtailing of aid depended upon the liberalization of trade. He pledged to continue the search for ways to enlarge the outward flow of private capital, but he warned:

It must be recognized, however, that when American private capital moves abroad it properly expects to bring home its fair reward. This can only be accomplished in the last analysis by our willingness to purchase more goods and services from abroad in order to provide the dollars for these growing remittances. This fact is a further compelling reason for a fair and forward-looking trade policy on our part.[12]

Thus the position of the executive branch in 1954 and 1955 was that reduction of American trade barriers was desirable as a means of spurring private investment abroad and thereby reducing the need for governmental aid.

IMPROVEMENT OF "INVESTMENT CLIMATE"

With regard to economic growth in underdeveloped areas, Dulles indicated his belief that "the business of government is primarily to help create an investment climate such that private capital does the job."[13] In order to induce foreign governments to create such an environment the United States again employed advice, blackmail, and diplomacy.

Spokesmen for the United States rarely ignored an opportunity to advise underdeveloped nations on the advantages of the private enterprise system in general and especially on the benefits of relying on private investment to promote economic development. In 1954 Secretary of the Treasury George M. Humphrey told a gathering of finance ministers in Brazil, "I think that every one of us here can agree that in this field our greatest opportunity and our greatest responsibility lies in creating in our several countries those conditions which will give maximum access to the great reserves

11 *Ibid.*

12 *New York Times,* January 11, 1955, p. 16.

13 "Economic Assistance to Underdeveloped Areas," *Department of State Bulletin,* December 20, 1954, p. 958.

of private-investment capital that are available throughout the world."[14] We may rest assured that not everyone at the meeting agreed, but this did not deter Humphrey from pointedly informing the delegates that "economic development in those countries which have successfully established access to the world's supplies of private capital is going ahead with a rapidity that is astonishing."[15] On several other occasions American representatives also used international forums to advise underdeveloped nations on the desirability of adopting policies which would attract private foreign investment.[16]

Besides advice, the United States used blackmail. Those who cannot ignore the value connotations of "blackmail" may think of this as the specific refusal to provide alternative sources of capital for economic development, the rationale being that if underdeveloped nations could not obtain capital elsewhere, they would be forced (encouraged) to rely on private capital. The United States opposed creation of the SUNFED and a proposed inter-American development bank during the 1954–57 period. This policy of refusing to provide an alternative to private capital, however, was less important between 1954 and 1957 than it had been at any time since the end of World War II. During this period the United States was reluctantly making public capital available to an increasing degree through the Mutual Security Program, PL 480, the Development Loan Fund, and the International Finance Corporation.

In addition to advice and refusal to provide alternative sources of capital, the United States used diplomacy to bring about an improvement in foreign "investment climates." In his 1954 message on foreign economic policy, President Eisenhower promised to "give full diplomatic support, through our activities here and through our missions and representatives in the field, to the acceptance and understanding by other nations of the prerequisites

[14] "Economic Cooperation in the Americas," *Department of State Bulletin*, December 6, 1954, p. 866.

[15] *Ibid.*, p. 867.

[16] See the following statements made before organs of the United Nations: Roger W. Straus, "Benefits of Foreign Investment," *Department of State Bulletin*, January 3, 1955, pp. 19–22; and "Statement by Mr. Jacoby on the Financing of Economic Development," *Department of State Bulletin*, September 23, 1957, pp. 502–4.

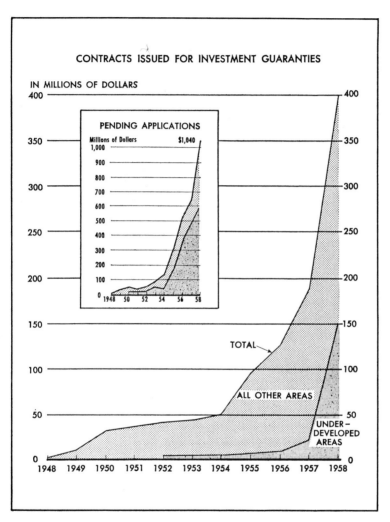

FIG. 3.—Contracts issued for investment guaranties by United States government. Source: Ralph I. Strauss, *Expanding Private Investment for Free World Economic Growth,* a special report prepared at the request of the Department of State, April, 1959, p. 61.

for the attraction of private foreign investment."[17] The 1955 message contained a similar pledge.[18]

INVESTMENT GUARANTY

During the 1954–57 period the United States continued its investment guaranty program begun in the 1949–53 period. Again it served not as a means for improving the "investment climate" but as compensation to private investors for the lack of a favorable "climate." We can see from Figure 3 that the applications pending for investments in underdeveloped areas rose sharply beginning in 1954, indicating that this technique was increasing in importance relative to the previous period.

Furnishing of Capital through Public Channels

Between 1954 and the end of 1957 the importance of the technique of furnishing public capital in order to promote economic development abroad grew rapidly. The Mutual Security Program was revamped in 1954, and the Agricultural Trade Development and Assistance Act (PL 480) was passed in the same year. The United States abandoned its opposition to the proposed International Finance Corporation (IFC) and in 1957 set up a $300 million fund to make soft loans for economic development. In delivering his final report, as the Foreign Operations Administration (FOA) ceased to exist, Harold Stassen described as one of the FOA's substantial achievements the squelching of the "illusion that private investment alone can supply, during the next few years, all of the foreign capital needs of the underdeveloped areas."[19] And Secretary of State Dulles declared in 1956 that risks in much of the world were such that private investors were reluctant to take them. "If capital is to be found," he cautioned, "a substantial part must be provided on a public basis which spreads the risk so that it is not appreciable in terms of any particular individual."[20]

[17] New York Times, March 31, 1954, p. 18.

[18] New York Times, January 11, 1955, p. 16.

[19] Harold E. Stassen, "The Progress of the Mutual Security Program and a Look Ahead: Excerpts from the Final Report to the President on the Foreign Operations Administration," Department of State Bulletin, August 15, 1955, p. 267.

[20] New York Times, February 27, 1957, p. 6.

Despite the greater emphasis on public capital the guiding principles of United States policy regarding this technique remained: (a) to keep the size small, (b) to insure decisive control by Americans, and (c) to avoid offending private investors. These principles must be regarded merely as standards to be approximated, not as goals to be actually implemented. The size of public capital movements was increasing; the United States did not insist on total control of all of its aid; and public capital always offends some private investors.

WHICH CHANNELS?

In expanding the transfer of capital through public channels the United States preferred bilateral as opposed to multilateral channels. New bilateral programs launched during the 1954–57 period included PL 480, the Development Loan Fund (DLF), and the soft lending provisions of the Mutual Security Act of 1954. In addition to these new programs the United States continued operation of its bilateral technical assistance program and the Export-Import Bank.

The IBRD retained its position as the American policy makers' favorite multilateral channel for distributing public capital. In 1954 President Eisenhower reiterated the United States position that the International Bank was "the primary institution for the public financing of economic development."[21] And in November of the same year the administration announced that it would support the proposal for the establishment of the IFC as an affiliate of the IBRD.[22]

Regarding multilateral channels other than the IBRD the United States still lacked enthusiasm. It did contribute to the United Nations Expanded Program of Technical Assistance, and in November, 1957, the United States proposed a new United Nations fund with about $100 million to spend on technical assistance each year. This fund eventually became the United Nations Special Fund. But the amount of American capital flowing to under-

[21] *New York Times*, March 31, 1954, p. 18.

[22] For a thorough discussion of the American policy see B. E. Matecki, *Establishment of the International Finance Corporation and United States Policy* (New York: Praeger, 1957).

developed areas through these United Nations channels did not begin to compare with the amounts moving in bilateral and IBRD channels. American opposition to expanding the flow of public capital through multilateral channels other than the IBRD was also indicated by its refusal to support proposals for the SUNFED and an inter-American development bank.[23] In submitting its views on the SUNFED proposal in 1954 the United States suggested that the United Nations might want to consider linking the proposed institution more closely with the IBRD or the IMF.[24]

ON WHAT TERMS?

During most of the 1954–57 period hard loans were the major form of public capital favored by American policy makers, but the establishment of the DLF in 1957 marked a clear increase in the importance of soft loans. Grants, too, continued as a technique for transferring capital to less developed areas.

Hard Loans

The American insistence throughout most of the 1954–57 period that the World Bank be regarded as the primary institution for public financing of economic development meant that conventional lending was of major importance. The new IFC also was set up as a "hard" lender, demanding dollar earnings on investments and refusing to make capital available on "bargain terms or at cut rates."[25] Other restrictions on IFC operations included the following:

1. IFC invests only in enterprises which are essentially private in character.

2. IFC invests only in association with private investors; it never finances all costs alone.

3. IFC will not invest if sufficient private capital is available on reasonable terms.

4. IFC will assume no management responsibilities.[26]

[23] See: "U.S. Position on Proposed Inter-American Bank," *Department of State Bulletin,* July 25, 1955, p. 140.

[24] United Nations, General Assembly, *Comments of Governments on the report of the Committee of Nine, submitted in accordance with General Assembly resolution 724 B (VIII)* (A/2646/Add.1, May 25, 1954), pp. 13–17.

[25] Matecki, p. 27.

[26] These are drawn from Matecki, pp. 25–27.

The effective limits on IFC operations, however, were not imposed by the above requirements; they were provided by three other factors. First, the organization was affiliated with the IBRD, an institution in which the United States wielded much power. If the United States did not like the IFC operations, it could do something about it through the IBRD. Second, IFC operations were unlikely to offend the United States since a conservative American businessman, R. L. Garner, was the president of IFC. It was not the charter limitations cited above that would limit IFC operations but Garner's interpretation thereof.[27] The third effective restriction on IFC activities resulted from the fact that its authorized capital amounted to only $100 million. In short, precautions had been taken with regard to IFC hard loan activities to keep it limited in size, keep it under American control, and minimize interference with private capital.

The Export-Import Bank was another major source of public capital on "hard" terms. Although its operations had been severely restricted by Secretary of the Treasury Humphrey in 1953, these restrictions were lifted in 1954 with President Eisenhower's announcement that the Export-Import Bank was once again in the development financing business and that the Bank would "consider on their merits applications for the financing of development projects, which are not being made by the International Bank, and which are in the special interest of the United States, are economically sound, are within the capacity of the prospective borrower to repay and within the prudent loaning capacity of the bank."[28] One-half billion dollars were added to the Bank's lending authority in 1954, bringing its total authorization to $5 billion. In 1955 the Assistant Secretary of State for Inter-American Affairs further emphasized the role of the Export-Import Bank:

We have assured the other American Republics that through the Export-Import Bank we shall do our utmost to satisfy all applications for sound economic development loans where the funds are not reasonably available from private sources or from the International Bank. This important commitment means simply that no economic develop-

---

[27] Matecki fails to point this out. He discusses the issue as if Garner really were bound by the ambiguous language in the IFC Charter. Cf. pp. 25–29.

[28] *New York Times,* March 31, 1954, p. 18.

ment loan is going to be turned down for lack of funds. The level of governmental lending for this purpose in the hemisphere is going to be determined largely by Latin America itself, because it will depend upon the volume of sound loan applications which are filed.[29]

Grants

In 1954 President Eisenhower subscribed to the "principle that economic aid on a grant basis should be terminated as soon as possible consistent with our national interest."[30] Although grant aid for economic development was available throughout the 1954-57 period, its days appeared to be numbered. The United Nations Expanded Program of Technical Assistance, the Mutual Security Program, and Public Law 480 were the main sources of grant aid during this period. The Mutual Security Program decreased the amount of economic aid given in the form of grants from 94 per cent for the period beginning in July, 1952, and ending in July, 1955, to 78 per cent for the period between July, 1955, and July, 1958.[31]

Soft Loans

The most significant innovation in American techniques for spurring economic development during this period was soft lending. Although, as Robert Asher has pointed out, loans repayable in inconvertible currency were not unknown before 1954, they acquired new respectability about that time.[32] Whereas the United States policy makers had previously denounced soft loans, during the 1954-57 period they began to argue that loans repayable in foreign exchange, such as those made by the IBRD and the Export-Import Bank, could not meet many "development needs"; and they concluded that "for the time being at least, there is room for grants

[29] Henry F. Holland, "U.S. Relations With the American Republics," *Department of State Bulletin*, April 11, 1955, p. 603.

[30] *New York Times*, March 31, 1954, p. 18.

[31] Derived from U.S., Congress, House, Committee on Foreign Affairs, *Background Material on Mutual Defense and Development Programs: Fiscal Year 1965*, 88th Cong., 2d sess., 1964, Committee Print, p. 24.

[32] Robert E. Asher, *Grants, Loans, and Local Currencies: Their Role in Foreign Aid* (Washington: Brookings Institution, 1961), p. 50.

and local-currency loans as well."[33] The three most important soft loan programs were those connected with the Mutual Security Act of 1954, PL 480, and the Development Loan Fund.

Mutual Security Program.—Two provisions of the Mutual Security Act of 1954, sections 402 and 505, furnished the legislative authority for much of the American soft lending during this period. Section 505 authorized the executive branch to accept repayment of loans in foreign currencies; and in addition, it required that not less than $200 million of the Mutual Security funds be made available only for loans. Section 201 of the Act specifically required that 30 per cent of the development assistance to Bolivia, India, the Near East, and Africa take the form of loans. Thus the Mutual Security Act of 1954 both required the use of loans and authorized the acceptance of inconvertible currency in lieu of foreign exchange as repayment.

In 1955 Dulles indicated that "pretty good progress" had been made in moving from the grant to the loan concept, and he noted that a standardized formula calling for repayment in local currencies had been adopted for loans under the Mutual Security Program.[34] Loans under section 505 were available on the following terms: (1) The borrower could take up to forty years to repay. (2) Repayment in local currency at 4 per cent interest or in dollars at 3 per cent was possible. (3) No payments of interest or principal were required during the first three years of the loan.[35]

The requirement that a minimum of $200 million be loaned was retained until the DLF was established by the Mutual Security Act of 1957. In 1955, however, the section 201 loan requirement was lifted in response to arguments by executive branch spokesmen that the legislative requirement made it more difficult to get other nations to accept loans since they tended to regard the 30 per cent figure as a maximum rather than a minimum. However, when John B. Hollister, director of the International Cooperation

[33] Robert R. Bowie, "United States Foreign Economic Policy," *Department of State Bulletin,* July 23, 1956, p. 141.

[34] U.S., Congress, Senate, Committee on Foreign Relations, *Hearings, Mutual Security Act of 1955,* 84th Cong., 1st sess., 1955, pp. 34–35. Cited hereafter as Senate Committee on Foreign Relations, *Mutual Security Hearings, 1955.*

[35] See the testimony of Harold Stassen, *ibid.,* p. 47; see also *New York Times,* April 14, 1957, p. 48.

Administration (ICA), admitted in 1956 that the results of efforts to increase the volume of loans under the Mutual Security Program had been "disappointing,"[36] Congress responded by inserting a requirement that at least 80 per cent of development assistance be loans.

Another provision of the Mutual Security Act of 1954 which authorized soft loans was section 402. This section replaced a similar provision in the Mutual Security Act of 1951 as amended in 1953, known as section 550. Section 402 of the Mutual Security Act of 1954 required the executive branch to use no less than $350 million of the funds allocated for Mutual Security to purchase surplus agricultural commodities. These commodities could then be granted or "sold" for inconvertible currencies to other nations in alleged furtherance of the goals of the Mutual Security Program. The local currencies derived from such sales could be granted or loaned to nations participating in the Mutual Security Program. Insofar as the over-all transactions under section 402 resulted in the transfer of real goods and services from the United States to other nations in return for I O U's payable in local currency the requisites for calling such actions soft lending were fulfilled. Insofar as the local currency proceeds of "sales" were granted to foreign nations, the total transaction must be considered a transfer of real goods in return for nothing—a grant.[37]

The amount earmarked for use under section 402 fell in 1955 to $300 million, in 1956 to $250 million, and in 1957 to $175 million. The executive branch indicated that it was finding it increasingly difficult to get underdeveloped nations to accept surplus agricultural commodities in lieu of dollars which they could spend in a number of ways. It even became necessary to require each recipi-

---

[36] U.S., Congress, Senate, Committee on Foreign Relations, *Hearings, Mutual Security Act of 1956*, 84th Cong., 2d sess., 1956, p. 116. Cited hereafter as Senate Committee on Foreign Relations, *Mutual Security Hearings*, 1956.

[37] Raymond F. Mikesell notes that under the PL 480 program "the acceptance of foreign currencies in exchange for surplus agricultural commodities is in itself a credit transaction." Mikesell, however, fails to distinguish between transactions in which local currency is loaned with the expectation that the same currency will be used in making repayment and transactions in which real goods and services are transferred in return for local currency. By using the term "soft loan" to apply to both types of transactions Mikesell needlessly confuses the issue. Raymond F. Mikesell (ed.), *U.S. Private and Government Investment Abroad* (Eugene: University of Oregon Press, 1962), pp. 292–93.

ent nation to take specified amounts of aid in the form of surpluses. Despite such measures, the ICA reported in 1956 that it had been unable to meet its minimum section 402 quota for fiscal year 1956 (year ending July 1, 1956).[38]

Public Law 480.—The summer of 1954 also marked the passing of the Agricultural Trade Development and Assistance Act, which authorized additional "sales" of surplus agricultural commodities for soft currency. The PL 480 program was conceived primarily as a surplus disposal program rather than as a foreign aid program, but it rapidly became an important technique of United States policy for promoting economic development. Initially this act authorized "sales" of surplus agricultural commodities valued at $700 million in terms of CCC investment costs over a three-year period ending in June, 1957, but this authorization for local currency "sales" was increased in July, 1955, to $1.5 billion and in July, 1956, to $3 billion. The most significant difference between PL 480 and section 402, from the point of view of the executive branch, was that Congress did not appropriate additional money to cover the purchase of surplus commodities under section 402 but instead provided that funds appropriated for the Mutual Security Program should be used.[39] PL 480, on the other hand, constituted an addition to existing foreign aid funds.

The major component of the PL 480 program was the "sale" of surplus commodities for local currencies. During this period over half of the local currency proceeds were loaned to foreign nations on terms allowing repayment in local currency.[40] Insofar as the United States ended up with local currency repayable I O U's, in return for a transfer of real resources to other nations, soft lending had occurred.

[38] This writer has found no discussion of these problems which is more useful than that contained in a statement submitted to Congress by the ICA, "Effect of Surplus Agricultural Commodity Legislation on the Mutual Security Program," Senate Committee on Foreign Relations, *Mutual Security Hearings,* 1956, pp. 951–71. The above discussion of section 402 draws on this memorandum.

[39] ICA Memorandum, Senate Committee on Foreign Relations, *Mutual Security Hearings,* 1956, p. 952.

[40] U.S., Congress, Senate, *Foreign Aid Program: Compilation of Studies and Surveys,* prepared under the direction of the Special Committee to Study the Foreign Aid Program, Study No. 5, "Agricultural Surplus Disposal and Foreign Aid," prepared by the National Planning Association, 85th Cong., 1st sess., 1957, Senate Doc. 52, p. 388.

We should be careful in evaluating the amount of "foreign aid" involved in surplus commodity disposal programs. We can identify at least four plausible measurements for such aid, the first of which is valuation at CCC investment costs. This is the most commonly used, and it results in the highest estimate of foreign aid costs, since it is based on the artificially supported prices paid to American farmers. The second concept values them at current world market prices, which are lower than CCC costs. Indeed, if the goods could be sold on the world market above CCC costs, there would be no need for the CCC price support program. A third concept, resulting in an even lower valuation of surplus commodity "aid," is based on an estimate of the world market prices that would have prevailed if American surplus commodities had been sold on world markets. And the fourth way is in terms of "opportunity costs"—the cost measured in terms of the sacrifice of alternatives involved in carrying out disposal programs. This raises the startling possibility of a zero cost since much of the money spent as "foreign aid" in the form of surplus commodities would have been spent by the CCC even in the absence of a foreign aid program.[41] When savings on storage costs are accounted for, it is even conceivable that such "foreign aid" costs could be negative. In other words, the United States might actually save money by getting rid of such commodities under certain circumstances. Thus, we must be wary in attaching significance to estimates of the magnitude of surplus disposal programs in terms of dollars.

Development Loan Fund.—Since the DLF was established by the Mutual Security Act of 1957, we could argue that it should be discussed as part of that program. Its separate consideration here is not intended to divorce it from the Mutual Security Program but merely to emphasize its importance as a foreign policy technique. With the establishment of the DLF the United States became firmly committed to the proposition that soft lending was to be a major technique for stimulating foreign economic develop-

41 For discussion of the problems of evaluating agricultural surpluses as foreign aid see Asher, pp. 58–59; and John A. Pincus, *Economic Aid and International Cost Sharing* (Baltimore: Johns Hopkins Press, 1965), pp. 113–45. In 1959 the President's agricultural special assistant admitted that "it may cost approximately as much to prevent the production of a bushel of wheat as it does to grow the bushel and move it abroad even if no payment is received." Don Paarlberg, "Food for Peace," *Department of State Bulletin,* November 9, 1959, p. 675.

ment. The DLF, as it finally emerged from the Congressional battleground, was a $300 million fund under State Department con-
trol authorized to make loans, credits, or guaranties, or to engage
in "other financing operations or transactions" excluding the making of grants.[42] It was understood, however, that the bulk of DLF
activities would consist of lending dollars and being repaid in inconvertible currencies.

In accordance with the American principle of keeping public
capital small, Congress appropriated only $300 million instead of
the $500 requested by the administration and authorized by the
foreign affairs committees in the House and Senate—a 40 per cent
cut. Administration efforts to expand the flow of public capital via
the DLF were also stymied by Congressional rejection of a plan
for circumventing the appropriations committees, traditional
"guardians" of the public treasury.[43] In 1957 Congress further
dimmed prospects for bigger DLF operations by ignoring a request for $750 million for fiscal year 1960 and reducing the amount
authorized in response to a request for $750 for fiscal year 1959 to
$625 million.

The terms on which the DLF was to provide public capital were
as follows: Loans repayable in local currency were to be the
primary technique. Such loans were not to be made if "other free
world sources" were willing to provide financing on "reasonable
terms." The Mutual Security Act of 1957 also required that the
fund be administered "so as not to compete with private investment capital, the Export-Import Bank or the International Bank
for Reconstruction and Development." The act admonished the
fund's administrators to consider the "economic and technical
soundness of the activity to be financed." Presumably this ruled
out financing perpetual motion machines, "sky hooks," and the
like; what else was eliminated by such ambiguous criteria is anyone's guess. A third legislative criterion for allocating DLF funds

[42] For texts and legislative history of the Mutual Security Acts and Public Law
480 see U.S., Congress, House and Senate, Committee on Foreign Affairs and Committee on Foreign Relations, *Legislation on Foreign Relations: With Explanatory
Notes*, 86th Cong., 2d sess., 1960, Joint Committee Print. Cited hereafter as *Legislation on Foreign Relations*, 1960.

[43] Cf. Richard F. Fenno, Jr., "The House Appropriations Committee as a Political System: The Problem of Integration," *American Political Science Review*, LVI
(June, 1962), 310–24.

limited financing to activities giving "reasonable promise of contributing to the development of economic resources." Since the executive branch was to be the judge of what constituted alternative sources of capital on "reasonable terms," "economic and technical soundness," and "reasonable promise" of contributing to economic growth, the practical limits on administration of the DLF were the size of the appropriations and the expectations of the administrators regarding the effect of current operations on future appropriations.

SUMMARY

Although reliance on local efforts and stimulation of private investment remained important foreign policy techniques during the 1954–57 period, their importance relative to the transfer of public capital was less than it had been at any time since World War II. Between January, 1954, and December, 1957, the United States steadily increased its emphasis on moving capital through public channels in order to promote economic development in less developed areas. Hard loan activities were expanded by the establishment in 1956 of the IFC. The most significant change in American policy, however, was the adoption of soft lending as a major technique for financing economic growth. The United States developed soft loan operations during this period under sections 505 and 402 of the Mutual Security Act of 1954, under Public Law 480, and under the provisions of the Mutual Security Act of 1957 setting up the DLF. By the end of 1957 soft loans were well established among the techniques of American foreign policy for promoting economic development.

III. WHY TECHNIQUES WERE CHOSEN OR REJECTED

EXTERNAL SETTING: 1954–57

GENERAL INTERNATIONAL SITUATION

The most important change in the international milieu of American foreign policy makers during this period was the shifting strategy of the Communist nations. Soon after the death of Stalin there were signs that the U.S.S.R. would increase its use of economic techniques of foreign policy. Trade agreements, loans, and technical assistance were the three main elements in the new economic strategy.

At the close of 1953 Communist bloc trade agreements with other countries numbered 113, but by the end of 1957 this figure exceeded 200.[44] The interest of the Communists in the less developed areas was indicated by the concentration of these new agreements in such areas. Whereas in 1953 only one-third of the bloc trade agreements were with underdeveloped nations, this had increased to more than one-half by late 1956.[45] The willingness of the Soviet bloc to export to non-Communist countries items of capital equipment such as machinery and railroad equipment represented a departure from previous export policy.

A second aspect of the new economic strategy was the adoption of a technical assistance program. At the beginning of the 1954–57 period the U.S.S.R. abandoned its policy of boycotting the United Nations technical assistance activities and, in addition, began to experiment with bilateral technical assistance. Technical assistance programs, according to a State Department estimate, brought over 2,300 bloc technicians to nineteen less developed countries during the last half of 1957, while another 2,000 technicians and students from such countries went to the bloc for study during 1957. Soviet bloc technical assistance tended to concentrate on a few nations, with about 80 per cent of all bloc technicians in Egypt, Syria, India, Indonesia, and Afghanistan.[46]

Besides trade agreements and technical assistance, the Com-

[44] Information on the expansion of trade agreements is drawn from U.S., Congress, Senate, *Foreign Aid Program: Compilation of Studies and Surveys,* prepared under the direction of the Special Committee to Study the Foreign Aid Program, Study No. 8, "Foreign Assistance Activities of the Communist Bloc and Their Implications for the United States," prepared by the Council for Economic and Industry Research, 85th Cong., 1st sess., 1957, Senate Doc. 52, pp. 619–766. Cited hereafter as "Foreign Assistance Activities of the Communist Bloc," Study No. 8, *Senate Studies on Foreign Aid Program,* 1957.

[45] During the 1954–56 period the Communist bloc signed trade agreements with Afghanistan, Iran, Egypt, Argentina, India, Greece, Lebanon, Uruguay, Iceland, Yugoslavia, Burma, Syria, Yemen, Pakistan, and Indonesia. *Ibid.,* p. 639.

[46] U.S., Department of State, *The Sino-Soviet Economic Offensive in the Less Developed Countries,* European and British Commonwealth Series, No. 51, 1958, p. 29.

munist bloc began to use loans to woo the underdeveloped nations. Early in 1958 the State Department reported that since 1954 the Soviet bloc had concluded long-term loan agreements with fourteen underdeveloped countries outside the bloc which provided for the extension of $1.9 billion for purchase of goods and services from the bloc.[47] About $1 billion of this represented loans for economic purposes to countries other than Yugoslavia. Soviet bloc aid usually took the form of loans repayable at 2.5 per cent interest over a period ranging from ten to thirty years. As with technical assistance, bloc aid focused on a few "key" areas, as is indicated by the concentration of more than 95 per cent of bloc credits in Yugoslavia, India, Afghanistan, Egypt, Syria, and Indonesia during this period.[48] Although loans by the bloc were not usually repayable in local currency, as were those from the American DLF, the bloc was willing to accept repayment in goods and services, a move which the United States found it difficult to imitate because of Congressional hostility to an influx of foreign products.[49]

The significance of the new Communist interest in economic techniques of statecraft for the evolution of American policy toward underdeveloped nations lay in its effect on the perceptions by American policy makers of the nature of the Communist "threat" and in its effect on the efficacy of the American techniques of statecraft then in use. These effects will be discussed later.

UNITED NATIONS

Between January, 1954, and January, 1958, the United Nations continued to provide forums for the underdeveloped nations to press their demands for establishment of an international organization which would expand the flow of public capital to such nations on terms more lenient than those offered by either the IBRD

[47] Ibid., p. 21.　　　　　　　[48] Ibid.

[49] For further discussion of economic aid from the Soviet bloc see Joseph S. Berliner, Soviet Economic Aid (New York: Praeger, 1958); Charles Wolf, Jr., Foreign Aid: Theory and Practice in Southern Asia (Princeton, N.J.: Princeton University Press, 1960), pp. 383–400; and Alvin Z. Rubinstein, The Soviets in International Organizations: Changing Policy Toward Developing Countries, 1953–1963 (Princeton, N.J.: Princeton University Press, 1964).

or the Export-Import Bank. Throughout this period the underdeveloped nations continually reminded the richer nations, especially the United States, of the alleged "need" for such an institution; and although we could hardly imagine an increase in the vigor with which they pressed their demands relative to the 1949–53 period, neither can we detect less vigor during the 1954–57 period.

The United States and other rich nations were able to beat back the effort to set up the SUNFED at the eighth session of the General Assembly in 1953, but the proponents of the SUNFED had pushed through a resolution asking governments to reconsider their positions and appointing Raymond Scheyven to survey governments and report to the General Assembly in 1954.[50] In submitting its comments to Scheyven the United States stated little other than its belief that the time was "not propitious for the establishment of such a fund."[51] The United States did not want to appear committed to the SUNFED by commenting on specific aspects of it, but insisted instead that efforts to delineate the organization and administration of such a fund were "premature."[52]

In his report to the General Assembly, Scheyven argued that "many forms of infrastructure investment *have to be regarded* as non-self-liquidating," and that since the "bulk of the infrastructure investment *cannot* be financed out of private capital," the assistance of "public capital *will have to be* called in."[53] He supported the SUNFED proposal and pointed out that the nations fell into three groups with respect to their positions on the fund. The first, including Canada, the United States, West Germany, Sweden,

[50] United Nations General Assembly Resolution 724 B (VIII), December 7, 1953.

[51] United Nations A/2646/Add.1, May 25, 1954, p. 13.

[52] *Ibid.*, p. 14. In debate in the Second Committee of the General Assembly in the fall of 1954, the United States showed a similar reluctance to discuss specific aspects of the SUNFED proposal. United Nations A/C.2/SR. 302, October 25, 1954, pp. 77–78.

[53] United Nations General Assembly, Ninth Session, *Official Records*, Supplement No. 19, "Special United Nations Fund for Economic Development," Final Report by Raymond Scheyven, Prepared in Pursuance of United Nations General Assembly Resolution 724 B (VIII), (A/2728, 1954), p. 9. Italics mine. Note the concealing of the issue of governmental attitudes toward private capital in underdeveloped nations by the use of the italicized words. He is assuming that such attitudes are not likely to change, an assumption which United States business and governmental circles were still reluctant to accept.

United Kingdom, and New Zealand, insisted on internationally supervised world-wide disarmament as a prerequisite to the establishment of the SUNFED. A second group, including most of the potential recipients of aid, supported the proposal without qualification. And a third group represented a split in the solid front of potential net contributors to the fund. It included such nations as Denmark, Italy, Norway, Netherlands, France, Japan, Belgium, and Luxembourg. These nations indicated that they were willing to consider the SUNFED proposal without waiting for universal disarmament.[54] Although some of these nations may have been counting on American intransigence to allow them to curry favor with underdeveloped nations without cost, the result was still further isolation of the United States in its opposition to the SUNFED. Just how embarrassing this was to the United States is difficult to judge, however, since any attempt by the United States to divert attention from itself by pointing to other nations' opposition to the SUNFED was likely to be about as effective as an elephant trying to hide in a flock of chickens.

In December, 1954, the United States changed its position on the IFC proposal but maintained its opposition to the SUNFED. The proponents of the fund refused to accept the IFC as a substitute for the fund, and they succeeded in mustering support for a resolution which: (a) expressed hope that the SUNFED would be set up as soon as practicable, (b) extended the appointment of Scheyven for another year, (c) urged governments to review their positions with regard to extending material support to the SUNFED, and (d) asked Scheyven to prepare a further report giving a full and precise picture of the form, functions, and responsibilities which such a special fund might have and to present it to the tenth session of the General Assembly.[55]

In March, 1955, Scheyven gathered another committee of experts, including the distinguished Dutch economist Jan Tinbergen, to re-examine the SUNFED proposal "in a spirit of realism."[56] The

[54] *Ibid.*, pp. 15-16.

[55] United Nations General Assembly Resolution 822 (IX), December 11, 1954.

[56] United Nations General Assembly, Tenth Session, *Official Records,* Supplement No. 17, "Special United Nations Fund for Economic Development," Report Prepared in Pursuance of United Nations General Assembly Resolution 822 (IX), (A/2906, 1955), p. 1.

guiding considerations of the committee were the recognition of the United Nations interest in the SUNFED, the difficulty of securing the necessary financial resources, and the hostility of several governments to creation of a new international bureaucracy. In a report exhibiting a level of economic sophistication which was unusually high for literature on this subject emanating from the United Nations, the committee recommended two major changes in the SUNFED as proposed by the Committee of Nine in 1953. In the first place, they favored emphasis on grants instead of loans, and they specifically objected to the loans on indefinite terms proposed by the Committee of Nine. They considered it "inadvisable to retain the provision made for flexibility and renegotiation of loans" contained in the original report.[57] The committee did, however, look with more favor on loans with definite terms of repayment which could be serviced in local currency. They emphasized that a particularly important aspect of such loans was that "contributions might be more readily given if the Fund made loans of this type"—a thinly veiled indication that they were well aware of the attitude of American legislators toward grants and soft loans.[58] They therefore recommended that contributing nations be allowed to specify whether they wished their contributions to be used to give grants or loans repayable in local currency.[59]

The second major change in the 1953 report advocated by the Scheyven committee concerned control of the organization. Perceiving that underdeveloped nations disliked voting arrangements weighted according to financial contribution, such as those used by the IBRD, as much as the richer nations preferred such arrangements, the Scheyven committee tried to compromise by retaining the provision for equal representation on the executive board of big contributors and likely recipients, while at the same time establishing closer links with the IBRD. Not only did the committee retain the original recommendation that the president of the IBRD should attend all meetings of the executive board in an advisory capacity, but also it added a proposal for a joint committee, composed of the Secretary-General of the United Nations, the Director-General of the Fund, and the president of the IBRD, to co-ordinate fund activities with the IBRD. When the Scheyven

[57] *Ibid.*, p. 10.   [58] *Ibid.*, p. 9.   [59] *Ibid.*

committee supported integration of IBRD and SUNFED operations on the grounds of a more economic use of resources, they
demonstrated political acumen. They noted that one advantage of
having the president of the IBRD participate in administering the
SUNFED was that he could satisfy contributors that the SUN-
FED was not competing with private capital.[60] In other words,
they acknowledged the possibility, to use the language of social
science, that the conservative IBRD management could perform
a "legitimizing" function vis-à-vis the SUNFED.

The United States again opposed the SUNFED proposal in
1955.[61] Noting, as it had in 1952, that 1956 was an election year in
the United States, the General Assembly established an *ad hoc*
committee composed of representatives of sixteen nations, to be
appointed by the President of the General Assembly, to study the
matter of the SUNFED further and to deliver a final report to the
twenty-third session of the ECOSOC, which would be after the
eleventh session of the General Assembly in 1956.[62] Thus, the General Assembly would not get to consider this report until its twelfth
session in the fall of 1957.

As the fall of 1957 approached there were signs of growing im-
patience by the underdeveloped nations with the United States
refusal to support the SUNFED. Until that time they had been
willing to postpone establishment of the institution in hopes that
the United States could be persuaded to support it. In July, 1957,
however, debate in the ECOSOC indicated that SUNFED supporters were prepared to go ahead with or without American help.
A resolution was passed urging the General Assembly to take the
necessary steps to establish the fund.[63]

In the Second Committee of the General Assembly the United
States fended off the SUNFED drive by offering a compromise
measure calling for establishment of a Special Projects Fund as an

[60] *Ibid.*, pp. 14–16. On the recommendations of the Scheyven Committee in 1955
see also Scheyven's statement before the Second Committee of the General Assembly, United Nations A/C.2/187, October 28, 1955, pp. 2–13.

[61] See statement by Congressman Brooks Hays before the Second Committee of
the General Assembly, United Nations A/C.2/SR. 370, November 8, 1955, pp.
122–23.

[62] United Nations General Assembly Resolution 923 (X), December 9, 1955.

[63] United Nations ECOSOC Resolution 662 B (XXIV), July 31, 1957.

integral part of the Expanded Program of Technical Assistance by January, 1959. Although the SUNFED advocates suspected that the United States was trying to give them a watered-down substitute for their pet project, they acquiesced and voted approval of a United Nations Special Fund—with the condition that "as and when the resources prospectively available are considered by the General Assembly to be sufficient to enter into the field of capital development, principally the development of the economic and social infrastructure of the less developed countries, the Assembly shall review the scope and future activities of the Special Fund and take such action as it may deem appropriate."[64] As the 1954–57 period ended, it was clear that the less developed nations were not going to let the richer nations, especially the United States, forget about their development problems; nor were they going to abandon efforts to set up an international grant and soft loan disbursing institution.

INTERNATIONAL BANK

The activities of the World Bank will be discussed in terms of its general lending policies, its role as critic of American policy, and its position regarding soft loans.

Eugene Black continued as president of the IBRD from 1954 to 1957, and the broad outlines of Bank policy were similar to those of the preceding years. On several occasions Bank officials indicated that strategic nonlending was still important in Bank operations. The *Ninth Annual Report* stated that the Bank was interested in more than merely being repaid: "The Bank's interests . . . go considerably beyond those of the more usual type of lending institution, and the achievement of its objectives cannot be ensured by safeguards dealing only with questions of debt service."[65]

The paternalistic attitude of the Bank, which was necessarily part of its strategic nonlending policy, continued to cause resentment on the part of potential loan recipients. The annual meeting of the board of governors in 1956 provided some especially heated debate on this subject. One of the Bank's governors criticized the

[64] United Nations General Assembly Resolution 1219 (XII), December 14, 1957.

[65] International Bank for Reconstruction and Development, *Ninth Annual Report, 1953–1954,* p. 9.

Bank for refusing to lend to countries in default—he accused the IBRD of becoming an "international debt collector."[66] Others objected to the Bank's policy of insisting on changes in internal policies as a condition for the granting of loans. Black flatly rejected all of these criticisms by saying, "We do not think it is the Bank's role to help governments postpone the difficult decisions needed to mobilize local resources."[67]

From the viewpoint of the underdeveloped nations such an attitude amounted to an attempt to blackmail them into "mobilizing local resources" in the way Mr. Black thought most desirable. And Black made it clear that he still regarded private enterprise as the best means of mobilizing local resources. "Governments must cease just tolerating private business," he told a conference of businessmen. "They must welcome its contribution and go out of their way to attract it. And there must be a fundamental reversal of the traditionally hostile attitude by Government and peoples alike toward the profit motive."[68]

In brief, the attitudes of Bank officials toward state ownership, inflation, default, and private enterprise, as they appeared in public statements, furnished little evidence of change in the IBRD policy of strategic nonlending.

The IBRD also continued to criticize American commercial policy with regard to its effects on long-term economic development. Black announced to the Ninth Annual Meeting of the Board of Governors: "I share the disappointment of many of you that the United States Government did not find it possible to put into effect this year the trade liberalization features of its foreign economic policies, and I welcome the President of the United States' recent statement, . . . that it is his intention to give high priority to them in next year's legislative program."[69] We should also note that, as in previous years, this statement amounted to approval of executive proposals and condemnation of Congressional handling of such proposals.

[66] *New York Times*, September 28, 1956, p. 38; and September 26, 1956, p. 49.

[67] International Bank for Reconstruction and Development, Eleventh Annual Meeting of the Board of Governors, *Summary Proceedings*, 1956, pp. 12–13.

[68] Quoted in *New York Times*, October 15, 1957, p. 45.

[69] International Bank for Reconstruction and Development, Ninth Annual Meeting of the Board of Governors, *Summary Proceedings*, 1954, p. 11.

During the 1949–53 period IBRD officials had repeatedly deprecated soft lending as a technique for stimulating economic development.[70] The Bank's position on soft loans gradually changed in the 1954–57 period. Before presenting his 1955 report to the General Assembly, Raymond Scheyven contacted Black and asked for his views on aspects of the SUNFED proposal.[71] In his reply Black reiterated both his belief that "normal international lending" should play an important role in promoting economic development and his fear that "a widespread program of long-term, low-interest-rate foreign exchange loans would, by blurring the distinction between loans and grants, inevitably tend to impair the integrity of international financial obligations, to discourage normal lenders and thus to deprive the development process of the support it should receive from this source." Having thus summarized his basic position, Black admitted that the debt-servicing capacity of some underdeveloped nations was such that they "could not bear the burden that would be imposed on their balance of payments if all external assistance needed for their development took the form of normal loans." He stated his belief that some grants would be necessary if these nations were to achieve "a reasonably satisfactory rate of development" and indicated that combining normal loans and grants "in the right proportions" was the "best means of adjusting the total service burden on the balance of payments to the circumstances in the particular country." Noting, however, that legislatures in capital-exporting nations were often reluctant to provide assistance in the form of grants, he cautiously observed that loans repayable in local currency "might be a useful tool in the field of international aid" if used judiciously and carefully integrated with lending by the IBRD.[72]

We need not be especially adept at "reading between the lines" to detect two important points in this letter. First, Black was saying that soft lending might not be so bad if done under the auspices of the IBRD. And second, he was basing his tentative approval of soft loans on a rather obvious reference to his expecta-

[70] See previous discussion, pp. 96–98.

[71] Black's reply to Scheyven, dated August 25, 1955, is reprinted in United Nations A/C.2/187, October 28, 1955, pp. 5–7.

[72] *Ibid.*

tions regarding the form of aid the American Congress was likely to make available.[73] Students of the role of Congress in foreign policy would do well to note Black's candid admission that he was changing his position on the loan-grant question primarily because of his perception of probable Congressional behavior. Those who would explain the shift from grants to soft loans in terms of a new awareness of the advantages of loans over grants—other than ease in getting appropriations—should also study this statement by the president of the World Bank. Not many elected officials can afford to be so frank.

By the end of the 1954–57 period it was generally accepted that Black favored increased use of soft loans under certain conditions. He saw the alternative as: (a) forcing default on conventional loans, (b) grants, or (c) soft loans. Since he judged the "temper" of Congress to be against outright grants, he favored soft loans.[74]

INTERNAL SETTING: 1954–57

DOMESTIC SITUATION IN GENERAL

Domestic agricultural problems still plagued the United States. The government price support program resulted in a buildup of CCC stocks in inventory and stocks pledged against outstanding loans and purchase agreements of 18 per cent during 1954 and 20 per cent in 1955. A peak of $9.1 billion was reached in February, 1956. Although this figure had been whittled down to $7.6 billion by June, 1957, the disposal of agricultural commodities which could not be sold at prices which would give American farmers incomes considered adequate by the government remained a problem.[75]

Some hoped that the Soil Bank Plan would contribute to diminishing the CCC stocks within the next few years, but most agricultural economists were skeptical. American farmers had shown a "remarkable ability to maintain output, despite acreage reduc-

[73] This is a good example of Friedrich's "rule of anticipated reactions." Carl J. Friedrich, *Constitutional Government and Democracy* (Boston: Little, Brown & Co., 1941), pp. 589–91.

[74] *New York Times*, April 19, 1957, p. 44; and June 13, 1957, p. 49.

[75] Figures are from Bruce F. Johnston, "Farm Surpluses and Foreign Policy," *World Politics*, X (October, 1957), 1–23.

tions, by securing higher yields per acre, by concentrating production on the best land, and by optimum timing of planting," among
other ways.[76]

Another domestic development was the steady increase in gross
national product during this period. The GNP rose from $363 bil-
lion in 1954 to $408 billion in 1957 (see Figure 4).[77] In every year
except 1954 the GNP exceeded that of the previous year. Thus, the
United States was steadily increasing its economic capability for
giving foreign aid.

[76] *Ibid.*, p. 4.

[77] In constant 1954 dollars.

Billions of dollars

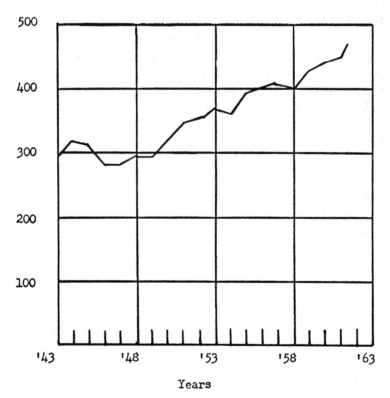

Years

Fig. 4.—United States Gross National Product in 1954 dollars, 1943–62. Source:
The Economic Almanac: 1964 (New York: National Industrial Conference Board,
1964), p. 116.

BUSINESS ELITE

Although important changes in the views of the business elite had come about by 1957, the business community in general still favored emphasis on private investment and opposed public capital transfers. In 1954 the Department of Commerce made public the results of a study designed to discover the obstacles to increased private foreign investment. Nearly four hundred business concerns were canvassed, and the replies indicated that businessmen wanted stronger backing by the United States government when they were in a foreign country and that they wanted the foreign aid program cut or eliminated in order to force foreign nations to rely on private capital.[78]

The United States Chamber of Commerce habitually advocated curtailment of foreign aid.[79] Clement Johnston, Chairman of the Board of the United States Chamber of Commerce, told the Special Senate Committee to Study the Foreign Aid Program:

Despite any contrary impressions that may have been entertained, the time is clearly at hand to start a prompt and rapid tapering off of United States aid, both military and economic, if the countries are ever to learn to stand on their own feet.

Unpleasant as the process may be, it will be a real kindness to certain of these countries if we "talk tough" and give them the real unvarnished facts of economic existence.[80]

During 1957 the views of those business leaders opposed to foreign aid received their most articulate airing up to that time in a study submitted to Congress.[81] The basic argument of this report was that American private investment would furnish most of the necessary capital for economic development abroad if foreign governments would just create the proper conditions. The report specifi-

---

[78] U.S., Bureau of Foreign Commerce, *Factors Limiting U.S. Investment Abroad (Part 2): Business Views on the U.S. Government's Role* (Washington: U.S. Government Printing Office, 1954), pp. 14–16, 23–25.

[79] See, for example, *New York Times,* April 29, 1954, p. 26; and Senate Special Committee to Study the Foreign Aid Program, *Hearings,* 1957, p. 665.

[80] *Ibid.,* p. 194.

[81] U.S., Congress, Senate, *Foreign Aid Program: Compilation of Studies and Surveys,* prepared under the direction of the Special Senate Committee to Study the Foreign Aid Program, Study No. 7, "American Private Enterprise, Foreign Economic Development, and the Aid Programs," prepared by the American Enterprise Association, 85th Cong., 1st sess., 1957, Senate Doc. 52, pp. 539–618.

cally cited hopes by foreign governments of receiving large-scale public aid as tending to "induce foreign governments to be less receptive to private capital."[82] The report also expressed approval of the IBRD policy of strategic nonlending:

The International Bank For Reconstruction and Development is to be congratulated for withholding loans from countries which are in default on publicly held foreign debt and for sometimes refusing to lend to countries which pursue unsound policies with respect to budgetary and power rate policies.[83]

The National Foreign Trade Convention reiterated at each of its annual conventions during the 1954–57 period its belief that (1) foreign economic development should be financed primarily by private capital; (2) the United States government should seek to impress upon foreign governments the importance of creating "favorable investment climates"; (3) the United States should not contribute to the SUNFED or similar schemes. In 1954 the convention stated its opposition to "our having a part in any mechanism, national or international, designed to finance through grants or 'soft loans' any economic development projects which lack sufficient intrinsic merit to attract private capital or to meet the standards of existing lending institutions."[84] The convention approved, as the American Enterprise Association study did later, the policy of strategic nonlending without actually calling it "blackmail." The convention held in 1955 that "neither the United States Government nor any international agency should provide funds for development projects whose financing will not, because of . . . governmental shortcomings . . . be undertaken by private capital."[85] The

---

[82] *Ibid.*, p. 548.   [83] *Ibid.*, p. 614.

[84] "Final Declaration of the Forty-First National Foreign Trade Convention," *Report of the Forty-First National Foreign Trade Convention* (New York: National Foreign Trade Council, 1955), p. xxv. For statements repeating the basic position of the Convention see the following: *Ibid.*, pp. xix–xxv; "Final Declaration of the Forty-Second National Foreign Trade Convention," *Report of the Forty-Second National Foreign Trade Convention* (New York: National Foreign Trade Council, 1956), pp. xix–xxi; "Final Declaration of the Forty-Third National Foreign Trade Convention," *Report of the Forty-Third National Foreign Trade Convention* (New York: National Foreign Trade Council, 1957), pp. xvi–xix; "Final Declaration of the Forty-Fourth National Foreign Trade Convention," *Report of the Forty-Fourth National Foreign Trade Convention* (New York: National Foreign Trade Council, 1958), pp. xv–xvii.

[85] *Report of the Forty-Second National Foreign Trade Convention*, p. xx.

"governmental shortcomings" were constituted by the "unwillingness of the government of a host country to permit a level of earnings and remittances adequate to attract the capital necessary for
the establishment and maintenance of such projects."[86]

Split in the Business Community

Despite the prevalent business hostility to foreign aid, there
were signs of change within the community.[87] The main vehicle
for the expression of liberal business opinions was the Committee
for Economic Development (CED). In April, 1957, the CED published a statement on national policy, prepared by its Research
and Policy Committee, which made the following points: (1) Economic growth in underdeveloped areas should be an important
goal of United States foreign policy. (2) Private investment will
probably be inadequate to achieve the rate of growth which is desirable from the standpoint of American foreign policy; therefore
public capital for economic development should be provided at a
rate of $1 billion per year in addition to the economic aid level
then current—which would have brought total economic aid levels
to over $2 billion. (3) Development assistance should be put on a
long-term basis, perhaps by allowing borrowing from the Treasury.
(4) Development assistance should be primarily bilateral. (5) Although some grants will be desirable, primary emphasis should be
on loans, even though some would have to be repayable in local
currency.[88]

Caution is appropriate in assessing the significance of the diver-
gent views on foreign economic policy among the business elite. It
is rarely recognized that the net impact of the views of business
leaders on foreign economic policy may depend on their opinions
on seemingly unrelated matters. What businessmen say about
taxes may be a more important determinant of foreign aid levels
than what they say about foreign aid. Even the liberal CED was
interested in "fiscal responsibility." In the same report in which

[86] Ibid.

[87] The development of the split within the business community is traced by
David S. McLellan and Charles E. Woodhouse, "The Business Elite and Foreign
Policy," Western Political Quarterly, XIII (March, 1960), 172–90.

[88] Committee for Economic Development, Economic Development Assistance,
1957, pp. 7–29.

they recommended more public funds for economic development they called for "economy in Federal expenditures to prevent inflation, and to permit important tax reductions and tax reforms."[89] The CED clearly implied that development assistance should take priority over less important budget items. The trouble with the CED approach was that it was based on a faulty estimate of the flexibility of the American budgetary process. Arthur Smithies has pointed out—in a study financed by the CED, ironically enough— that the priorities in American budgeting are relatively fixed:

> Expenditures for agricultural price support, veteran's compensation and benefits, and grants to the states for public assistance, highway construction, and other purposes are all largely determined by the basic legislation setting up these programs and are therefore largely exempt from budgetary scrutiny. The interest bill is regarded as a contractual obligation which must be paid ahead of everything else. The President classified $14.1 billion of expenditures for fiscal 1955 as "relatively uncontrollable" on these grounds. *The existence of these budgetary priorities means that the brunt of cuts in the budget must be borne by the national-security program and by the unprotected non-defense programs.*[90]

Since there are few programs more vulnerable to budget cutting than foreign aid, a plea for a balanced federal budget is frequently tantamount to calling for curtailment of foreign aid. Considering the interest of most business leaders, conservatives and liberals alike, in "fiscal responsibility," we should be wary of descriptions of the split within the business community which depict one side as "for" and the other as "against" foreign aid.

Businessmen and Legitimacy of Aid

The transfer of capital through public channels had always been an activity which American businessmen were reluctant to approve. According to the American business creed such public financial dealings were justifiable only under exceptional circumstances. The idea of providing public capital for economic development on a long-term basis was anathema to the traditional business outlook on the role of governments in economic affairs.

[89] *Ibid.*, p. 21.

[90] Arthur Smithies, *The Budgetary Process in the United States* (New York: McGraw-Hill, 1955), pp. 10–11. Italics mine.

The process by which foreign aid was gradually acquiring legitimacy in the eyes of the business elite is worth examining.

In the first place, influential portions of the business community, allied for the most part with the CED, were beginning to perceive the postwar world situation as composed of a semipermanent set of "exceptional circumstances." This group was willing to change its view of "proper" techniques of statecraft in accordance with its perceptions of the rapid changes taking place throughout the world—economically, politically, and technologically.[91] Thus, by 1957 the CED represented an articulate part of the business elite which was beginning to regard public capital movements, possibly including soft loans, as legitimate techniques of statecraft.

Congressmen were well aware of business attitudes on public capital movements, and they often tried to get business leaders to give their stamp of approval (or disapproval, depending on the congressman's attitude toward foreign aid) to foreign aid as a technique of statecraft. A good example is provided by Senator Fulbright's attempt to secure the business seal of legitimacy from Benjamin Fairless in 1957:

I think sometimes this whole business of foreign aid, as we call it, beginning with the Marshall Plan, has been condemned by those who oppose it as a giveaway and a softheaded, unrealistic, humanitarian gesture.

Now it is not often we have an opportunity to ask an industrialist of your standing questions along this line, and all I am trying to do is to have you emphasize you do not believe this is a visionary scheme of a long-haired professor; that you think it is good business, as former president of the United States Steel Co. Is that right?[92]

In addition to getting business leaders to endorse foreign aid, there was a second means by which the friends of foreign aid sought to promote its legitimization in the eyes of the business elite. Briefly put, it amounted to letting members of the business elite administer the foreign aid program. Such business leaders as Paul Hoffman, Clarence Randall, Benjamin Fairless, Nelson Rockefeller, Eric Johnston, and Eugene Black were involved in planning

[91] On the views of these "progressives" as they developed from 1944 to 1957 see McLellan and Woodhouse, *Western Political Quarterly*, XIII, 172–90.

[92] Senate Special Committee to Study the Foreign Aid Program, *Hearings*, 1957, p. 378.

or administering public capital transfer programs. The ICA was placed under the direction of John B. Hollister, a former law partner of Senator Robert A. Taft. Presumably close association with the right wing of the Republican Party compensated for his lack of business experience in assuring businessmen that the ICA would be "soundly" run. Associating business leaders with the planning and programming of public capital movements was designed to allay the traditional business suspicions regarding bureaucratic inefficiency and corruption. It was supposed to assure them that foreign aid programs would be run on a "sound, business-like basis."

Businessmen occupied not only important foreign aid posts but also an increasing number of more general foreign policy making positions. In surveying the occupational background of holders of the top civilian foreign policy making posts, one study found that the percentage of businessmen had jumped from eight in 1938 to twenty-three in 1948 and to forty-seven in 1956.[93] This study observed that "by all odds the most significant trend in the profile of foreign policy decision-makers is the importance assumed by business and financial figures."[94]

One former member of the business elite commanded special respect from many of his former cohorts. By 1957 the IBRD, under the leadership of Eugene Black, had established itself as a "respectable, business-like" institution in the eyes of the business community. After more than a decade there were few business leaders who did not approve of the IBRD and its president. Thus, when Black began to favor increased public capital in the form of soft loans, an important step in the process of legitimizing soft lending took place.

In summary, although the prevailing view of the business community during the 1954–57 period still favored positive promotion of private enterprise and specific avoidance of public capital transfers, there were signs that foreign aid was gaining acceptance. These signs were furnished primarily by the statements of the CED and by the growing numbers of businessmen involved in

[93] David S. McLellan and Charles E. Woodhouse, "Businessmen in Foreign Policy," *Southwestern Social Science Quarterly,* XXXIX (March, 1959), 285.

[94] *Ibid.*

making and administering foreign policy. The outlook for soft loans was brightened by the approval of such techniques expressed by Eugene Black and by committees composed of business leaders.[95]

CONGRESS

The attitudes of Congress toward administration proposals on trade liberalization and foreign aid resembled those of the 1949–53 period.

Congress and Trade Liberalization

Although executive branch spokesmen tried to convince the legislators that failure to liberalize trade would result in increased demands for economic aid, the Congress continued to resist both reduction of trade barriers and increases in foreign aid. In January, 1954, the Randall Commission presented its report, which recommended a three-year renewal of the Reciprocal Trade Agreements Act and authorization for an additional 15 per cent reduction in tariff rates.[96] The inclusion of several protectionist members on the commission—for example, Senator Eugene D. Millikin, Representative Daniel A. Reed, and Representative Richard A. Simpson—had insured that the report would not be a free trade manifesto. It was not. It advocated only moderate tariff reductions, a moderate extension of the Reciprocal Trade Agreements Act, and retention of the peril point and escape clause provisions which so irritated free traders. The *New York Times* reported that the commission's recommendations were "just about the minimum program most European governments . . . considered possible for the United States to undertake if the economy of the West" was not to be "hopelessly split into dollar and nondollar blocs."[97] The fact

[95] See the following: International Development Advisory Board, *A New Emphasis on Economic Development Abroad: A Report to the President of the United States on Ways, Means and Reasons for U.S. Assistance to International Economic Development,* March, 1957 (cited hereafter as IDAB, *A New Emphasis on Economic Development Abroad,* 1957); and CED, *Economic Development Assistance.* The International Development Advisory Board was chaired by Eric Johnston, and among committee members were J. Peter Grace and Harvey S. Firestone, Jr.

[96] Commission on Foreign Economic Policy, *Report to the President and the Congress* (Washington: U.S. Government Printing Office, 1954), p. 50.

[97] *New York Times,* January 25, 1954, p. 1.

that the Randall Commission report was far from radical was also indicated by the reaction of a conference of scholars which discussed the report in February, 1954. They expressed disappointment at what they believed to be a serious compromise of the liberal trade position and unanimously found the report wanting as a basis for formulating long-range economic policy for the United States.[98]

Despite the moderate tone of the Randall Commission's recommendations, and despite the fact that his own party controlled Congress, President Eisenhower failed to get Congress to implement the commission's recommendations. He got instead only a one-year, stopgap extension of the Reciprocal Trade Agreements Act. In 1955, with the Democrats in control of Congress, the administration was able to win a three-year extension of the Trade Agreements Act. One observer, however, noting that in the House a motion from the Committee on Rules to take up the bill passed by a margin of one and that on final passage the bill survived with a margin of only seven votes, concluded that "in 1955 the Trade Agreements Program came nearer to defeat than any time in its history."[99] Clearly, the prospects for a vigorous program of trade liberalization were dim. Although the battle for renewal of the Trade Agreements Act did not have to be fought again until 1958, the administration suffered defeats at the hands of the protectionists in both 1956 and 1957 in its efforts to secure legislative approval for United States participation in a proposed Organization for Trade Cooperation (OTC), which was designed to place the General Agreements on Tariffs and Trade on a more viable basis. And in 1957, on the eve of the 1958 drive for extension of the Trade Agreements Act, Senator Aiken remarked to Benjamin Fairless during hearings on foreign aid: "I presume you are aware that it has been a long time since Congress has been under such pres-

[98] Klaus Knorr and Gardner Patterson (eds.), *A Critique of the Randall Commission Report on United States Foreign Economic Policy* (Princeton, N.J.: International Finance Section and Center of International Studies, Princeton University Press, 1954). Participating in the conference were such scholars as Clair Wilcox, Jacob Viner, Thomas C. Schelling, Robert Triffin, John K. Galbraith, William Diebold, Jr., Harlan Cleveland, Stacy May, and Wilfred Malenbaum.

[99] James A. Robinson, *Congress and Foreign Policy-Making* (Homewood, Ill.: Dorsey Press, 1962), p. 60.

sure to reduce quotas and increase tariffs as we are at the present time."[100]

Congress and Foreign Aid

Congressional attitudes toward the use of loans in foreign aid and the agricultural disposal programs will be discussed. Since the establishment of the DLF has given rise to an unusual hypothesis about the role of Congress in foreign policy making, attention will also be given to this problem.

Congress and surplus disposal.—Professor John D. Montgomery has observed that "the use of agricultural surpluses as a means of augmenting aid was conceived jointly by Congress and the Department of Agriculture."[101] Insofar as Montgomery is trying to illustrate that Congress has introduced "positive innovations in foreign aid practice,"[102] he is correct; but his statement carries the misleading implication that Congress was motivated by a desire to augment the aid program. It would be more accurate to describe Congressional activities as "augmentation of aid as a means of disposing of agricultural surpluses" instead of the other way around. Congress was interested, as it had been since World War II, in cutting, not augmenting, the dollar appropriations required for foreign aid.

The surplus disposal programs under PL 480 and section 402 were first and foremost a means by which Congress sought to relieve itself of embarrassing and costly storage of the CCC inventories, which had mounted rapidly between 1952 and 1956. Two reasons for believing this come readily to mind. First, it accords well with the proposition that Congress tends to be more interested in domestic than in foreign problems. Montgomery furnishes no evidence in support of the proposition that Congressional attitudes toward surplus disposal were an exception to this rule. In the absence of evidence to the contrary, it would seem prudent to explain legislative attitudes in terms of typical behavior on similar issues in the past. The PL 480 legislation was routed through the

---

[100] Senate Special Committee to Study the Foreign Aid Program, *Hearings,* 1957, p. 362.

[101] John D. Montgomery, *The Politics of Foreign Aid* (New York: Praeger, 1962), p. 220.

[102] *Ibid.*

agriculture, not the foreign affairs, committees; and State Department witnesses were not even heard.[103]

The second reason for believing that concern for emptying CCC storage bins was uppermost in the minds of legislators is that several congressmen who had been active supporters of surplus disposal legislation frequently expressed a desire to see the cost of the agricultural price support program minimized—even at the expense of inflating the apparent costs of foreign aid.[104] By transferring the costs of surplus commodities from the books of the Agriculture Department to State Department books, the legislative friends of agriculture hoped to squelch some of the criticism of the costly agricultural support program. The State Department was hardly enthusiastic about having agricultural disposal charged as a cost against the aid program. In the first place, it might have been able to promote its objectives more effectively with dollars than with wheat. In the second place, even assuming that it were desirable to provide wheat to foreign nations, the State Department could have secured wheat from other sources more cheaply than it could in the American market, with its artificially supported prices. The major reason for buying in the United States

---

[103] On this point see C. David Hartmann, "Local Currency Programs and United States Foreign Policies" (Ph.D. dissertation, Columbia University, 1962), pp. 28–32.

[104] See comments by Senator Hubert Humphrey: "I resent being told that these agricultural commodities cost $1 billion a year because somebody doesn't know how to keep books." U.S., Congress, Senate, Committee on Foreign Relations, *Hearings, Mutual Security Act of 1957*, 85th Cong., 1st sess., 1957, p. 508. (Hereafter cited as Senate Committee on Foreign Relations, *Mutual Security Hearings*, 1957.) See also Senator Bourke Hickenlooper's statement: "The point I hope to be able to bring out here is that a great many people have the idea that a billion and a half dollars a year is going, we might say, down the rathole in order to dispose of surpluses, and that we are practically giving them away and taking foreign currencies for those things that are just piling up." He later added: "There has been a great tendency, I think, to charge agriculture with large expenditures when other agencies are getting the benefit of that in one way or another in these countries on the whole.

"I think it is an idea that we have to dispel, that agriculture is costing the country for the disposal of surplus products, say a billion and a half dollars a year. . . . It simply isn't true." Senate Special Committee to Study the Foreign Aid Program, *Hearings*, 1957, pp. 69–70. In 1957 Senator Humphrey was allowed to chair hearings on the relationship between PL 480 and foreign policy. Examples of his desire, and that of others, to minimize the apparent costs of the agricultural program abound in these hearings. U.S., Congress, Senate, Committee on Agriculture and Forestry, *Hearings, Policies and Operations under Public Law 480*, 85th Cong., 1st sess., 1957, pp. 54–55 *et passim*.

instead of Canada would be in order to help the CCC dispose of its wheat. The State Department did not mind so much helping the Agriculture Department rid itself of its surpluses, but it did resent being told that it should pay for this dubious privilege out of its own funds. In 1957, for example, Dulles told a legislative committee, in effect, that he did not mind helping dispose of agricultural surpluses as long as it was recognized that he was doing Congress and the Department of Agriculture a favor by disposing of surplus that was costing a lot to store and would probably rot anyway. He disliked the idea that they were doing him a favor, one for which he should pay.

> We have found that our surplus commodities can serve as a very important aid to our foreign policy in ways which are relatively economical, because they dispose of our surpluses which if otherwise not disposed of, to some extent, at least, just rot away and cost the taxpayer a large amount of money.
> I think we are spending close to a million dollars a day on storage charges. After you store some of these commodities, like wheat, long enough, it just becomes worthless. So you have paid your storage for nothing and dump it out as waste.[105]

To the degree that Montgomery implies that surplus disposal was viewed by Congress as a means of increasing the aid program his statement is at least misleading, if not false. There is substantial evidence that Congress viewed the section 402 and PL 480 programs as means by which the dollar appropriations for foreign aid could be curtailed, not expanded. Congress made it clear with regard to section 402 that "foreign currencies arising from the sale of commodities under this section are to be used so far as practicable for the same purpose for which the dollars used to finance the purchase of the commodities were originally programed."[106] By requiring the executive branch to allocate part of its foreign aid funds for purchase of agricultural commodities, Congress was, in effect, substituting wheat for dollar appropriations. Administration

[105] U.S., Congress, House, Committee on Foreign Affairs, *Hearings, Mutual Security Act of 1957*, 85th Cong., 1st sess., 1957, p. 530. Cited hereafter as House Committee on Foreign Affairs, *Mutual Security Hearings*, 1957.

[106] U.S., Congress, Senate, Committee on Foreign Relations, *The Mutual Security Act of 1954*, 83rd Cong., 2d sess., 1954, Report No. 1799, p. 76. Cited hereafter as Senate Committee on Foreign Relations, *Mutual Security Report*, 1954.

spokesmen stressed again and again that dollars and surplus commodities were not equally useful as instruments of foreign policy. In 1956 John Sherman Cooper, Ambassador to India, complained about the tendency of Congress to substitute commodities for foreign aid dollars. He expressed his hope that when action was taken on renewal of PL 480, Congress would keep in mind that surplus grains would "not meet India's need for foreign exchange to purchase capital supplies."[107]

Another indication that Congress saw PL 480 and section 402 as ways to save money on foreign aid was the frequency with which legislators asked administration spokesmen why they did not make greater use of the local currencies rapidly accumulating under both programs. In confronting the legislature with requests for foreign aid authorizations and appropriations, the executive branch was invariably asked, at some time during the proceedings, why it could not use local currency instead of dollars. The interchange between ICA Director Hollister and Senator Capehart regarding the DLF proposal was typical:

SENATOR CAPEHART: What I am talking about is that here we have— you want $2 billion for this new fund, and you have $2 billion—

MR. HOLLISTER: We haven't $2 billion. Unfortunately, we have $2 billion worth of all kinds of currencies.

SENATOR CAPEHART: I understand that.

MR. HOLLISTER: Yes, but you keep calling it $2 billion.

SENATOR CAPEHART: It was originally $2 billion.

MR. HOLLISTER: But when it stops being $2 billion and is $2 billion of something else, that is a different value than it had before, and we can't substitute that for dollars.[108]

[107] Senate Committee on Foreign Relations, *Mutual Security Hearings*, 1956, p. 376.

[108] Senate Committee on Foreign Relations, *Mutual Security Hearings*, 1957, p. 468. For other examples of the Congressional desire to substitute local currencies generated by "sale" of surpluses for foreign aid dollar appropriations see: U.S., Congress, House, Subcommittee of the Committee on Appropriations, *Hearings, Mutual Security Appropriations for 1958*, 85th Cong., 1st sess., 1957, pp. 111–12, 118, *et passim* (cited hereafter as House Committee on Appropriations, *Mutual Security Hearings*, 1957); and U.S., Congress, House, Committee on Government Operations, *Review of the Budget Formulation and Presentation Practices of the International Cooperation Administration*, 85th Cong., 1st sess., 1957, Report No. 449, pp. 13–14, 18; and U.S., Congress, House, Committee on Appropriations, *Mutual Security Appropriation Bill*, 1958, 85th Cong., 1st sess., 1957, Report No. 1172, p. 4.

In sum, Congressional attitudes toward disposal of agricultural surpluses during the 1954–57 period evinced: (*a*) relatively greater interest in domestic problems than in foreign policy, (*b*) a high degree of ignorance regarding the economic aspects of "local currency sales," and (*c*) a desire to curtail dollar appropriations for foreign aid.

Congress and loans.—During the 1954–57 period Congress exerted unrelenting pressure on the executive branch to extend foreign aid, especially that for economic development, on a loan basis. Later developments in American foreign aid policy should be understood in the context of the executive-legislative struggle over loans and grants. When the executive branch was acquiescing to legislative demands for greater emphasis on loans, it did not advertise the fact since it is considered politically inexpedient to present to Congress a program which is admittedly second choice. It is apparently believed necessary to present each year's foreign aid program as the greatest invention since the wheel. In 1957, therefore, the administration's acquiescence was clothed in a much-heralded proposal for establishment of a new lending agency, the DLF. The administration sought to compensate for its concession to Congress on loans by: (*a*) increasing the total dollar appropriation for economic development, (*b*) securing authority to make soft loans of the local currency type, and (*c*) insulating part of the foreign aid program from the annual authorization-appropriation cycle. Thus, a memorandum setting forth the administration's position on the DLF described the proposed change in the method of financing as "the major change involved in establishing the fund" and added that setting up a fund "without making this change would be essentially a contradiction in terms."[109]

In spite of the well-publicized feud between Congress and the executive branch on loans versus grants dating from World War II, some observers, such as Professor Raymond F. Mikesell, maintain that the adoption of soft lending as a technique of foreign policy resulted from "the genuine preference on the part of both the

[109] Senate Committee on Foreign Relations, *Mutual Security Hearings,* 1957, p. 615. Congress evinced its hostility to all foreign aid by emasculating the DLF proposal. It decreased the proposed dollar appropriation and refused to permit circumvention of the appropriation process.

Congress and the Administration for loans over grants."[110] Such a view ignores the bargaining aspects of executive-legislative relations, and it also ignores the political history of foreign aid legislation since World War II. We should at least consider the hypothesis that the executive branch continued to favor grants but believed it would get bigger appropriations from Congress if it pretended to prefer loans. Without such a hypothesis it is difficult to explain the following: (1) Between 1954 and 1957 several administration spokesmen expressed wariness of loans and preference for grants.[111] (2) During this period executive spokesmen indicated that they regarded the loan requirement in Mutual Security legislation as onerous. In this connection they often noted that they were unaware of the alleged preference of governments in recipient nations for loans instead of grants.[112] (3) Throughout the 1954–57 period those administration spokesmen who did speak favorably of loans as opposed to grants usually referred to the type of soft loan which most resembles a grant, the local currency loan.

In 1954 the House Committee on Foreign Affairs noted its desire "that our Government and recipient governments get to thinking more about loans instead of grants."[113] The committee report quoted approvingly from a statement submitted by Representative John M. Vorys, the leading protagonist in the drive to put foreign aid on a loan basis:

A Nation such as ours, with constantly diminishing natural resources, should make loans, not gifts, from these resources wherever this is possible. We do not need to be repaid next year, or the year after. We

[110] Mikesell, p. 344.

[111] U.S., Congress, House, Committee on Foreign Affairs, *Hearings, The Mutual Security Act of 1954*, 83rd Cong., 2d sess., 1954, pp. 492–94, 515, 522 (cited hereafter as House Committee on Foreign Affairs, *Mutual Security Hearings,* 1954); U.S., Congress, Senate, Committee on Foreign Relations, *Hearings, Mutual Security Act of 1954*, 83rd Cong., 2d sess., 1954, pp. 68–69 (cited hereafter as Senate Committee on Foreign Relations, *Mutual Security Hearings,* 1954); *Senate Committee on Foreign Relations, Mutual Security Hearings,* 1956, p. 116; Senate Special Committee to Study the Foreign Aid Program, *Hearings,* 1957, p. 484.

[112] Senate Committee on Foreign Relations, *Mutual Security Hearings,* 1955, pp. 34–35; Senate Committee on Foreign Relations, *Mutual Security Hearings,* 1956, p. 116; Senate Special Committee to Study the Foreign Aid Program, *Hearings,* 1957, p. 467.

[113] U.S., Congress, House, Committee on Foreign Affairs, *Mutual Security Act of 1954*, 83rd Cong., 2d sess., 1954, Report No. 1925, Part 1, p. 95. Cited hereafter as House Committee on Foreign Affairs, *Mutual Security Report,* 1954.

can wait for a number of years, when we will be importing an increasing amount of scarce materials. We can defer payment on our loans, if necessary, to make other loans more "bankable," as many individuals and companies did here in our country during the depression—and were finally repaid. But a Nation with 6 per cent of the world's resources, half the production, and double the debt of the rest of the world, should be making more loans, and fewer gifts.

Those who oppose all aid and those who want nothing but gifts join in saying that aid loans are substantially gifts anyway and cause bad feelings. Experience shows that both groups are wrong in these arguments.

This committee has required a whole series of loans in aid bills. All of them were opposed by the executive branch. None of the loans were ever turned down by the other countries involved. None of these loans have been defaulted. None of them have caused hard feelings.[114]

Although the Senate Committee on Foreign Relations reduced the House committee's loan requirement, its report made it clear that the Senate committee sympathized with the goal of replacing grants with loans—even soft loans.[115]

In 1955, despite a recommendation from the Hoover Commission advising use of grants in cases where prospects of repayment were dim, Congress reaffirmed its preference for loans.[116] Both of the foreign affairs committees in Congress again urged the executive to make the maximum possible use of loans in the aid program, and the House committee pointedly allowed Representative Vorys to append a statement on loans to the main committee report on Mutual Security.[117] The Democrats, who had won control of Congress in the 1954 elections, were no less in favor of loans than their Republican predecessors.

In 1956 ICA Director John B. Hollister reported to Congress that the "attempted substitution of a loan for a grant has frequent-

114 *Ibid.*, p. 46.

115 Senate Committee on Foreign Relations, *Mutual Security Report*, 1954, pp. 71-72.

116 Commission on Organization of the Executive Branch of the Government, *Overseas Economic Operations*, A Report to the Congress, June, 1955, pp. 54, 57-58.

117 U.S., Congress, Senate, Committee on Foreign Relations, *Mutual Security Act of 1955*, 84th Cong., 1st sess., 1955, Report No. 383, p. 22; and U.S., Congress, House, Committee on Foreign Affairs, *Mutual Security Act of 1955*, 84th Cong., 1st sess., Report No. 912, 1955, pp. 18, 82-85.

ly, either for political or economic reasons, been impracticable."[118] The House Committee on Foreign Affairs responded by recommending that *all* development assistance, except that used to buy agricultural surpluses and that related to projects involving more than one nation, be in loan form.[119] The Senate Committee on Foreign Relations modified this stand by recommending a requirement of only 75 per cent but warned that it had seriously considered a 100 per cent requirement. [120] The final compromise figure was 80 per cent. In the fall of 1956 the retiring chairman of the House Committee on Foreign Affairs, James P. Richards, held hearings on foreign aid in general. On the basis of these hearings he submitted in December, 1956, a report recommending that economic aid take the form of dollar loans repayable over long time periods at low interest rates either in dollars or local currency.[121]

The year 1957 represented the culmination of legislative efforts to place development assistance on a loan basis.[122] The Senate set up a Special Committee to Study the Foreign Aid Program, which in turn gathered an impressive collection of expert opinions and held comprehensive hearings. This committee favored loans for economic aid and gave qualified approval to the administration's soft loan proposal.[123] The "qualifications," however, were little more than signs of Congressional naïveté, more in the category of wishful thinking than qualification. The committee warned that

[118] Senate Committee on Foreign Relations, *Mutual Security Hearings*, 1956, p. 116.

[119] U.S., Congress, House, Committee on Foreign Affairs, *Mutual Security Act of 1956*, 84th Cong., 2d sess., Report No. 2213, 1956.

[120] U.S., Congress, Senate, Committee on Foreign Relations, *Mutual Security Act of 1956*, 84th Cong., 2d sess., Report No. 2273, 1956.

[121] U.S., Congress, House, Committee on Foreign Affairs, *Report on Foreign Policy and Mutual Security*, Report by James P. Richards, 85th Cong., 1st sess., 1957, Report No. 551, pp. 43R–44R. (Cited hereafter as House Committee on Foreign Affairs, *Report on Foreign Policy and Mutual Security*, 1957.) According to Montgomery (p. 271) this report was neither endorsed nor followed by the committee.

[122] For a detailed description of legislative foreign aid activities in 1957, see H. Field Haviland, Jr., "Foreign Aid and the Policy Process: 1957," *American Political Science Review*, LII (September, 1958), 689–724.

[123] U.S., Congress, Senate, Special Committee to Study the Foreign Aid Program, *Foreign Aid*, 85th Cong., 1st sess., 1957, Report No. 300, pp. 15–16, 27. (Cited hereafter as Senate Special Committee to Study the Foreign Aid Program, *Foreign Aid Report*, 1957.)

soft loans must not be allowed to resemble grants nor to compete with other sources of capital—as if legislative warnings would make economic facts evaporate.

Congress typically resents being considered merely as a source of funds for the executive. It wants to supervise the day-to-day execution of policy by the executive; yet it lacks the time, organization, and competence required for such an undertaking. Its policy advice, therefore, usually takes the form of the advice contained in the 1957 report on Mutual Security by the House Committee on Foreign Affairs: "If it is important for the United States to promote the growth of less developed countries, it is essential that we seek to do this in a sound businesslike way, which will insure a full value for each dollar expended."[124] Such vague pronouncements make the legislators feel that they are participating in policy making. The legislators have, in a general way, indicated that they think loans are more "sound" and "business-like" than grants, but they have also exhibited ignorance regarding the economics of international capital transfers. Thus, in discussing the operations of the proposed DLF, the House committee observed that the local currencies received in repayment of loans could be increasingly "used to acquire resources of value to the United States as the borrowing countries' development goes forward."[125] Such currencies, however, *by definition,* could not be used to any great extent to transfer resources to the United States. In considering the question of whether soft loan programs might undermine hard lending, the committee could find no evidence of such interference.[126] Just what kind of "evidence" the committee considered relevant is difficult to imagine. It is obvious, however, that they failed to recognize that soft lending always competes with hard lending because hard loans are always available on some terms and in the long run.

If legislators failed to comprehend the limitations on the use of local currency acquired through repayment of soft loans, it was not entirely their fault. In defending the soft loan repayable in local currency, administration spokesmen often exaggerated the

[124] U.S., Congress, House, Committee on Foreign Affairs, *Mutual Security Act of 1957,* 85th Cong., 1st sess., 1957, Report No. 776, p. 21.

[125] *Ibid.,* p. 22.

[126] *Ibid.,* p. 23.

usefulness of such currencies.[127] Secretary of State Dulles, for example, emphasized the positive aspects of local currency accounts:

... Of course when you get local currency ... that does not mean you get something that is valueless, because there are often ways in which that local currency can be spent which relieves the Treasury of other financial burdens—travel, the expenses of our foreign Embassies, and a good many things of that sort.

Local currency can often be spent or sometimes be spent for local products which we wish and desire to have. Proceeds from any transactions like these could be placed in the fund to relieve the burden of putting up new money.[128]

Such statements were to haunt administration spokesmen in later appearances before Congress. In explaining to Congress why local currencies generated by DLF loans and agricultural surplus "sales" could not substitute for dollar appropriations, administration witnesses had to deprecate the usefulness of such currencies. Even the less perceptive legislators could feel the wool sliding over their eyes.

In sum, legislative attitudes on loans reflected the general hostility of Congress to all foreign aid. As William S. White phrased it in 1957, "If there has been one central and dominant desire at the Capitol for five or six years it has been for the eventual liquidation of foreign aid, and never for its more or less permanent lodgment in this country's high policy."[129] Congress also exhibited a lack of understanding regarding the international lending process. Some of the most confusing testimony in legislative history is that relating to the legislators' attempts to understand soft loans. The reasoning of many legislative supporters of soft loans was no more sophisticated than the following: "Any sort of loan is preferable to just giving them the money."

Congress and the DLF.—It is generally agreed that Congress rarely exercises initiative in the formulation of American foreign

---

[127] See for example, Senate Committee on Foreign Relations, *Mutual Security Hearings,* 1957, pp. 27–28; House Committee on Appropriations, *Mutual Security Hearings,* 1957, pp. 106, 804–5; and Senate Special Committee to Study the Foreign Aid Program, *Hearings,* 1957, pp. 422 *et passim.*

[128] Senate Special Committee to Study the Foreign Aid Program, *Hearings,* 1957, p. 422.

[129] *New York Times,* April 14, 1957, Part 4, p. 3.

policy; yet the establishment of the DLF has been cited by several scholars as a conspicuous exception to this rule.[130] Robinson and Montgomery have cited this "exception" to the rule in support of their contention that Congress can, under certain circumstances, take initiative in foreign policy. Some consideration of their unusual hypothesis, therefore, seems warranted.

Since none of the proponents of this hypothesis has defined "initiative," we must assume they are using a standard dictionary definition referring to "responsibility for originating" some act or idea. The question, of course, arises as to whether they are thinking of origination of the "act" or the "idea." Let us take first the formal legislative act of establishing the DLF. Had the proposed "Bricker Amendment" succeeded in passing Congress, we would have referred to it as an instance of legislative initiative in foreign policy because the bill was proposed by a congressman without administration support. The DLF, however, had little in common with the procedure by which the Bricker proposal entered the legislative machinery. The DLF proposal was first presented to Congress in a statement by Secretary of State Dulles before the Senate Special Committee to Study the Foreign Aid Program.[131] In its report recommending the establishment of such a fund the committee referred specifically to the proposal by Dulles: "The committee acknowledges the view of the Secretary of State that a new means, such as a revolving development fund, is needed to provide development assistance to other nations."[132] The DLF proposal was further refined and presented as an administration proposal under the Mutual Security Act of 1957. The executive branch, thus, introduced and defended the DLF proposal as its own. On the surface, therefore, the DLF proposal does not appear to be an instance of Congressional initiative. However, we must admit the possibility of initiative having been exercised in a subtle fashion.

Perhaps key members of Congress actually masterminded the

[130] Robinson, pp. 192–93, 211; Montgomery, pp. 219–21; and Richard P. Stebbins, *The United States in World Affairs, 1957* (New York: Harper & Bros., 1958), p. 67.

[131] Senate Special Committee to Study the Foreign Aid Program, *Hearings, 1957,* pp. 394–426.

[132] Senate Special Committee to Study the Foreign Aid Program, *Foreign Aid Report,* 1957, p. 15.

DLF proposal by feeding the idea to the executive and encouraging them to back it. Let us look at the history of the DLF idea. The three basic elements of the DLF were: (*a*) a fund under American control, (*b*) authority to make soft loans for economic development, and (*c*) long-term financing for the fund provided by some modification of the annual authorization-appropriation process. In the first place, discussion in previous chapters has described several proposals for both bilateral and multilateral agencies for making soft loans for economic development. The general idea was quite familiar in governmental circles by 1957. In the first year of the Eisenhower administration, Mutual Security Director Harold Stassen received a report suggesting the establishment of a new United States institution to make soft loans for economic development and based on a recognition of development financing as a long-run interest of the United States.[133] There were other signs that the executive branch was considering a proposal similar to the DLF. In January, 1956, Secretary of State Dulles told a news conference that he had supported such a proposal as early as 1955:

... The concept of finding a way to make this economic assistance both more flexible and to get a greater continuity is one which I have favored for some time. We have thought about various ways of doing it. I remember I had considerable discussion, I think it was last year, about the possibility of creating a new finance institution with sufficient capital so it could draw on it year by year, somewhat as the Export-Import Bank does. That particular project did not win favor that year.[134]

We might argue that the "Richards Report" in December, 1956, provides evidence of Congressional suggestion of the basic DLF ideas.[135] This document, however, was primarily a personal report to Congress by James P. Richards. Besides that, those who view the DLF as a product of legislative initiative do not refer to this document but point instead to the Senate Foreign Relations Com-

[133] *Economic Strength for the Free World,* A Report to the Director for Mutual Security by the Advisory Committee on Underdeveloped Areas, May, 1953, pp. 22–32.

[134] *New York Times,* January 12, 1956, p. 10.

[135] House Committee on Foreign Affairs, *Report on Foreign Policy and Mutual Security,* 1957, pp. 43R–44R.

mittee as the promoter of the DLF.[136] Robinson reports that "it has become customary in the Senate to attribute the initiative for this proposal [DLF] to the Committee on Foreign Relations and especially to one of its senior members [Senator J. W. Fulbright]."[137] He admits that "a similar proposal was contained in the Johnston committee report,"[138] but proceeds to treat this as insignificant and to insist that what has become a customary senatorial belief is true. The report of the International Development Advisory Board (IDAB), chaired by Eric Johnston, was made public on March 8, 1957, about two weeks before the Senate Special Committee to Study the Foreign Aid Program began to hold hearings. The IDAB recommended establishment of an "International Development Fund" under the auspices of the ICA and the State Department with authority to make soft loans for economic development. The report also recommended that legislative appropriations permit the fund to operate for at least three years without requiring additional financing.[139] This proposal was almost identical with the DLF proposal submitted to Congress by the administration.

Furthermore, during the Mutual Security appropriations hearings in 1957, Representative Otto Passman expressed interest in learning the origin of the DLF proposal. The administration witness he was questioning in this regard gave no indication that the DLF was in any way a product of legislative initiative.[140] And when Passman pressed Dulles with a similar line of questioning, Dulles replied: "While I do not claim any monopoly on the idea [of long-term financing], I am prepared to say that I, myself, strongly sponsored the idea. Indeed, I had suggested it within the executive department for several years."[141]

It appears from the above discussion that Congress was not responsible for originating either the DLF or the idea behind it.

---

[136] Montgomery refers only to "Congress" and does not designate a subordinate element as of primary importance.

[137] Robinson, p. 58.   [138] Ibid.

[139] IDAB, A New Emphasis on Economic Development Abroad, 1957, pp. 15–18. This is sometimes referred to as the "Johnston committee report."

[140] House Committee on Appropriations, Mutual Security Hearings, 1957, pp. 541–43.

[141] Ibid., p. 137.

Until more evidence is provided in support of the hypothesis that the DLF resulted from Congressional initiative, we will do well to view establishment of the DLF as yet another example of Congressional passivity relative to the executive in formulating foreign policy.

Perception of the Situation and Selection of an Alternative

RELIANCE ON LOCAL EFFORT

The decision to rely on local efforts to spur economic growth in underdeveloped areas was based on two main perceptions by the foreign policy makers. First, they believed that self-sustaining economic development could only result from domestic efforts. In this respect the policy makers' concept of the development process coincided with the views being voiced by foreign statesmen and by American academic circles in the rapidly growing literature on economic development.

Secondly, the foreign policy makers could hardly have failed to perceive that Congress was unlikely to increase appropriations for providing alternatives to relying on local efforts. Businessmen also made it fairly clear that they were reluctant to increase their foreign investment radically because of the attitudes of foreign governments toward private foreign investors. In short, no large-scale capital, either public or private, was likely to be forthcoming; therefore the United States policy makers counseled reliance on domestic efforts.

PRIVATE CAPITAL FLOW

The decision to stimulate private foreign investment in order to promote economic development abroad likewise rested on the perception that alternative sources of capital were limited. If capital on the order of magnitude of $10 billion annually were needed by the developing nations, it would have to come primarily from private sources.

Reliance on private investment was not only necessary but desirable as well from the policy makers' viewpoint. Promotion of economic development through private investment would have three advantages in their eyes: (1) Private investment was an effective way of combining technical assistance and capital in the right proportions. (2) American businessmen stood to profit from foreign investment. (3) Economic development based on private enterprise was believed to be more compatible with American ideology than economic development based on government enterprise. Ideologically, economically, and politically, stimulation of private enterprise was viewed as a desirable technique for spurring economic development.

Both the desirability and necessity of stimulating private capital movements were stressed in the Randall Commission's report, which President Eisenhower received approvingly in 1954.[142] Another report, submitted to the President in 1957, gave similar emphasis to the role of private foreign investment in foreign economic development.[143] Although this report was not so warmly received by the President, it indicated that some high-level advisers were thinking in these terms.

PUBLIC CAPITAL

It is difficult, although not impossible, to describe "the executive branch position" regarding the use of public capital as a technique of statecraft during the 1954–57 period. It is difficult because the administration was not of one opinion on the issue, but it is possible—and useful—because we can identify a viewpoint which eventually won out.

The Eisenhower administration had come to office in 1953 proclaiming its intention to balance the budget and cut out wasteful foreign "giveaways." In 1953 the Truman administration's proposed budget was trimmed by over $9 billion, with the deepest cuts in the most vulnerable place—foreign aid. By early 1954, however, there were signs that some in the administration were reappraising the usefulness of public capital movements in statecraft. During Mutual Security hearings in 1954 Senator Capehart asked Dulles about the relationship between activities of the IBRD and Export-Import Bank and the cold war. Dulles replied:

[142] Commission on Foreign Economic Policy, *Report to the President and the Congress*, pp. 16–18.

[143] *Report to the President by the President's Citizen Advisers on the Mutual Security Program*, March 1, 1957, p. 8. Cited hereafter as the Fairless Committee Report.

I think you put your finger on what is the most difficult aspect of our foreign relations at the present time: That the United States, in my opinion, is not taking a sufficiently broad viewpoint with reference to its responsibilities as the greatest economic unit in the world, and almost the only source of funds, capital funds, which could be loaned abroad.[144]

As 1954 drew to a close it was obvious that fundamental changes in administration attitudes on foreign policy were taking place. As *New York Times* columnist James Reston phrased it:

What has happened here is that the Republican Administration has gone full circle in its first two years in office. It started off by emphasizing the military aspects of the cold war and proclaiming a "policy of liberation" and it is ending the first half of its term trying to "contain" the Communists through economic policies which it originally minimized.[145]

It was well known that Secretary of the Treasury George M. Humphrey was one of Eisenhower's most trusted advisers, and it was also well known that Humphrey was interested in balancing the budget and opposed proposals to expand public capital movements. It is hardly surprising, therefore, that the *New York Times* reported a split between Dulles and Stassen on the one hand and Humphrey on the other over the role of a proposed long-range program of economic grants and loans.[146] In 1955 the split continued, and the press labeled the participants in the dispute "Young Turks" and "the 4-H Club," the latter term referring to initials of last names. The "Young Turks" conceived economic development abroad as important to the United States and viewed the expansion of public capital movements to that end as desirable. Included in this group were Harold Stassen, Nelson Rockefeller, and Vice-President Nixon. Dulles also tended to share the views of this group. The members of the "4-H Club," on the other hand, emphasized the military as opposed to the economic aspects of the cold war and lacked enthusiasm for foreign aid for any purpose other than short-run military security. This group included Secretary of the Treasury Humphrey; John B. Hollister, Director

[144] Senate Foreign Relations Committee, *Mutual Security Hearings,* 1954, p. 26.

[145] *New York Times,* November 28, 1954, Part 4, p. 8.

[146] *New York Times,* December 4, 1954, p. 1.

of ICA; Herbert Hoover, Jr., Undersecretary of State; and Rowland R. Hughes, Director of the Bureau of the Budget. The victory of the "Young Turk" point of view was indicated not only by the increasing emphasis on economic aspects of the cold war during 1956 and 1957 but also by the fact that the resignation of Hollister as ICA chief in July, 1957, meant the last of the "4-H Club" members had vacated his government post. Unless otherwise indicated, subsequent references to "administration" points of view will refer to the group which eventually prevailed. We should, however, bear in mind that the administration "position" was not monolithic.

Channels for Public Capital

It was noted above that the United States preferred bilateral to multilateral channels for moving public capital to underdeveloped nations during this period. Although this is an accurate description of American policy, it fails to make a distinction which is important to an understanding of the evolution of foreign aid policy in later years—that between the International Bank and other multilateral organizations.

In the first place, Congress had indicated since 1949, in various ways, that it took a dim view of letting the Russians have a say in determining how American aid would be distributed. State Department officials were probably reluctant to suggest channeling American aid through the United Nations at a time when the Senate Internal Security Subcommittee was challenging the loyalty of a former official of the International Monetary Fund on the basis of a memorandum he circulated while with the IMF which advocated a similar measure.[147] The subcommittee counsel delivered the coup de grâce by pointing out that the United Nations delegate from Poland had taken a similar position.

The American preference for bilateral channels indicated opposition to a particular multilateral channel rather than to all. The particular one was the United Nations. President Eisenhower announced in 1956 that he intended to use bilateral channels and "associations" other than the United Nations for distributing

[147] *New York Times*, May 16, 1956, p. 17. Cf. also comments by Jacob Javits on attitude of Congress toward channeling American aid through the United Nations. *New York Times*, October 4, 1956, p. 24.

American aid, saying that "in actual practice we are quite certain that as of today, and you know the character and difficulties of the United Nations, as well as I do, you couldn't keep out politics."[148] In a similar vein Secretary of State Dulles explained his views on United Nations aid to Congress by noting that "it is important to remember that the United Nations, like every other organization, is not an abstraction. It operates through human beings like every organization does, and you have to measure it by the people, by the governments who play the role."[149] Thus, the public statements by American foreign policy makers indicated that they opposed sending American aid through multilateral organizations —such as the United Nations—to which the Russians belonged. Such a position is consistent with the administration view of the world situation in terms of competition between the "free world" and the Communist nations. The administration emphasis on a cold war rationale for economic aid makes it desirable for us to distinguish between those multilateral agencies which could be useful tools in the cold war and those which could not. If we make this distinction, we are less likely to regard the subsequent American support for the International Development Association and the Inter-American Development Bank as a complete reversal of previous policy on multilateral aid since neither of these institutions included Communist nations as members.[150]

Hard Loans

The conventional loan was still regarded as a valuable technique of statecraft. Of all the forms of public capital movement this one aroused the least domestic opposition. From the business community's point of view it was the least likely to undermine private international lending. And from the Congressional viewpoint it was one of the least costly forms of techniques of statecraft involving the movement of public capital. With regard to the establishment of the IFC, August Maffry told an interviewer that, hav-

---

[148] *New York Times,* May 5, 1956, p. 8.

[149] Senate Committee on Foreign Relations, *Mutual Security Hearings,* 1956, pp. 43–44.

[150] Such a distinction is seldom made by scholars. See for example Mikesell, p. 349; Montgomery, pp. 274–76; and Benjamin Higgins, *United Nations and U.S. Foreign Economic Policy* (Homewood, Ill.: Irwin, 1962), pp. 84–87 *et passim.*

ing decided in principle to make a gesture toward the underdeveloped nations, "the government looked around for the cheapest thing to do, and the cheapest thing to do was the IFC."[151] Given the domestic popularity of hard loans relative to either soft loans or grants, there can be little doubt that policy makers would have been quite content to rely exclusively on them if they thought that their objectives could be attained in this way.

Grants

Previous discussion pointed out that from 1954 to 1956 there were occasional references by executive branch spokesmen to the danger of soft loans. It was also indicated that neither Congress nor the business elite liked grants as a technique of statecraft. We must conclude, therefore, that the continued importance of grants during the 1954–57 period reflected an administration belief that grants were more effective in attaining the goals of American policy than either hard or soft loans. However, throughout the period grants were often publicly deprecated by the executive branch and a desire to abandon them was often expressed. The fact that this desire was not reflected in actual policy operations leads us to suspect that the homage paid to the loan principle was by way of pacifying Congress and the business community. In any event, the disparagement of grants reached a peak in 1957 when the executive submitted its DLF proposal. In 1957 the executive almost exceeded Congressional vigor in its denunciation of grants. "Experience has shown," Douglas Dillon noted, "that it is far better to extend development assistance in the form of loans than as grants. This is true even in cases where it becomes necessary to make loans on unusually generous terms."[152]

Soft Loans

Soft lending represented an innovation in American foreign policy during the 1954–57 period and was perceived as such by policy makers. Milton S. Eisenhower, for example, describes the creation of the DLF to make soft loans as "a sharp departure from

[151] Quoted in Matecki, p. 149.

[152] Douglas Dillon, "Encouraging Economic Growth in Less Developed Countries of the Free World," *Department of State Bulletin,* July 1, 1957, pp. 32–33.

traditional policy."[153] Why did the governmental decision makers change their minds about this technique of statecraft in this period? It will be argued that the increased emphasis on soft loans resulted from changes in the foreign policy makers' perception of: (a) the importance of the foreign policy goal of promoting economic growth abroad relative to other goals, (b) the domestic political feasibility of soft loans relative to other techniques of statecraft, and (c) the effectiveness of other techniques in stimulating growth.

Importance of economic development.—Beginning in 1954 there were indications that the administration was increasing the importance it attached to economic development as a foreign policy goal. Two appointments in December 1954 were significant in this respect. Nelson Rockefeller, who was known to have a special interest in economic aspects of the cold war, was appointed as White House Administrative Assistant for foreign policy. Four days later the President appointed Joseph M. Dodge, his former Budget Director, as head of a Council of Foreign Economic Policy and charged him to help develop strategy for economic phases of the cold war.

Other evidence of a change in policy makers' perceptions of economic growth was furnished by the persistent recurrence of newspaper stories describing the administration's belief that the cold war was settling down to a long period of competitive coexistence and that the main battleground was likely to be in the field of economic development.[154] James Reston claimed that the National Security Council had reviewed cold war policies in November, 1954, and had found them wanting with regard to economic aspects of policy. He noted that the council was worried about the speed of Communist China's economic development relative to that of India, the Russian foreign aid program, and the failure of the United States and its allies to meet this challenge.[155]

We would hesitate to take such newspaper reports seriously were it not for their subsequent confirmation by public statements

[153] Milton S. Eisenhower, *The Wine Is Bitter: The United States and Latin America* (Garden City, N.Y.: Doubleday, 1963), p. 252.

[154] See *New York Times*, November 24, 1954, p. 1; November 28, 1954, Part 4, p. 5; December 4, 1954, p. 1; December 8, 1954, p. 1; December 12, 1954, p. 1.

[155] *New York Times*, November 28, 1954, Part 4, p. 8.

and actions. In December, 1954, Secretary of State Dulles announced plans to increase economic aid to Asia, and he noted that both he and the President agreed that the cold war was becoming a long-term economic struggle.[156] President Eisenhower stressed the importance of economic growth in underdeveloped areas in his message to Congress on foreign economic policy in January, 1955.[157] And in his "State of the Union" message in January, 1956, he pointed out that "Communist tactics against the free nations have shifted from reliance on violence and the threat of violence to reliance on division, enticement and duplicity."[158] Dulles also made public statements outlining his conception of the changing nature of the Communist threat.[159] State Department perceptions of the changing nature of the cold war during the 1954–57 period were reflected in a publication released early in 1958—*The Sino-Soviet Economic Offensive in the Less Developed Countries*. This publication described the new Communist tactic of "economic penetration" as the "most dangerous of all."[160] And the foreword by Douglas Dillon, then Deputy Undersecretary of State for Economic Affairs, gave a clear statement of the thinking which had preceded the publication:

. . . In 1953, following the death of Premier Stalin, the new leadership of the Kremlin had launched a different and unannounced offensive against the free nations—a massive program of trade, aid, and technical assistance aimed at the world's less developed countries. The nature of the major aid agreements which the Sino-Soviet bloc has concluded with these "target" countries and the intensity with which the bloc has pursued its trade-aid campaign in the last 3 years have helped to underscore the statements of Nikita Khrushchev, now Premier of the U.S.S.R., who declared in 1955: "We value trade least for economic reasons and most for political purposes."

It is of great importance that the American people, now well aware of the technical and scientific challenge posed by the Communist world, understand and rise to meet the equally great, and perhaps more subtly

[156] *New York Times,* December 8, 1954, p. 1.

[157] Text reprinted in *New York Times,* January 11, 1955, p. 16.

[158] Text reprinted in *New York Times,* January 6, 1956, p. 10. On this point see also, Sherman Adams, *Firsthand Report* (New York: Harper & Bros., 1961), p. 395.

[159] See for example two speeches reprinted in *New York Times,* December 9, 1955, p. 8; and February 27, 1956, p. 6.

[160] P. 1.

dangerous, offensive which the Sino-Soviet bloc has vigorously launched in the less developed areas. This offensive represents an attempt by the Sino-Soviet bloc to employ its growing economic and industrial capacities as a means for bringing the newly developing free nations within the Communist orbit.[161]

Besides the decision makers' changing estimate of the nature of the Communist threat, there was another reason for the increased importance of economic development. The underdeveloped nations never let the United States representatives forget about their problems. As in the 1949–53 period the American representatives perceived that they were under constant pressure from these nations. In explaining the background of the United States decision to support the IFC proposal, Senator H. Alexander Smith noted that "the matter was presented to the United States Delegation [to the United Nations] in the light of the insistent demands of the underdeveloped countries for some kind of economic development program such as SUNFED. The Delegation believed that it was unwise to continue to say 'no' to such requests. . . ."[162]

In sum, the United States policy makers were less likely in the 1954–57 period to be satisfied with foreign growth rates which had been judged acceptable in previous years. They were more likely to want to push economic development at a rate faster than that which reliance on hard lending would make probable.[163]

Political feasibility of soft loans.—The increased interest in stimulating economic growth abroad does not tell us why policy makers turned to soft loans instead of grants. One reason was that soft lending was more feasible in terms of domestic politics than it had been in earlier periods. In the first place, the business community was beginning to show signs of softening its traditional hostility to all forms of foreign aid, especially soft loans. It was noted in earlier discussion that a liberal element in the business community, represented by the Committee for Economic Development, approved of foreign aid and, to some extent, of soft loans.

---

[161] *Ibid.*, p. iii.   [162] Quoted in Matecki, p. 146.

[163] Note that this situation is described in terms of probable rates of growth. We often find this phrased in terms of the rate "permitted" by hard lending. This is unfortunate since it implies that hard lending necessarily places a limit on the growth rate, an implication which is true only if one makes a *ceterus paribus* assumption. If governmental policies are not assumed to be fixed, hard lending, per se, is not so restrictive on the growth rate as is often implied.

In addition, the large number of businessmen in administrative posts tended to hasten legitimation of foreign aid in general. And the fact that the respected Eugene Black approved of soft lending gave policy makers even more evidence of the softening of business opposition to soft loans.

Besides the increasing legitimacy of soft loans in the eyes of businessmen, there were Congressional attitudes which increased the feasibility of soft lending. The Congressional desire to dispose of agricultural surpluses opened the possibility of additional resources being made available to foreign policy makers. However, it also made possible the substitution of such surpluses for dollar appropriations, an alternative which the executive branch opposed throughout the 1954-57 period. The intensity of the legislators' interest in the agricultural surplus disposal programs was so great that it would have been impolitic for the State Department to oppose them.[164] Therefore, we can say that insofar as the disposal programs involved soft loans, the foreign policy makers embraced them mainly to please Congress.

The basic problem confronting the executive branch was how to pry dollar appropriations out of a Congress which was hostile to foreign aid. The policy makers were well aware that Congress disliked grants more than it disliked loans. Until 1957, however, the attitude of the policy makers toward the legislative loan requirements had resembled that of a small boy taking castor oil. In 1957 an administration spokesman described the alternatives as perceived by the policy makers: (a) continued reliance on grants, (b) reduction of aid and consequent elimination of some foreign policy objectives, or (c) soft lending via the DLF.[165] Given the attitude of Congress toward grants, it is not surprising that the administration chose the third alternative. The fact that the executive branch conceived soft loans primarily in terms of the short-run goal of securing appropriations from Congress rather than in terms of their greater effectiveness relative to grants was illustrated by Secretary Dulles' comments during appropriations hearings on the DLF:

[164] On Dulles' antipathy toward PL 480 see Adams, pp. 389-91.

[165] House Committee on Appropriations, *Mutual Security Hearings*, 1957, pp. 542-43.

MR. DENTON: Do you not think that it will cause hard feeling later when the soft loans come due and cannot be paid, if that is the case?

SECRETARY DULLES: It may, but I do not care about that. If the making of these loans saves a country from communism, a people, an area, the loss of which to communism would be bad for the United States, I do not care whether they like us or hate us. We will have accomplished our purpose.

MR. DENTON: What I am thinking about, you are accomplishing it now, but what will be the effect when the loan comes due and you cannot pay the soft loan? Will we accomplish our purpose then?

SECRETARY DULLES: I do not know. That will be a problem for some other Secretary of State, not me.[166]

Commenting on the prospects for the foreign aid bill in 1957, the *New York Times* noted that observers generally agreed that one reason for the generally favorable outlook for the foreign aid bill was the willingness of the executive to shift economic aid to a loan basis.[167] Even the stalwart foe of foreign aid, Senator Capehart, announced that he would support the DLF proposal, the first time he had ever voted for a foreign aid bill.

The executive's concern for securing appropriations was also reflected in its emphasis on the circumvention of the appropriations process and on the type of soft loan most like a grant—that repayable in local currency. From a strictly economic point of view, the type of lending envisioned for the DLF resembled grant operations more than it did conventional loan operations. Although it acquiesced to the Congressional desire for loans, the executive sought to facilitate future access to funds by securing authorization to borrow directly from the Treasury. In this connection Dulles argued that the annual authorization-appropriation cycle was really the "heart of the problem" of foreign aid.[168] The fact that the administration's shift from cool tolerance of soft loans to enthusiastic advocacy was linked with an attempt to bypass the annual authorization-appropriation cycle leads us to suspect that the executive was motivated more by a desire to enlarge its foreign aid appropriations than by a sudden awareness of the merits of soft lending as a technique for promoting economic development.

[166] *Ibid.*, p. 120.

[167] *New York Times,* May 24, 1957, p. 9.

[168] House Committee on Foreign Affairs, *Mutual Security Hearings,* 1957, p. 515.

Be that as it may, there must have been little doubt in the minds of executive branch policy planners that Congress would receive a request for foreign aid funds more warmly if the funds were to be lent on soft terms than if they were to be given away.

The increase in the political feasibility of soft loans relative to other techniques was partially the counterpart of the decreasing political feasibility of trade liberalization as a technique for promoting growth. In both 1954 and 1955 the administration warned Congress that failure to liberalize trade would lead to greater demands for economic aid.[169] But in both 1954 and 1955 Congress made it clear that it was not going to tolerate the launching of a vigorous program of trade liberalization. The executive branch, therefore, behaved exactly as it had predicted it would; it intensified its efforts to increase economic aid in 1956 and 1957. From the viewpoint of the executive, Congress had, in effect, vetoed its proposal to reduce trade barriers as a means of stimulating foreign economic growth, and it was threatening to veto the use of grants for the same purpose.

Effectiveness of other techniques.—For over a decade the executive branch had been warning Congress that failure to reduce trade barriers would reduce the effectiveness of other techniques for promoting economic growth, such as reliance on domestic effort, hard loans, and private investment. The executive branch was well aware that servicing hard loans—public or private— would be more difficult without reduction of American tariffs, that potential private foreign investors would be more willing to invest if American tariffs were lowered, and that foreign domestic efforts would be more effective if foreign exchange could be earned by selling in the American market. In 1954 President Eisenhower stressed that his proposals to curtail aid, expand trade, and increase private foreign investment were all interdependent, that each required the other; yet Congress refused to treat the program as an organic package.

The policy makers also had other reasons to believe that hard loans, private investment, and reliance on local effort were unlikely to be effective enough to satisfy them. All three of these tech-

---

[169] See President Eisenhower's messages to Congress on foreign economic policy reprinted in *New York Times*, March 31, 1954, p. 18; and January 11, 1955, p. 16. On Eisenhower's view of trade as an alternative to aid see also, Adams, pp. 381–82.

niques were based on an attempt to elicit a change in the policies of foreign governments. American policy makers were becoming increasingly aware of the strength of the nationalistic feeling in many underdeveloped nations and the consequent reluctance to adopt governmental policies necessary to make hard loans, reliance on local effort, and private investment effective.

In addition, American policy makers realized that underdeveloped nations were less susceptible to pressure to change their policies since the Soviet Union had begun to provide an alternative for them. No longer could the United States present the underdeveloped nations with the alternatives of creating a "favorable investment climate" or going without capital. The underdeveloped nations' incentive to rely on local effort, to take hard loans, and to welcome private investors was considerably reduced by the Soviet willingness to provide aid on a soft loan basis.

During the 1954-57 period the executive branch was exposed to arguments stressing the limited effectiveness of hard loans, private investment, and reliance on local effort in reports originating in academic circles. The most influential of these, prepared by the Center for International Studies at the Massachusetts Institute of Technology (MIT), was known as the "Millikan-Rostow report."[170] This report, according to the *New York Times*, circulated at the highest government levels and was known to have been considered by the National Security Council in the spring of 1956.[171] Later that year the MIT group prepared for the Special Senate Committee to Study the Foreign Aid Program a study containing the same basic ideas and lines of argument. Scattered throughout the views expressed by the MIT group we find references to what private investors "cannot"[172] do, to projects which "by their very nature"[173] are not attractive to private investors, and

[170] Max F. Millikan and W. W. Rostow, *A Proposal: Key to an Effective Foreign Policy* (New York: Harper & Bros., 1957).

[171] *New York Times*, May 20, 1956, p. 1.

[172] U.S., Congress, Senate, *Foreign Aid Program: Compilation of Studies and Surveys*, prepared under the direction of the Special Senate Committee to Study the Foreign Aid Program, Study No. 1, "The Objectives of United States Economic Assistance Programs," prepared by the Center for International Studies, Massachusetts Institute of Technology, 85th Cong., 1st sess., 1957, Senate Doc. 52, pp. 40–41. (Cited hereafter as "The Objectives of United States Economic Assistance Programs," Study No. 1, *Senate Studies on Foreign Aid Program*, 1957.)

[173] *Ibid.*

to limits on the ability of the IBRD and Export-Import Bank to expand their activities.[174] Such concepts involve an implicit assumption of governmental policies in recipient nations as fixed. If we do not make this assumption, and the possibility of governmental subsidies, for example, is held open, we cannot find projects which *cannot* be financed by private investors. The MIT group concluded that in the early stages of economic development capital "must" be supplied in the form of grants and soft loans.[175] This frequent use of such words as "must," "need," "necessary," and "cannot," instead of more restrained terms involving probabilities and desires, reminds us of the soft loan polemic in United Nations publications. The MIT group emphasized the desirability of using a variety of loan and grant forms and of maintaining "maximum flexibility between grants and loans."[176] It is not intended here to provide a critique of the MIT approach, but rather to show that foreign policy makers were exposed to academic reports stressing the limited effectiveness of hard loans, private investment, and reliance on local effort and emphasizing the usefulness of grants and soft loans.[177] The point to note here is the possible effect of such arguments on executive branch perceptions of the situation and selection of alternatives.

Summary

In sum, the situation as perceived by the foreign policy makers was one in which they believed that promotion of economic development had increased in importance as a goal of policy; therefore they wanted to increase the effectiveness of the United States policy for promoting such development. In surveying the techniques of statecraft which could be used to spur economic growth they could see that both grants and trade liberalization were not feasible in terms of domestic politics. They also believed that hard

---

[174] *Ibid.*

[175] Millikan and Rostow, pp. 52–53.

[176] "Objectives of United States Economic Assistance Programs," Study No. 1, *Senate Studies on Foreign Aid Program,* 1957, pp. 40–41.

[177] The writer has submitted the basic concepts of the MIT approach to critical review elsewhere. See: P. N. Rosenstein–Rodan, "International Aid for Underdeveloped Countries," *Review of Economics and Statistics,* XLIII (May, 1961), 107–38; and David A. Baldwin, "International Aid for Underdeveloped Countries: A Comment," *Review of Economics and Statistics,* XLIV (May, 1962), 213.

loans, reliance on domestic efforts, and stimulation of private investment were unlikely to be effective enough to bring about a growth rate judged by the policy makers to be satisfactory. The policy makers were thus left with soft lending as the technique of statecraft which they believed best combined effectiveness with domestic political feasibility.

IV. EFFECTIVENESS OF POLICY: 1954–57

RELIANCE ON DOMESTIC EFFORT

An additional limitation on the efficacy of relying on local efforts appeared in the 1954–57 period. If the United States advised underdeveloped nations to rely on their own efforts, these nations could turn to the alternative of accepting help from the Soviet Union. Thus, a refusal by the United States to give aid might encourage an underdeveloped nation to ask help from the Soviet Union instead of encouraging it to strengthen its domestic development efforts.

STIMULATION OF PRIVATE INVESTMENT

Trade Liberalization

The attempt to stimulate private foreign investment by reducing trade barriers lacked effectiveness largely because of the mildness of the trade liberalization measures taken during the 1954–57 period. The administration had to fight hard to prevent reversal of the slow trend toward freer trade. The most important limitation on trade liberalization, to put it bluntly, was that there was not enough of it to make much difference.

Improvement of the "Investment Climate"

Private foreign investment did increase during this period, but a large portion of it went to Canada instead of to underdeveloped nations. Also, a large portion was invested in the petroleum industry. Political scientists often seem to believe that investment in extractive industries, such as petroleum, does not promote economic development. There is nothing, however, necessarily unproductive about such investments. What should be noted is that the petroleum industry often engages in political activities which underdeveloped nations find offensive.[178] This has led some underdeveloped nations—Brazil, for example—to oppose foreign investment in their petroleum industry.

A number of other factors also restricted the efficacy of American attempts to induce other nations to change their policies toward private investment. First, the American failure to reduce trade barriers made underdeveloped nations wary of the possibility that foreign investors' future desires to convert their earnings into dollars might cause a strain on the balance of payments. The Canadian ambassador to the United States warned of this possibility in December 1954:

> Much has been written about the necessity, as United States foreign aid comes to an end, for underdeveloped countries, . . . to create a domestic climate that will attract foreign, and principally American investment.
>
> Less has been said about the corollary that overseas countries will be reluctant to welcome dollar investment unless they can see a fair prospect of ultimately earning an increased volume of dollars from the United States.[179]

The effectiveness of the United States attempt to get other governments to improve their "investment climates" was further reduced by the increase in the alternative sources of capital, other than private investment, available to underdeveloped nations. To the extent that underdeveloped nations had alternatives available, the efficacy of the American threat to avoid providing alternatives was curtailed.[180] During the 1954–57 period alternative sources of capital were provided by the Soviet Union, and the United States itself was stepping up its economic aid to underdeveloped nations, thus undermining its own attempts to blackmail such nations into improving their "investment climates."

In addition to the increase in alternative sources of capital available to underdeveloped nations, another factor limited the willingness of governments in such nations to change their policies

[178] Evidence of the political aspects of the activities of the petroleum industry is scarce. The most perceptive analysis is by Robert Engler, *The Politics of Oil* (New York: Macmillan, 1961).

[179] Quoted in *New York Times*, December 3, 1954, p. 43.

[180] Cf. Thomas C. Schelling, *The Strategy of Conflict* (Cambridge, Mass.: Harvard University Press, 1960), p. 6.

toward private capital—the lack of credibility of the American threat to avoid providing alternatives to reliance on private investment. The credibility of the American threat was impaired in the following ways: (1) The underdeveloped nations could perceive that the United States interest in their economic development was related to the cold war, and they therefore tended to take the American threat less seriously.[181] (2) The fact that the United States did in fact launch several new aid programs, such as the DLF, the IFC, and PL 480, during this period strengthened the underdeveloped nations' belief that American policy on provision of public capital was subject to change. (3) The number of governmental studies and avowed reappraisals of problems connected with foreign aid during this period added to the strength of this belief. (4) The vague criteria by which American aid was distributed and the reluctance of Congress to make long-term commitments increased the uncertainty of the underdeveloped nations regarding the intentions of the United States. This lack of a clear demarcation of American intentions gave potential aid recipients a "disincentive" to husband their resources.[182] Congress had, after all, given them reason to believe that those nations with the biggest "crises" would get the most aid. And the executive branch could not make firm advance commitments because it never knew what Congress was going to do during the authorization-appropriation process.

Nationalism continued to be an important force in underdeveloped nations, and its emphasis on industrialization, government planning, and anti-colonialism once again increased the reluctance of governments to improve their treatment of foreign private investors.

In sum, governments in underdeveloped nations hesitated to improve their "investment climates" because of: (*a*) the existence of alternative sources of capital, (*b*) the lack of credibility of the

[181] In discussing bargaining situations, Thomas C. Schelling refers to the possibility that the threatened punishment will hurt the threatener as much as it will the one threatened, perhaps more. He notes that "there is an analogy between a parent's threat to a child and the threat that a wealthy paternalistic nation makes to the weak and disorganized government of a poor nation in, say, extending foreign aid and demanding 'sound' economic policies . . . in return." *Ibid.*, p. 11.

[182] "This fear of a 'disincentive' is a real one wherever the limits to U.S. intentions . . . cannot be made clearly visible in advance." Thomas C. Schelling, "American Foreign Assistance," *World Politics*, VII (July, 1955), 609.

United States threat to avoid providing more alternatives, (c) the failure of the United States to lower tariffs, and (d) the strength of nationalist feelings in such nations.

PUBLIC CAPITAL

Hard Loans

The combination of previous hard lending and American refusal to lower tariffs restricted the efficacy of hard loans as a technique for spurring economic growth. The existence of debt contracted in earlier years and the difficulty of earning foreign exchange with which to service this debt made underdeveloped nations reluctant to take on more hard loans and made hard lenders less anxious to lend. In bankers' jargon, the underdeveloped countries' debt-servicing capacity was decreasing.[183] But it would be more accurate to say that the underdeveloped nations were reaching a point where servicing of more conventional loans would require sacrifices which would be politically unpopular.

Another reason for the hesitancy of governments in underdeveloped nations to implement measures necessary to qualify for hard loans was that their incentive to do so was lessened by their expectations regarding the increasing availability of soft loans from the United States and the Soviet Union. Why should they effect politically unpopular internal reforms in order to qualify for hard loans if they could get soft loans without such measures? The president of the Export-Import Bank noted in 1957 that he feared his hard loan standards would be undermined by establishment of the DLF.[184] The rationale behind soft lending was, after all, the adaptation of loan terms to the conditions in the underdeveloped nations instead of requiring adaptation of the conditions in these countries to the terms of the loan. Douglas Dillon argued in 1957 that the fact that the terms of DLF loans would be less strict than those of IBRD or Export-Import Bank loans would "help to insure

[183] On this point see Dragoslav Avramovic, assisted by Ravi Gulhati, *Debt Servicing Capacity and Postwar Growth in International Indebtedness* (Baltimore: Johns Hopkins Press, 1958); Dragoslav Avramovic and Ravi Gulhati, *Debt Servicing Problems of Low-Income Countries, 1956–1958* (Baltimore: Johns Hopkins Press, 1960); and Dragoslav Avramovic et al., *Economic Growth and External Debt* (Baltimore: Johns Hopkins Press, 1964).

[184] Senate Special Committee to Study the Foreign Aid Program, *Hearings*, 1957, pp. 531–34, 538–40.

that its financing complements, rather than substitutes for, the financing available from these other sources."[185] It was, however, precisely this difference in the strictness of terms that gave potential recipients an incentive to try to substitute soft loans for hard. Mr. Dillon's assertion to the contrary is incorrect.

It was widely recognized that soft lending might undermine hard lending, but it was argued that this effect would be minimized by close co-ordination of the activities of the IBRD, Export-Import Bank, and the DLF. In 1957 ICA Director Hollister assured Congress that he worked closely with the IBRD and the Export-Import Bank in order to prevent competition among them.[186] But in an interchange with Senator John F. Kennedy he indicated ignorance regarding IBRD loan terms:

SENATOR KENNEDY: As I understand it, the World Bank provides for repayment in the currency which is given to the country; is that right?

MR. HOLLISTER: The World Bank makes its loans you say in currency which is advanced to it?

SENATOR KENNEDY: Provides for repayment in currency in which the loan is made?

MR. HOLLISTER: I think so, though I am not an authority on it.[187]

One wonders how effective co-ordination could have taken place when the head of the ICA did not even know on what terms the IBRD lent its money.

Grants

Grants were an effective means of transferring capital to underdeveloped nations without imposing a balance of payments strain. Given the United States tariff policy we could make a good case for using grants, which raised few debt-servicing problems. A common argument against grants is that they may actually impede economic growth by encouraging the recipients to waste resources. The validity of this argument is weakened, however, by Robert Asher's observation that in most foreign aid operations the ulti-

[185] Douglas Dillon, "Our Mutual Security Programs," *Department of State Bulletin*, July 15, 1957, p. 117.

[186] Senate Special Committee to Study the Foreign Aid Program, *Hearings*, 1957, p. 499.

[187] *Ibid.*, p. 484.

mate aid recipient is unaware of the technique by which the capital transfer was effected.[188]

A more likely limitation on grants is the possibility that governments in recipient nations will tend to become dependent on grants and will slacken their own efforts. Much empirical research would be required to make even a rough estimate of the extent to which this happened during the 1954–57 period. We can point out, however, that the governments in underdeveloped nations have more incentive to slacken their efforts if there is reason to believe that grant aid might be increased accordingly than they do if the donor has clearly defined his intentions regarding future aid and has convinced potential recipients that not one additional penny will be made available for any reason. American intentions regarding future foreign aid were anything but clear during the 1954–57 period.

Soft Loans

It is difficult to evaluate the efficacy of soft lending during the 1954–57 period since the total process of loan and repayment was not completed within this period. Most of the soft loans during this period had not begun to be repaid by 1957. Repayments in local currency were supposed to begin flowing in large quantities in fiscal year 1959, and ICA officials were reportedly worried about possible uses of such currency.[189]

The immediate effect of soft loans during this period was to transfer resources to underdeveloped nations. In this respect such loans were more effective than lending them their own currency. But we can only determine the net impact of soft lending on the basis of estimates of the degree to which hard loans, public or private, would have actually been made in the absence of soft lending. For reasons noted above there was good reason to suspect that underdeveloped nations would not have changed their policies toward private investors much in the absence of soft loans during this period. We would also have to estimate the effect of soft loans

188 Asher, pp. 14–16, 24–25. "In short, there is no necessary connection between the form of the intergovernmental transaction and the financial terms on which the capital or the commodities obtained subsequently become available to business enterprises and private citizens in the country aided" (p. 25).

189 *New York Times*, April 14, 1957, p. 48.

—actual and *expected*—on the governmental policies in recipient nations.

The ultimate effect of soft lending during this period depended upon what was done with the local currency repayments in later years. To the extent that this currency was spent for American embassy expenses and other expenses which the United States would have incurred even in the absence of soft loans, no dollars were available to underdeveloped nations which would not have been available anyway. A second possible use was to loan such currency back to the underdeveloped countries ad infinitum or just give it back to them. In either case the economic effect of the soft loan would be similar to that of a grant. A third possibility was to let the currency pile up and try to ignore it—known as the "ostrich approach." Two possible ramifications of this approach related to economic development. First, the piling up of these currencies in the hands of the American government could affect the behavior of governments in underdeveloped nations because of their expectations regarding American use of it. And second, a later release of these currencies could, if not properly co-ordinated with policies in the home country, cause inflation. Fear of such a move might impede development planning efforts in underdeveloped nations.[190]

Public Law 480

Operations under PL 480 involved some difficulties justifying special attention here. Three major limitations on the efficacy of surplus commodity disposal arise from the nature of the initial transfer of resources, the effect on dollar receipts in the recipient nation, and the use of local currencies by the United States. The first limit is the inflexibility of the initial transfer of resources relative to an initial transfer of dollars to be used in any way the recipient sees fit. This operation is like the owner of a small grocery who gives his son an allowance but insists that it be spent in the store—and specifically on some canned goods which have not been selling very well. The reaction of the recipients of PL 480 aid often resembles that of the receiver of such an allowance.

We should not make the mistake of dismissing food on the grounds that what developing nations need is capital. Since we are

[190] For an example of such a situation in Indonesia see Higgins, p. 192.

using a definition of capital as that which is not consumed in order to expand productive capacity, we must consider surplus agricultural commodities as capital inasmuch as Americans abstained from consuming them, and underdeveloped nations could conceivably use them to increase productive capacity. How? Well-fed workers are more productive than ill-fed ones in many situations. The relevant question relates to the extent to which additional food facilitates an increase in the productive capacity of underdeveloped nations. Two possible ways come immediately to mind. The nation receiving food can release some of its domestic food producers to do other work. The problem here is that in many less developed nations. Two possible ways come immediately to mind. There is also the possibility that the additional food will allow previously undernourished persons to eat enough to enter the labor force. Again the problem is that many underdeveloped nations do not have enough jobs for the willing workers *before* the additional food is made available.

It is also possible that the government in a developing nation is having difficulty in generating tax revenues, possibly to control inflation. If this is the case, the sale of food by the recipient government may be a useful tool for alleviating inflationary pressure.

If the developing nation needs capital equipment, such as machinery, obtainable only from richer nations, then receipt of extra food may be no help at all in solving its problems. Additional food could only help get a tractor, for example, if the food freed domestic resources which could be used for the importing or domestic production of tractors. In short, the most important limitation on surplus food in spurring economic development is that food has fewer uses than dollars.

A second major limit on the usefulness of PL 480 is based on its net effect on the availability of dollars to the recipient nation. This problem can be broken into four elements: (1) Does the recipient of PL 480 food receive fewer dollars under the Mutual Security Program than it otherwise would have? In discussing Congress above it was noted that less developed nations probably do receive fewer dollars from Mutual Security Programs. A precise estimate of the degree to which this is true is hindered by the fact that the size of Congressional appropriations for Mutual Security was probably affected by legislative expectations regarding use of the funds to dispose of surplus food. (2) Is the expenditure of local currencies generated by agricultural disposal programs to pay United States obligations in the recipient nation an expenditure which would have been made in the absence of the availability of such currencies? To the extent that local currency is used instead of dollars for expenses which would have been incurred anyway, the underdeveloped nation has been induced to spend its (potential) dollars on American agricultural exports. We can assume that at least the expenditures for embassy expenses and military procurement would have been made even in the absence of PL 480 funds. (3) Would the underdeveloped nations have purchased the food anyway? Insofar as they would have, the receipt of PL 480 aid would allow them to conserve dollars. There is little evidence, however, that many underdeveloped nations give high priority to importing food in allocating their limited supply of foreign exchange. (4) Do PL 480 activities in third countries reduce the foreign exchange earning capacity of a developing country? Again, it is difficult to estimate this, but we do know that (a) American surplus disposal involves exporting agricultural commodities, (b) most underdeveloped nations rely on exports of agricultural products to earn foreign exchange, and (c) nations receiving cotton under PL 480 from the United States are probably going to spend less to import cotton from other sources. It is probable that, to some extent, American PL 480 activities in country X do tend to reduce the exports of country Y to country X.

A third limit on the efficacy of surplus disposal programs depends on what is done by the United States with the local currencies generated by such programs. As with the currencies coming in under other soft loan programs, the two most important ways in which economic development could be impeded by such currencies were causing of inflation by untimely release of the currency and damage to development planning from the expectations of such a release.

The major limitations on surplus disposal programs in promoting economic development may be summarized as follows: (1) Surplus agricultural commodities are less effective means of spurring development than dollars. (2) The net impact of providing surplus commodities may have resulted in a decrease in the availability of dollars to developing nations. (3) There was the possibility that the United States would use the local currencies in such a way as to impair the development effort.

POPULATION

The population "explosion" in underdeveloped nations again constituted the major threat to economic growth. The magnitude of this problem was becoming so great as to threaten to cancel even the most vigorous efforts of the developed and underdeveloped nations.

V

Adoption and Refinement of Soft Loans
1958–62

I. WAS ECONOMIC GROWTH A GOAL OF UNITED STATES POLICY?

During the 1958–62 period United States policy statements evinced a desire to stimulate economic growth in underdeveloped areas for three main reasons. Growth was viewed as: (a) a requisite for peace in the long run, (b) a requisite for internal political stability, and (c) an alternative to dependence on the Communist bloc. The linking of economic development with a vague concept of long-run peace had been a continuing thread in American policy since World War II. Undersecretary of State Dillon noted in 1959 that one of the basic premises of American foreign economic policy was that "satisfactory economic progress in all countries is one of the preconditions to the achievement of a durable peace."[1] The concept of economic development as vital to the long-run security of the United States was echoed by the Kennedy administration. U. Alexis Johnson, Deputy Undersecretary for Political Affairs, pointed out in 1962 that "these emerging nations may well hold the key to the world of tomorrow. Our ability to identify ourselves with their aspirations, indeed our ability to permit this revolution to unfold and not be turned back by communism, is crucial to our own future."[2]

The second reason for American interest in foreign economic development was that the United States wanted to help less developed nations to attain internal political stability without re-

[1] Douglas Dillon, "American Foreign Economic Policy," *Department of State Bulletin,* November 23, 1959, p. 739.

[2] U. Alexis Johnson, "The Emerging Nations of Asia," *Department of State Bulletin,* January 8, 1962, p. 53.

sorting to totalitarian forms of political organization. In 1960 a spokesman for the Eisenhower administration put it thus:

The countries of Asia, Africa, and Latin America are part of the free world, but they are not committed irrevocably to freedom. They *are* committed to economic growth. The question is whether they can achieve the economic growth they so urgently desire in an environment of freedom or whether, overwhelmed by massive problems, they turn to totalitarian rule at home and aggression abroad.[3]

Secretary of State Dean Rusk voiced a similar view in 1962 when he remarked that "in today's world, only a nation which is making steady economic progress, which is offering hope and a realization of that hope to its people, can maintain the political stability essential to the maintenance of its national integrity and political liberty."[4]

The United States policy makers also wanted to spur foreign economic development in order to reduce the probability that recipient nations would join the Communist bloc. "These peoples," President Eisenhower observed, "desperately hoping to lift themselves to decent levels of living must not, by our neglect, be forced to seek help from, and finally become virtual satellites of, those who proclaim their hostility to freedom."[5] The rationale was that less developed nations were less likely to become dependent on the Communist bloc if alternative methods of promoting economic growth were available. The United States was thus concerned with providing some alternatives.

II. HOW TO PROMOTE ECONOMIC GROWTH: TECHNIQUES

The major changes in American techniques during the 1958–62 period were trends toward increased emphasis on public capital transfers in general and increased emphasis on soft loans in particular.

[3] Edwin M. Martin, "Aspects of U.S. Foreign Economic Policy," *Department of State Bulletin,* February 29, 1960, p. 341.

[4] Dean Rusk, "The Alliance for Progress in the Context of World Affairs," *Department of State Bulletin,* May 14, 1962, pp. 789–90.

[5] "The State of the Union," address of the President to Congress reprinted in *Department of State Bulletin,* January 25, 1960, p. 112.

RELIANCE ON DOMESTIC EFFORT

Although the United States adopted several new techniques for helping the less developed nations to grow economically, the order of magnitude of all the programs combined was so small that it was obvious that reliance on local effort was again to be important in American policy.[6] Policy statements by both the Eisenhower and Kennedy administrations frequently noted the importance of domestic efforts in stimulating economic development and the relatively limited contribution which external aid could make.[7] We should note, however, that the increased emphasis on public capital movements during this period meant a relative decline in the degree of reliance on domestic efforts.

STIMULATION OF PRIVATE CAPITAL FLOW

TRADE LIBERALIZATION

Although trade was not in fact liberalized much in the 1958–62 period, the United States executive branch pressed hard throughout the period for greater use of this technique of statecraft. In 1959 Undersecretary of State Dillon noted that "the prosperity and

---

[6] Current orthodoxy in the literature on economic aid should not be allowed to blind us to "reliance on local effort" as a technique available to policy makers. This technique gets relatively little attention, if I may speculate, because it is regarded as a limit on decision makers rather than an alternative regarding which a decision must be made. We suspect that the consensus among students of foreign aid is that the policy maker *must* rely on domestic effort. Those who doubt the usefulness of describing "reliance on local effort" as a technique of statecraft should consult Frederic Benham: "If a country is prepared to accept outside help, virtually everything it needs for a project could be imported. This happened during the war. For example, the American Army drained a swamp to provide a base in Trinidad. It imported all the equipment it needed, all the skilled workers it needed, the houses (prefabricated) for them to live in, the food for them to eat; it built roads and imported the jeeps and cars, and so forth. This kind of thing could be done almost anywhere. Resources may be limited, but not 'absorptive capacity.'" Frederic Benham, *Economic Aid to Underdeveloped Countries* (New York: Oxford University Press, 1961), p. 116. A decision to refrain from undertaking operations such as those described in Trinidad is thus a decision to rely on domestic effort.

[7] For example, see President Eisenhower's remarks in his 1960 "State of the Union" address emphasizing that development "is no mere matter of obtaining outside financial assistance" and that an "indispensable element in this process is a strong and continuing determination on the part of these nations to exercise the national discipline necessary for any sustained development period." *Department of State Bulletin*, January 26, 1960, p. 113. Compare this with Dean Rusk's observation that "no nation can develop unless it possesses its own inner determination to progress" and that external aid can give only a "marginal boost" to development efforts. "The Alliance for Progress in the Context of World Affairs," *Department of State Bulletin*, May 14, 1962, p. 791.

the economic well-being of the nations and their peoples will be fostered and furthered if artificial obstacles to world trade are held to the practicable minimum. We are convinced that liberal trade policies are essential to the raising of standards of living throughout the world."[8] Dillon added in 1960 that the "problem of world trade goes hand in hand with the complex and difficult problem of stimulating growth in the newly developing countries."[9] The Kennedy administration's view of trade liberalization as a means of stimulating growth was summarized in 1962:

In the lesser developed regions, . . . expanded trade will stimulate investment, provide more stable export markets and sources of supply, and thereby permit these countries to earn foreign exchange to supplement that now being received in the form of loans and grants. Eventually, of course, these earnings are expected to substitute for loans and grants as the lesser developed countries advance toward the ultimate goal of self-sustaining growth.[10]

A new aspect of American policy on reducing trade barriers appeared during the 1958–62 period. As prosperity increased in Europe, the United States began to bring diplomatic pressure to bear on other industrial nations to lower their trade barriers in order to help the underdeveloped countries.[11]

IMPROVEMENT OF "INVESTMENT CLIMATE"

During the 1958–62 period United States policy makers continued to feel that if an underdeveloped nation were to achieve self-sustaining growth in a "reasonable period of time, it must create conditions . . . conducive to private external investment, including assurances against discriminatory treatment and expropriation."[12] In order to encourage governments in developing nations to create such conditions, the United States again used the familiar techniques of advice, blackmail, and diplomacy.

[8] *Department of State Bulletin,* November 23, 1959, p. 739.

[9] Douglas Dillon, "A New Era in Free-World Economic Growth," *Department of State Bulletin,* March 14, 1960, p. 402.

[10] George C. McGhee, "Strategy of American Foreign Policy," *Department of State Bulletin,* April 23, 1962, p. 682.

[11] George Ball, "The Less Developed Countries and the Atlantic Partnership," *Department of State Bulletin,* March 12, 1962, p. 414.

[12] George Ball, "Sharing the Financial Burdens of a Changing World," *Department of State Bulletin,* October 15, 1962, p. 578.

Advice

In a report to the President, which was adopted as official policy, Milton S. Eisenhower offered the following pointers to less developed nations seeking private capital:

... avoidance of *discriminatory* restraints, the maintenance of *stable* financial and political policies within each country, the absence of *discriminatory* labor laws, *control* of inflationary forces, a *reasonable* return on the investment, ability to remit dividends to the lending country in the currency of that country, and above all, a *favorable* attitude toward private competitive enterprises which are to be financed with the private capital.[13]

The Kennedy administration also lectured the underdeveloped nations on the merits of economic development based on private enterprise. Some Kennedy supporters—and opponents—might be surprised to learn of a speech that the American ambassador to Mexico delivered in 1962 to a Latin American audience on the relevance of United States economic history to Latin American problems. This speech was liberally sprinkled with references to such "authorities" on economic development as Adam Smith, Ludwig Erhardt, John Chamberlain, Henry Hazlitt, and Ludwig Von Mises.[14] In the United Nations the American representative advised the underdeveloped nations that it was both necessary and desirable that they rely more on private foreign capital.[15] It was necessary, he argued, because public capital would be insufficient, and it was desirable because of the technical expertise which accompanies private investment. Without such expertise, he added, "nothing is easier than to build the wrong factory in the wrong place for the wrong product in the wrong market."[16]

[13] Milton S. Eisenhower, "United States–Latin American Relations, 1953–1958: Report to the President," *Department of State Bulletin*, January 19, 1959, p. 96. Italics mine. It should be noted that the potential private investor himself would decide what constituted "discriminatory" labor laws, "control" of inflation, "reasonable" returns, and a "favorable" attitude.

[14] Thomas C. Mann, "The Experience of the United States in Economic Development: Its Relevance for Latin America," *Department of State Bulletin*, November 19, 1962, pp. 772–77. It is interesting to note that President Johnson later elevated Mann to the third-ranking post in the State Department, Undersecretary for Economic Affairs.

[15] Adlai E. Stevenson, "United Nations Development Decade," *Department of State Bulletin*, August 6, 1962, pp. 228–30.

[16] *Ibid.*, p. 228.

Blackmail

The American threat to the underdeveloped nations consisted of three elements. First, there was the threat to suspend economic aid to governments which impaired their "investment climates" by expropriating American-owned property without making "equitable" compensation within six months after the event. The credibility of this threat was increased in 1962 when Congress amended the Foreign Assistance Act to make such action mandatory for the President.[17]

The second threat was to prevent the flow of capital through public channels for purposes for which private capital was available on "reasonable" terms. All of the major sources of public capital approved by United States policy operated under the proviso that they would provide capital only in the absence of the availability of private capital on "reasonable terms." These sources included the DLF, the IFC, the Export-Import Bank, the IBRD, the IDA, and the IADB. Credibility was lent to this threat by the United States preference for men with relatively conservative economic views as administrators of such organizations. The judgment of the administrators of each institution regarding the vague concept of "availability on reasonable terms" would, of course, determine the nature of the threat in any specific situation. It is therefore especially important to note that those in charge of public capital disbursing institutions usually shared an occupational background in business.

The third American threat was that to limit the total public capital flow to a size much smaller than the total amount of capital estimated as needed by the underdeveloped nations. This threat usually took the form of a warning to the less developed nations that public capital would not be forthcoming in sufficient amounts to meet all of their alleged needs. Credibility was lent to this threat by the fact that the total capital available from public sources *was* much smaller than the amount the underdeveloped

[17] See Foreign Assistance Act of 1961 as amended, section 620(e). On the development of American policy regarding suspension of aid as a means of improving "investment climates" see U.S., Congress, Committee on Foreign Affairs, *Expropriation of American-Owned Property by Foreign Governments in the Twentieth Century*, report prepared by the Legislative Reference Service, Library of Congress, 88th Cong., 1st sess., 1963, Committee Print, pp. 22–28, 40. Cited hereafter as House Committee on Foreign Affairs, *Expropriation of American-Owned Property*.

nations estimated that they needed in order to achieve a "satisfactory" rate of growth. In fact, there was widespread agreement that the amount of public capital likely to be forthcoming would be far less than *anyone's* estimate of the needs of the less developed nations. For example, Paul G. Hoffman worked out an estimate, on the basis of a number of independent studies, of the amount of capital which would be required to enable the less developed nations to increase per capita income at the rate of 2 per cent per year in the 1960's.[18] Although a 2 per cent growth rate would probably seem to be a modest enough goal to most people, Hoffman concluded that even the attainment of this goal would require $20 billion in addition to the public and private capital likely to be forthcoming from institutions existing in 1960.

Diplomacy

In addition to advice and threats to withhold public capital, the United States used diplomacy to encourage governments in less developed nations to improve their "investment climates." During the 1958–62 period the United States concluded two new treaties of friendship, commerce, and navigation with Pakistan and Vietnam. Diplomacy was also used on a day-to-day basis in an effort to improve the treatment of private capital. Secretary of State Rusk summarized this policy in the following manner:

We don't challenge in the strictest constitutional sense the right of a sovereign government to dispose of properties and peoples within its sovereign territory. . . . We do think that as a matter of policy it would be wise and prudent on their side to create conditions which will be attractive to the international investor, the private investor. So our influence is used wherever it can be and persistently, through our Embassies on a day-to-day basis, in our aid discussion and in direct aid negotiations, to underline the importance of private investment.[19]

INVESTMENT GUARANTIES

Besides trying to get other nations to improve their "investment climates," the United States continued to expand its investment guaranty program for compensating private investors in case gov-

[18] Paul G. Hoffman, *One Hundred Countries and One and One Quarter Billion People* (Washington: Albert D. and Mary Lasker Foundation, 1960).

[19] Quoted in House Committee on Foreign Affairs, *Expropriation of American-Owned Property*, p. 24.

ernments failed to improve "investment climates." Total investment guaranties in force rose from $157 million in 1958 to $796 million in 1962.[20] The emphasis on underdeveloped areas was sharpened in 1959 when the Mutual Security Act of 1959 excluded economically developed countries from coverage under the investment guaranty program.

In sum, the United States attempted to stimulate the flow of private capital by trade liberalization, improvement of "investment climates," and investment guaranties during the 1958–62 period. In this respect the period resembled the preceding two periods. It differed from preceding periods in that the importance of stimulating private capital was decreasing relative to that of furnishing capital through public channels.

FURNISHING OF CAPITAL THROUGH PUBLIC CHANNELS

In both words and deeds the Eisenhower and Kennedy administrations increased the emphasis on furnishing capital through public channels as a technique for promoting economic growth abroad in the 1958–62 period. In 1958 Douglas Dillon, then Deputy Undersecretary of State for Economic Affairs, stated the administration's view that although some of the external resources needed for economic development could come from new private investments and from established government sources, such as the IBRD and the Export-Import Bank, these sources would "fall considerably short of meeting the requirements."[21] The implication was that if capital to meet these "requirements" were to be forthcoming, it would have to come through public channels. The Kennedy administration also committed itself to augmenting the public capital flow. Shortly after taking office President Kennedy noted that "development assistance . . . must—and shall—take its place as a full partner in the complex of foreign policy."[22] Further evidence of the waxing importance of public capital movements dur-

[20] U.S., Congress, House, Committee on Foreign Affairs, *Background Material on Mutual Defense and Development Programs, Fiscal Year 1965*, 88th Cong., 2d sess., 1964, Committee Print, p. 26. Cited hereafter as House Committee on Foreign Affairs, *Background Material on Mutual Defense and Development Programs*, 1964.

[21] U.S., Congress, Senate, Committee on Banking and Currency, *Hearings, International Development Association*, 85th Cong., 2d sess., 1958, p. 100. Cited hereafter as Senate Committee on Banking and Currency, *IDA Hearings*, 1958.

[22] Text of a letter to Congress on foreign aid, *New York Times*, May 27, 1961, p. 2.

ing this period is furnished by the United States support for doubling the resources of the World Bank, creating the IDA and the IADB, expanding the lending authority of the Export-Import Bank, and establishing the Alliance for Progress to promote Latin American economic development. The guiding principles of American policy regarding furnishing American capital via public channels required, as they had since World War II: (*a*) keeping the total amount small relative to the private capital flow, (*b*) a substantial degree of American control, and (*c*) avoidance of competition with private capital.

WHICH CHANNELS?

In addition to the traditional question of bilateral versus multilateral channels for disbursing public capital, the United States faced a new question on channels during the 1958–62 period. The new question concerned the contribution of Europe and Japan to the development effort. Noting the increased prosperity in these nations, the United States attempted to get them to move more public capital through their own and multilateral channels. The United States used several techniques, including exhortation, threats, and inducement, to get Europe and Japan to increase their public capital aid to underdeveloped nations. Beginning about 1958, we find an increase in the frequency with which American spokesmen refer to the ability of Europe and Japan to expand their economic aid programs. President Eisenhower's remarks to the IBRD Annual Meeting in 1959 are typical: "The improved economic position of the industrialized countries provides the means whereby they can better do their part in assisting development elsewhere, both directly and through their participation in international institutions."[23] The Kennedy administration likewise "urged other industrialized countries to devote a larger share of their resources to the provision of capital to the less developed nations."[24]

[23] "Remarks by President Eisenhower," *Department of State Bulletin*, October 19, 1959, p. 532. See also "The State of the Union," address of the President to Congress, *Department of State Bulletin*, January 25, 1960, p. 112; and the statement by Undersecretary Dillon before the Special Economic Committee of the Organization for European Economic Cooperation (OEEC), *Department of State Bulletin*, February 1, 1960, p. 140.

[24] "Foreign Economic and Military Assistance Program for Fiscal Year 1963," message of the President to Congress, *Department of State Bulletin*, April 2, 1962,

In addition to such exhortations the United States threatened to curtail its own efforts if the other advanced nations would not accept a bigger share of the responsibility for aiding underdeveloped areas. The United States lent credibility to this threat in October, 1959, when it announced that "in view of the growth in the economic strength of the industrialized countries of the free world and their steadily increasing ability to assist the less developed countries," the United States would henceforth require that DLF loan funds be spent only in the United States.[25] As Professor Albert O. Hirschman observed, this was a bargaining move, signifying to Western Europe more forcefully than by mere advice that it ought to finance its own export surplus with the underdeveloped countries.[26] In addressing the annual meeting of the World Bank in 1962, President Kennedy noted that the United States found it difficult to sustain its foreign aid effort and maintain a balance of payments equilibrium at the same time. After exhorting other advanced nations to increase their foreign aid, he issued the following none-too-subtle threat:

Of course, the United States could bring its international payments into balance overnight if that were the only goal we sought. We could withdraw our forces, reduce our aid, tie it wholly to purchases in this country, raise high tariff barriers and restrict the foreign investment or other use of American dollars. Such a policy, it is true, would give rise to a new era of dollar shortages, free world insecurity and American isolation—but we would have "solved" the balance of payments.[27]

Besides exhortation and threats the United States sought to induce other nations to increase their public capital available for economic development by proposing a new multilateral institution, the IDA. On several occasions administration spokesmen alluded to the IDA as a technique for prying more public capital out of Europe and Japan.[28]

---

p. 550. See also George Ball, "The Less Developed Countries and the Atlantic Partnership," *Department of State Bulletin*, March 12, 1962, p. 414.

[25] Statement issued on October 20, 1959, by Vance Brand, reprinted in *Department of State Bulletin*, November 16, 1959, p. 708.

[26] Letter to the Editor, *New York Times*, November 9, 1959, p. 30.

[27] International Bank for Reconstruction and Development and International Development Association, 1962 Annual Meetings of the Boards of Governors, *Summary Proceedings*, 1962, p. 2.

[28] See, for example, Douglas Dillon, "Economic Growth in a Divided World," *Department of State Bulletin*, June 9, 1958, p. 971.

With regard to the traditional question of bilateral versus multi-lateral channels, the United States continued to prefer bilateral channels and multilateral channels with weighted voting arrangements favoring the United States. The American dislike for multi-lateral channels, such as the proposed SUNFED, was made clear by the American efforts to expand public capital movements in the 1958–62 period. The Export-Import Bank was strengthened, and the DLF funds were increased; both of these were bilateral channels. The establishment of the IDA in 1960 was an expression of the satisfaction of American policy makers with operations of the International Bank.[29] And the Inter-American Development Bank resembled the IBRD both in its exclusion of the Soviet bloc and in its inclusion of voting arrangements weighted according to financial contribution.

ON WHAT TERMS?

During the 1958–62 period the trend toward increasing em-phasis on soft loans continued. This is not to say that hard loan and grant activities were diminishing but only that they were not expanding so rapidly as soft loan activities.

Hard Loans

Financing of economic growth through conventional loans was supported by the United States in one bilateral institution, the Export-Import Bank, and in three multilateral ones, the IADB, the IBRD, and the IFC. The United States initiated a move in 1958 to double the lending capacity of the World Bank from $10 billion to $20 billion. It should be noted that the World Bank was raising most of its capital in private capital markets; therefore the dou-bling of its lending capacity required only an increase in "callable" capital guaranteed by member governments. What this boils down to is that the United States Congress did not have to appropriate money in order to double the United States subscription to the IBRD; it merely had to promise that money would be available in the future if the Bank got into financial trouble. Considering the

[29] During hearings on IDA Dillon reminded congressmen that "member countries are all free world countries. There are no Soviet bloc countries which are members of the World Bank or the Monetary Fund or this proposed institution, and on that basis political things cannot enter." U.S., Congress, House, Committee on Banking and Currency, *Hearings, International Development Association*, 86th Cong., 2d sess., 1960, p. 84. Cited hereafter as House Committee on Banking and Currency, *IDA Hearings*, 1960.

Bank's conservative administration and considering that the Bank had never had a default, the United States approval of expansion of IBRD subscriptions was not a very risky move. The net result, nevertheless, was to make available to underdeveloped nations more capital on conventional terms.

The International Finance Corporation, with nearly $100 million in subscribed capital, was also making capital available on hard terms. Its terms were in fact so hard that one student has even expressed doubts as to whether it should be considered a foreign assistance agency. He notes:

> Its loans have gone to credit-worthy private enterprises on rather onerous terms. Interest rates range from 5 to 10 per cent, and loans made at rates below 8 per cent typically carry some kind of profit-sharing clause as well. The maturities are medium-term rather than long-term, with maturities frequently ranging from about 5 to about 15 years on particular loans. In any case, the IFC's scale of operations is small. At the end of fiscal year 1960–1961 the total IFC investment amounted to only $44.4 million of which $34 million was in the Western Hemisphere.[30]

In addition to supporting existing hard loan institutions, the United States promoted the creation of a new one, the Inter-American Development Bank. In August, 1958, the United States reversed long-established policy and announced that it would support the establishment of such a bank. This move was appropriately described by one observer as "a step which Latin Americans had been urging for fifty or sixty years."[31] The IADB came into existence on December 30, 1959, with subscribed capital of nearly $1 billion, 85 per cent of which was to be available to Latin American countries on conventional loan terms. Although the United States share of hard loan capital was $350 million, only $150 million of this had to be paid in; the rest was callable.[32]

[30] Benjamin Higgins, *United Nations and U.S. Foreign Economic Policy* (Homewood, Ill.: Irwin, 1962), p. 89. Since the IFC provides equity capital, it is not, strictly speaking, a hard lender. For purposes of this study, however, it is enough like hard lending to be so described.

[31] Richard P. Stebbins, *The United States in World Affairs, 1959* (New York: Harper & Bros., 1960), p. 365.

[32] We should understand that the IADB did not actually have its capital on January 1, 1960. What it had were commitments to pay over a period of years. For texts of legislation and international agreements relating to IADB and for a "Comparative Chart of the Organization, Purpose, Financing, and Repayment Terms of Interna-

Besides the IBRD, the IFC, and the IADB, the United States used its own Export-Import Bank to disburse hard loans. This institution resembled the IBRD in its record of repayment, and it was popular with American businessmen engaged in foreign trade. The lending authority for the Export-Import Bank was raised from $5 billion to $7 billion in 1958. Since the Export-Import Bank is permitted to borrow directly from the Treasury, no appropriation was required. It should also be noted that the $7 billion was a limit on total outstanding debt at any one time; the Bank could lend money received in repayment of past loans without additional legislative authorization.

Grants

During the 1958–62 period there was a shift in emphasis from grants to loans in American policy. Evidence of this shift is furnished by: (a) the frequent expressions of a desire to shift from grants to loans by both the Democratic and Republican administrations, (b) the fact that new institutions created during this period were, with the exception of the United Nations Special Fund, loan institutions, and (c) the fact that economic aid under the American Mutual Security Program was 22 per cent loans in the 1956–58 period and 58 per cent loans in 1962.[33] The United States contributions constituted 40 per cent of the budgets of the United Nations Special Fund and the Expanded Program of Technical Assistance, each of which spent under $80 million yearly. This aid was distributed primarily on a grant basis. Other grant aid for economic development was made available by the United States through PL 480 at a rate of about $300 million (CCC cost) yearly and through the Alliance for Progress. Loans, however, were more important in the latter program than grants. The general trend during the 1958–62 period was to use grants for short-term goals, such as military aid to such nations as Taiwan, Korea, Vietnam, and Turkey, which bordered the Communist bloc, and

---

tional Lending Agencies," see U.S., Congress, House, Committee on Foreign Affairs, *Staff Memorandum on International Lending and Guaranty Programs,* 88th Cong., 2d sess., Committee Print, 1964.

[33] House Committee on Foreign Affairs, *Background Material on Mutual Defense and Development Programs,* 1964, p. 24.

to use loans for promoting the long-term objective of economic development.[34]

Soft Loans

In 1961 President Kennedy declared that although promotion of economic development required a flexible set of tools, "the instrument of primary emphasis—the single most important tool—will be long-term development loans at low or no rates of interest."[35] Soft loans had finally become a major technique of American statecraft. In the 1958–62 period the United States supported soft lending activities by the DLF, the IDA, the IADB, and by agencies involved in agricultural surplus disposal.

Development Loan Fund.—Although it was created by the Mutual Security Act of 1957, the DLF did not begin lending until 1958. The Mutual Security Act of 1958 enhanced the status of the DLF by establishing it as a permanent government corporation. Its funds were expanded from an appropriation of $300 million for fiscal year 1958 to $550 million for the following fiscal year, although the executive had to get a supplemental appropriation to reach the $550 million figure. In fiscal year 1960 the DLF received $550 million and in fiscal 1961, $600 million. In fiscal 1962, under a reorganization of the aid program in which the DLF lost its status as a permanent government corporation, $1,112 million was allocated for development loans.

There are a number of characteristics of DLF lending which should be noted. First, loans must be spent in the United States. This "tied loan" policy has been in effect since October, 1959. Second, DLF loans are repayable on a long-term basis—usually between twenty and forty years. Third, until 1961 DLF loans were repayable in local currency, and about 75 per cent of DLF lending was on this basis. In 1961, however, the Kennedy administration announced that DLF loans would henceforth be repayable in dollars at low or zero rates of interest.[36] The fourth characteristic of

[34] Cf. Robert E. Asher, *Grants, Loans, and Local Currencies: Their Role in Foreign Aid* (Washington: Brookings Institution, 1961), pp. 59–64, 72–77.

[35] "Foreign Aid: Message of the President to the Congress," *Department of State Bulletin*, April 10, 1961, p. 511.

[36] See Henry R. Labouisse, "Foreign Aid, a Constructive Element of U.S. Foreign Policy," *Department of State Bulletin*, August 21, 1961, pp. 320–22. From 1961 to 1963 AID loans were repayable over a maximum of forty years, with a ten-year

DLF operations is the familiar ban on competition with other sources of capital, public or private. As usual, the "requirement" is nothing but a vague admonition which depends for its effectiveness on the way it is interpreted. In stating his determination to avoid competing with private capital, Vance Brand, Managing Director of the DLF, observed pointedly that "a man cannot help bringing into any task his own background and experience, and my background happens to be that of a small-town banker, lawyer, and businessman."[37]

International Development Association.—In 1958 the United States took the initiative in promoting the creation of a new multilateral soft lending agency as an affiliate of the International Bank. In 1959 articles of agreement were drawn up and submitted for approval to members of the IBRD in January, 1960. The International Development Association came into official existence in September, 1960, but it made no loans until the following year. The IDA was to acquire about $1 billion in capital over a five-year period, with an American contribution of $320 million. Although the IDA was authorized to make any type of soft loan, including loans repayable in local currency, in practice it limited itself to dollar-repayable, interest-free loans. Such loans usually carried a ten-year grace period and could be repaid over fifty years. The IDA operated under the same prohibitions against consideration of political factors and competition with private capital as did the IBRD. As we might expect, the IDA quickly became a popular source of development capital, and by September, 1962, it had lent more than $200 million and was running out of funds. One of the main agenda items of the IBRD annual meeting in 1962 was expansion of IDA resources. By 1964 IDA members had pledged an additional $700 million to the organization, of which the United States' share was $312 million.

Inter-American Development Bank.—The IADB administered two soft loan funds. Although 85 per cent of the Bank's subscribed capital was for hard loan operations, the remaining 15 per cent,

---

grace period before repayment began, at .75% interest. For detailed description and analysis of AID lending terms during this period, see Agency for International Development, *Loan Terms, Debt Burden and Development,* April, 1965.

[37] Vance Brand, "The Future Course of the Development Loan Fund," *Department of State Bulletin,* November 2, 1959, p. 636.

amounting to about $150 million, went into a Fund for Special Operations, which makes soft loans, including those repayable in local currency. The United States contribution to the Fund for Special Operations was $100 million.

In his report to the President, later adopted as official policy, Milton Eisenhower advised, "There can be no doubt that 'soft' loans are needed in Latin America."[38] He supported this assertion by pointing out that although underdeveloped nations found it difficult to meet repayment schedules calling for dollars, "they could meet their obligations in local currencies."[39] Given the existence of managed currencies, this was like saying that an individual could meet his obligations with "rubber" checks.

The IADB also administered a soft loan fund on behalf of the United States. This fund, known as the Social Progress Trust Fund, was part of the Alliance for Progress program, which grew out of the Act of Bogotá of September 12, 1960. Of $500 million appropriated in 1961 for the Alliance, $394 million went to the Social Progress Trust Fund. Under an agreement with the United States government, the IADB was entrusted with administration of this fund. Loans from the Social Progress Trust Fund were to be repayable in whole or in part in the currency of the borrower.

Surplus disposal programs.—During the 1958–62 period section 402 of the Mutual Security Act continued to require that no less than $175 million of the Mutual Security funds be used to purchase surplus agricultural commodities. These commodities were usually "sold" for local currencies, and the local currencies were used to pay American obligations in the country and for grants or loans back to the country. The administration found, as it had in the previous period, that "the principal problem connected with section 402 has been the difficulty of locating aid-recipient countries *capable of absorbing* an amount of agricultural surpluses equal to the minimum which the Mutual Security Act requires be spent in the form of agricultural surpluses."[40]

[38] Milton S. Eisenhower, "United States–Latin American Relations, 1953–1958: Report to the President," *Department of State Bulletin,* January 19, 1959, p. 94.

[39] *Ibid.*

[40] Memorandum submitted by Douglas Dillon on "Foreign Currencies Owned or Controlled by the United States," U.S., Congress, House, Subcommittee of the Committee on Appropriations, *Hearings, Mutual Security Appropriations for 1960,* 86th Cong., 1st sess., 1959, p. 370. Italics mine. In order to compensate for bureaucratic concealment of the issue, substitute the following phrase for the italicized words: "willing to accept in lieu of dollars."

Public Law 480 retained its good standing in the eyes of Congress, and authorizations for purchase of CCC commodities for "sale" under Title I of PL 480 were increased as follows: $2.25 billion for use between July 1, 1958, and December 31, 1959; $3.0 billion for use between January 1, 1960, and December 31, 1961; an additional $2.0 billion for use during calendar year 1961; and $4.5 billion for use between January 1, 1962, and December 31, 1964.[41] As explained in the previous chapter, to the extent that surplus disposal operations had the net result of trading real resources for local currency I O U's, they were soft loan operations. To the extent that nothing was received in return, they were grant operations. And to the extent that the foreign currency was spent for payment of American obligations which would have been paid in dollars in the absence of surplus disposal programs, the United States was merely promoting the export of its embarrassing surplus commodities.

SUMMARY

In selecting techniques of statecraft for promoting economic growth in underdeveloped areas in the 1958–62 period, American policy makers tended to emphasize public capital movements more than they had in previous years. The year 1958 stands out as a turning point in this respect; in that year the following events occurred: (1) Lending authority for the Export-Import Bank was increased from $5 billion to $7 billion. (2) The United States initiated the creation of the IDA. (3) The United States acquiesced to Latin American demands for a regional institution to finance economic development. (4) The lending capacity of the International Bank was doubled. Within the category of public capital the most significant trend was that toward greater emphasis on soft lending. During the 1958–62 period the United States made increasing use of the DLF, expanded PL 480 operations, and supported creation of two new international institutions with authority to make soft loans. In the period between 1943 and 1962 the United States had come to adopt soft lending as a legitimate technique of statecraft—a technique which, at the beginning of the period, it had regarded as anathema.

[41] These figures exaggerate the value to recipients of American aid under PL 480, since the real goods purchased with this money are valued at CCC costs instead of at world market prices.

III. WHY TECHNIQUES WERE CHOSEN
OR REJECTED

EXTERNAL SETTING: 1958–62

GENERAL INTERNATIONAL SITUATION

In the 1958–62 period the Communist bloc continued to strengthen economic ties with the less developed nations. The Soviet Union's program of foreign assistance grew in size and geographic scope until in 1962 it encompassed twenty-five underdeveloped nations. During the 1959–61 period these nations received aid from the Soviet Union at an average rate of about $700 million annually. By June, 1962, the Soviet Union had extended $5.6 billion to underdeveloped nations, while other Communist nations had contributed $1.3 billion to such nations. Aid from the Communist bloc usually took the form of loans repayable over a period of twelve years or less at interest rates of about 2 per cent.[42]

In foreign trade the Communist bloc also increased its activity vis-à-vis the less developed nations. Through use of large-scale contracts the bloc had become the major trading partner of Guinea, Mali, Egypt, and Cuba by 1962. And between 1955 and 1962 the Soviet Union's commodity exchange with the underdeveloped nations grew at a rate of about 30 per cent a year.[43]

A second aspect of the general international situation which is relevant to the evolution of American soft loan policy is the improved economic position of Europe and Japan. Not until the 1958–62 period could we find widespread agreement that the period of postwar reconstruction was over. This economic recovery was signaled by the lifting of limits on currency convertibility on December 29, 1958, by Britain, France, West Germany, Italy, Sweden, Belgium, the Netherlands, Luxembourg, and Norway.[44] It could hardly have escaped the attention of American policy

[42] The facts about the Communist bloc aid program are drawn from U.S., Congress, Joint Economic Committee, *Dimensions of Soviet Economic Power*, "The Scope and Distribution of Soviet Economic Aid," a study prepared by George S. Carnett and Morris H. Crawford, 87th Cong., 2d sess., 1962, Joint Committee Print, pp. 457–74.

[43] Facts on foreign trade are drawn from Penelope Hartland Thumberg, "The Soviet Union in the World Economy," *ibid.*, pp. 409–38.

[44] Limitations on convertibility did remain for some purposes, but for most current account transactions funds could be easily converted into dollars.

makers that in 1948 American gold reserves were $24 billion and West Germany's were nil, but by 1960 American gold was down to $18.5 billion and West Germany's was up to $6.5 billion. It is little wonder that the United States began to prod the Europeans —especially the Germans—to provide more economic aid to poor areas.

A third relevant aspect of the international situation was Fidel Castro's rise to power in Cuba in January, 1959. Castro's activities vis-à-vis Russia and the United States served to focus the attention of many Americans on the problems of dealing with underdeveloped nations, especially in Latin America. We suspect that few governments in underdeveloped nations failed to note the increased interest in Latin American problems exhibited by the United States after the assumption of power by Castro.

UNITED NATIONS

In the United Nations the proposal for creation of the SUNFED or, as it was known in its prenatal stages, an International Development Authority, had become a symbol of the dissatisfaction of the underdeveloped nations with their lot and of their belief that the richer nations ought to do something about it. Between 1957 and 1960 the United States pre-empted these labels for use in two international agencies—the IDA and the United Nations Special Fund. Although the Special Fund appealed to less developed nations in terms of its organizational control devices, it did not have substantial financial resources. And although the IDA controlled more than $700 million, it was organized in such a way as to give big contributors more influence than big recipients.

The problem of United Nations pressure for the SUNFED was compounded by the addition of several new members, each with one vote and each with an underdeveloped economy. New members in the 1958–62 period included Guinea, Cameroun, Chad, Central African Republic, Cyprus, Dahomey, Gabon, Ivory Coast, Madagascar, Mali, Niger, Nigeria, Senegal, Somalia, Togo, Upper Volta, Mauritania, Tanganyika, Sierra Leone, and others.

The creation of IDA and the Special Fund presented the less developed nations with a dilemma. In the first place, the symbolic value of the words—or initials—was diminished. Secondly, they had been asking for a SUNFED with $250 million to disburse, not because they thought such a paltry sum would be adequate but because they thought that the prospects for creation of the SUNFED would be enhanced if it started on a small scale. The establishment of the IDA with resources exceeding those proposed for the SUNFED gave the richer nations the opportunity to describe the IDA as more than the SUNFED supporters had even asked for. The rich nations did not neglect the opportunity.[45]

It is ironic that the dilemma facing the underdeveloped nations was in part a result of the success of past efforts to get the developed nations to provide them with more public capital on soft loan or grant terms. Having succeeded in partial attainment of their goals, they wondered how to continue to dramatize the magnitude of their problems. Since 1958 the underdeveloped nations in the United Nations have striven in various ways to remind the richer nations that the problem of economic development is far from solved and that no approach has yet been devised which is likely to lead to a satisfactory solution.[46]

In the fall of 1958 the General Assembly established the Special Fund.[47] But in order to remind the developed nations of the inadequacy of such a fund, the General Assembly also decided to "continue to review, as a separate subject of its agenda, progress in the field of financing the economic development of the less developed countries, particularly progress towards the establishment of a United Nations capital development fund."[48] In the fall of 1959 the General Assembly voted to endorse the IDA proposal, but the debate in the Second Committee made it clear that the underdeveloped nations had no intention of relenting in their efforts to secure more public capital on easier terms from the de-

[45] See, for example, the following statements made in United Nations forums: George Meany, "Economic Development of Underdeveloped Countries," *Department of State Bulletin*, December 14, 1959, pp. 883–86; and Adlai E. Stevenson, "United Nations Development Decade," *Department of State Bulletin*, August 6, 1962, pp. 228–30.

[46] For an interesting perspective on this point see James S. Magee, "Structure and Substance: The Politics of Decentralization in the United Nations," *Journal of Politics*, XXVII (August, 1965), 518–35.

[47] United Nations General Assembly Resolution 1240 (XIII), October 14, 1958.

[48] United Nations General Assembly Resolution 1317 (XIII), December 12, 1958.

veloped nations.[49] A proposal for a United Nations capital development fund similar to the SUNFED was debated in the Second Committee in 1960, with arguments on both sides of the issue remaining about the same. And a resolution was passed which decided "in principle that a United Nations capital development fund shall be established."[50] The General Assembly also expressed a desire to "encourage, on a bilateral and multilateral basis, the extension as appropriate of long-term loans, grants, or credits on favourable terms, including interest-free loans at the lowest possible interest rates, the longest possible repayment periods and repayment in local currencies or in other beneficial forms."[51] The sixteenth session of the General Assembly in 1961 provided the occasion for the most extreme statement of desires by less developed nations up to that time. Acting probably from frustration with what they considered to be the indifference of the rich nations toward their problems, the less developed nations put the General Assembly on record as believing that "assistance should be of a kind and in a form consistent with the wishes of the recipients and should involve no unacceptable conditions for them, whether political, economic, military or other."[52] As one-sided as such a proposal may seem, it was probably no more so than the proposals for improving "investment climates" with which the United States had been bombarding the underdeveloped nations for years.

In sum, during the 1958–62 period the underdeveloped nations continued to use United Nations organs to apply pressure on the richer nations for more public capital on easier terms. The accretion of members from underdeveloped areas during this period reinforced this tendency.

INTERNATIONAL BANK

In the first decade of its operations the IBRD had stressed the importance of efforts by governments in underdeveloped nations to attract private enterprise, and it had tended to deflate the esti-

[49] See the following: United Nations A/C.2/SR. 618, November 13, 1959, p. 19; A/C.2/SR. 613, November 9, 1959, p. 6.

[50] United Nations General Assembly Resolution 1521 (XV), December 15, 1960.

[51] United Nations General Assembly Resolution 1524 (XV), December 15, 1960.

[52] United Nations General Assembly Resolution 1706 (XVI), December 19, 1961.

mates put forth by such nations of their need for public external capital. Although Bank officials continued to insist on the importance of "sound" governmental policies, the emphasis gradually shifted until, in the 1958–62 period, the Bank was a leading exponent of the expanded use of soft loans to promote economic growth. It was noted in the previous chapter that Eugene Black had approved soft loans in principle, provided they were "properly administered." In 1958 he pointed out to the members of the IBRD that some of the developing nations, "for reasons not directly attributable to poor financial and economic management, are approaching the limits of their present capacity to assume additional obligations which, like Bank loans, must be serviced on a fixed timetable and in scarce foreign exchange."[53] He later observed that there was "an unquestionable and real need in many countries for additional development investment capital on terms which impose little or no burden on their balance of payments."[54]

Black also indicated that there was a connection between his previously expressed opinions on commercial policies in industrial nations and the gradual change in his attitude toward soft lending. What he was saying, in effect, was that the United States should have lowered its trade barriers vis-à-vis the less developed nations and that the failure to do so was largely responsible for the decreased debt-servicing capacity in developing nations. In 1959 he pointed out that "aid today must be followed by trade tomorrow if the aid takes the form of loans which must be repaid."[55] And he made the charge more specific by noting: "Many trade restrictions today, particularly on agricultural products and industrial raw materials, already stand in obvious contradiction to the professed aim of the more advanced countries to aid the underdeveloped lands."[56] In 1960, 1961, and 1962 Black continued to argue for more public capital on soft loan terms for economic

[53] International Bank for Reconstruction and Development, 1958 Annual Meeting of the Board of Governors, *Summary Proceedings*, 1958, p. 13.

[54] *Ibid.*, p. 16.

[55] International Bank for Reconstruction and Development, 1959 Annual Meeting of the Board of Governors, *Summary Proceedings*, 1959, p. 10.

[56] *Ibid.*

development.[57] In fact, the man who had assumed the presidency of the IBRD detesting soft loans relinquished it with a farewell address devoted primarily to a plea for expanding the soft loan capacity of the IDA.[58] The unique position of Black as a conservative Wall Street banker, an "insider" in Washington governmental circles, and an international civil servant allowed him to espouse the soft loan cause effectively. He could give soft lending a stamp of legitimacy which it sorely needed.

INTERNAL SETTING: 1958–62

DOMESTIC SITUATION IN GENERAL

The two most important changes in the general domestic situation concerned the gross national product and the American balance of international payments. During the 1958–62 period the economic capacity of the United States to give aid was increased by a rise in the GNP from $401 billion (1954 dollars) in 1958 to $475 billion in 1962. The growth was steady; and in every year except 1958, the GNP exceeded that of the previous year.

Beginning about 1958, the United States began to have difficulty in maintaining equilibrium in its balance of payments. Basically this means that more money was being paid to foreigners by Americans than was being paid to Americans by foreigners. When such a situation occurs, a nation can make up the deficit by selling gold or by short-term borrowing. Although such expedients are effective as stopgap measures, they obviously cannot provide a long-run remedy since a nation's gold supply and its ability to borrow short term are limited. Whereas the United States had a balance of payments surplus of $.5 billion in 1957, it had a $3.5 billion deficit in 1958. In 1959 the deficit rose to $3.7 billion, and to a high point of $3.9 billion in 1960. This was followed by a deficit of $2.4 billion in 1961 and one of $2.2 billion in 1962. The solution to this problem lay in two areas: First, American payments to foreigners could be reduced by such methods as curtailing foreign aid, restricting imports, limiting foreign

[57] See Eugene R. Black, *The Diplomacy of Economic Development* (Cambridge, Mass.: Harvard University Press, 1960), p. 55; and International Bank for Reconstruction and Development and International Development Association, 1961 Annual Meetings of the Boards of Governors, *Summary Proceedings*, 1961, pp. 9–13.

[58] IBRD, *Summary Proceedings*, 1962, pp. 12–15.

lending, or by other means. Alternatively, the problem could be solved by increasing the payments by foreigners to Americans by such methods as requiring that foreign aid be spent on American products, increasing exports in other ways or by long-term borrowing. There was also, of course, the possibility of some combination of techniques. The main significance of the balance of payments problem for the American policy of promoting economic development was that it led to suggestions that the problem be solved by reducing economic aid.[59]

BUSINESS ELITE

The American business community remained split on a number of economic issues during this period. The liberal segment was associated with the Committee on Economic Development and "modern" Republicanism; whereas the conservative element was associated with the National Association of Manufacturers and the "Old Guard" Republicans. No detailed examination of business attitudes is planned here; it suffices to look at broad trends. In the first place, it should be noted that the attitudes ranged from outright hostility toward all forms of government efforts to stimulate long-term economic growth to a mild approval of the modest proposals advanced by the executive branch during the 1958–62 period. Throughout the period the National Foreign Trade Convention annually repeated its condemnations of government grants and soft loans for economic development and admonished the United States government to take more vigorous measures for promoting the role of private investment in the economic development of less developed nations.[60]

The attitude of most businessmen seemed to be one of willingness to tolerate aid programs on the grounds that "unusual" cir-

[59] On this problem see G. C. Hufbauer, "The United States Balance of Payments and Economic Aid," in *Public Policy, 1961* (Cambridge, Mass.: Harvard University Press, 1962), pp. 139–51.

[60] See: *Report of the Forty-Sixth National Foreign Trade Convention* (New York: National Foreign Trade Council, 1960), pp. xvi–xxiii; *Report of the Forty-Fifth National Foreign Trade Convention* (New York: National Foreign Trade Council, 1959), pp. xvii–xxii; *Report of the Forty-Seventh National Foreign Trade Convention* (New York: National Foreign Trade Council, 1961), pp. xvii–xxiv; *Report of the Forty-Eighth National Foreign Trade Convention* (New York: National Foreign Trade Council, 1962), pp. xviii–xxvi; and *Report of the Forty-Ninth National Foreign Trade Convention* (New York: National Foreign Trade Council, 1963), pp. xviii–xxiii, xxxvii–xxxix.

cumstances existed in the world. This lack of enthusiasm was exemplified by the statements submitted to Congress by the United States Chamber of Commerce "supporting" various aid programs. The Chamber of Commerce consistently supported an elusive concept known as "the principle of mutual security," but it also consistently recommended cuts in the amount of money allocated for this program.[61] In 1961, for example, the Chamber of Commerce statement "supporting" Mutual Security called for a reduction of President Kennedy's authorization request from $4.8 billion to $3.6 billion—with the bulk of the cut concentrated in the economic aid request.[62] The Chamber also opposed proposals to finance foreign aid through borrowing from the Treasury, thus ensuring that aid appropriations would be kept relatively small.

In the hearings on the IDA the Chamber of Commerce and other business spokesmen indicated a general wariness about soft lending as a technique for stimulating economic development, and they made it clear that they were approving United States membership in the IDA only because of their confidence in the "sound" judgment of Eugene Black.[63] The spokesman for the Chamber of Commerce noted that affiliation of the IDA with the IBRD would "assure that the administration of IDA would be governed by the sound banking judgment that has characterized the World Bank operations in the past."[64] The prospects for continued legitimacy of IDA operations in the eyes of the business elite were enhanced by President Kennedy's announcement in October, 1962, that the United States would nominate George D.

---

[61] For example, see U.S., Congress, Senate, Committee on Foreign Relations, *Hearings, Mutual Security Act of 1959*, 86th Cong., 1st sess., 1959, pp. 996–1005 (cited hereafter as Senate Committee on Foreign Relations, *Mutual Security Hearings*, 1959).

[62] U.S., Congress, Senate, Committee on Foreign Relations, *Hearings, International Development and Security*, 87th Cong., 1st sess., 1961, pp. 935–42 (cited hereafter as Senate Committee on Foreign Relations, *International Development and Security Hearings*, 1961).

[63] House Committee on Banking and Currency, *IDA Hearings*, 1960, pp. 62–63; and U.S., Congress, Senate, Committee on Foreign Relations, *Hearings, International Development Association*, 86th Cong., 2d sess., 1960, pp. 52–54, 87–89 (cited hereafter as Senate Committee on Foreign Relations, *IDA Hearings*, 1960).

[64] *Ibid.*, p. 89.

Woods, a Republican Wall Street banker, to succeed Black. The American nominee won—to no one's surprise.

CONGRESS

Although it should be understood that Congressional attitudes toward foreign aid and trade programs were not monolithic, the prevailing mood was, as it had been since World War II, one of a lack of enthusiasm for either trade liberalization or foreign aid —at least insofar as foreign aid required appropriations.

Congress and Trade Liberalization

Congressional behavior in the 1958–62 period gave the free traders little cause to rejoice. In 1958 President Eisenhower was able to secure renewal of the Reciprocal Trade Agreements Act for four years in the midst of a situation which prompted one student of American foreign policy to note: "Seldom had there been such a strong and well-organized protest against the admission into the American market of foreign-made goods. . . ."[65] Despite President Eisenhower's success in extending the life of the Reciprocal Trade Agreements Program, Congress inserted into the act for the first time a provision for legislative veto of tariff decisions by the President.

In 1962 the Kennedy administration concentrated its efforts on a substantial revision in the Reciprocal Trade Agreeements Act originally passed in 1934. President Kennedy attained the following goals: (1) The "peril point" section was removed. (2) The act renewed the tariff-cutting authority of the President for five years. (3) The President was given authority to cut tariffs by 50 per cent of levels prevailing in 1962. (4) Special authority for tariff reduction in negotiations with the European Economic Community were granted to the President. Although passage of the Trade Expansion Act of 1962 was hailed as Kennedy's greatest political victory, the compromises that were necessary to secure passage indicated that Congressional attitudes on trade liberalization were still negative. The main concessions to the protectionists were these: (1) The administration offered to negotiate an international agreement for voluntary restrictions on

[65] Richard P. Stebbins, *The United States in World Affairs, 1958* (New York: Harper & Bros., 1959), p. 113.

exports of textile products to the United States, and textile industries were further protected by promises of administration support for taxes on textile imports and tax allowances for domestic textile producers. (2) There was a promise to review the import quotas on oil and coal imports. (3) The "escape clause" was modified to make it more effective. (4) Any reduction of tariffs on oil, lead, zinc, and a score of other products was prohibited completely. The strength of protectionist sentiment in Congress was also indicated by the fact that the free traders were barely able to stave off an attempt to reinstate the "peril point" clause in the Senate; the vote was 38–40 against reinstatement.

Congress and Foreign Aid

Although a few congressmen, notably those on the Senate Foreign Relations Committee, were ardent supporters of economic aid as a technique for stimulating economic development, the prevailing attitude in the 1958–62 period was hostile to this technique. This hostility was signified in a number of ways. In the first place, executive branch requests for foreign aid funds were usually cut by about 20 per cent, with the largest cuts coming in the economic aid category. Secondly, the foreign aid appropriations bill was usually placed last on the legislative agenda, a situation which increased the probability that the administration would give way on foreign aid in order to secure approval of other legislation.[66] A third means by which Congress expressed its hostility toward foreign aid was its frequent investigations into the use of foreign aid funds in an atmosphere of impending exposé. Fourth, and probably most important of all, Congress steadfastly refused to approve long-term financing plans which would bypass the annual appropriation process. The Eisenhower administration had been rebuffed on this issue in 1957 and was reluctant to broach it again. In 1961 President Kennedy described long-term financing as the "key to the continuity and efficiency of the entire program,"[67] but his refusal to compromise on this issue resulted in one of his most resounding political defeats. The

[66] See, for example, Sherman Adams, *Firsthand Report* (New York: Harper & Bros., 1961), p. 379.

[67] "Foreign Aid: Message of the President to the Congress," *Department of State Bulletin,* April 10, 1961, p. 512.

fifth way Congress evinced its dislike of economic aid was by continual insistence that inconvertible currency be substituted for dollar appropriations in foreign aid programs.

The pressure to increase the use of local currencies, however, was more than a manifestation of legislative reluctance to appropriate dollars to give to foreigners. It also illustrated the widespread misunderstanding by congressmen of the nature of soft loans repayable in inconvertible currency. In response to Congressional suggestions that more local currencies be used, the executive branch repeatedly explained that "local currency cannot be used to provide additional physical resources for use in the country in which it is generated, because it cannot be used to import goods and services into that country."[68] Perusal of legislative hearings on foreign aid during the 1958–62 period provides scant evidence that congressmen increased their understanding of local currencies much during the period.[69]

Congressional Initiative

It has been suggested by several scholars that the creation of the IDA provides an example of legislative initiative in foreign policy making.[70] Since a major proposition here is that Congress is unlikely to take the initiative with regard to foreign aid, some attention must be given to examining the validity of this proposition. First, let it be understood that in terms of formal legislative history Senator Monroney did appear to provide the initial impetus. In 1958 he proposed a resolution (Senate Resolution 264 of the 85th Congress) calling for establishment of an International

[68] U.S., Congress, House, Committee on Foreign Affairs, *Hearings, Mutual Security Act of 1958*, 85th Cong., 2d sess., 1958, p. 247. Cited hereafter as House Committee on Foreign Affairs, *Mutual Security Hearings, 1958*.

[69] We should not conclude that failure to understand the nature of local currencies is a sign of Congressional ineptitude. Metzger has observed that "probably no subject in the current field of international finance is as much misunderstood as that of the uses and limitations of 'local currencies' of one country which are owned by another." Stanley D. Metzger, "The New International Development Association," *Georgetown Law Journal*, XLIX (Fall, 1960), 32. Cf. Asher, p. 120.

[70] James A. Robinson, *The Monroney Resolution: Congressional Initiative in Foreign Policy Making* ("Eagleton Foundation Studies in Practical Politics" [New York: Henry Holt, 1959]); James A. Robinson, *Congress and Foreign Policy-Making* (Homewood, Ill.: Dorsey Press, 1962); John D. Montgomery, *The Politics of Foreign Aid* (New York: Praeger, 1962), pp. 219–21; Raymond F. Mikesell (ed.), *U.S. Private and Government Investment Abroad* (Eugene: University of Oregon, 1962), p. 350.

Development Association. An institution with that name was subsequently set up. Although we could argue that the IDA actually established was not the one Monroney had in mind, it is not proposed here to dispute Senator Monroney's initiative in the formal legislative sense. His role as initiator in the broader perspective of the foreign policy decision making process as a whole will be questioned.

Regarding the role of Congress in the establishment of the IDA, Robinson draws these conclusions:

> It is not too much to say that the idea of such an organization occurred independently to Senator Monroney. Some other legislator might have put together the same elements which interested Monroney, but it is highly unlikely that the executive branch would have taken the initiative of this sort. Indeed, the Department of State actively opposed the resolution as it was first broached by the Senator. Although he made certain modifications in his original idea, in order to advance the basic principle which he had in mind, the resolution remained a clear-cut case of Congressional initiative.[71]

It will be argued that (1) it is "too much" to say that the idea occurred independently to Monroney; (2) there are good reasons to believe that the executive branch would have taken the initiative on a proposal of this sort; (3) it is misleading to say that the State Department "opposed" the resolution; (4) the modifications in his original idea were so significant that the creation of the IDA should not be considered a clear-cut case of Congressional initiative.

First, let us consider the idea that Senator Monroney originated the idea behind the IDA. In preceding chapters numerous proposals for a multilateral soft lending institution put forth between 1948 and 1956 were mentioned; yet Robinson claims that the idea occurred to Monroney in 1956.[72] Since Monroney had been a member of the Banking and Currency committees in the House and Senate since the time of Bretton Woods, it is difficult to believe that he was unaware of the various proposals for such an institution which had been put forth by Senator McMahon, Walter Reuther, Senator Javits, the United Nations, and the various

---

[71] *Congress and Foreign Policy-Making*, p. 62.

[72] *The Monroney Resolution*, pp. 1–2.

studies performed for the executive branch.[73] In fact, the *Atlantic Monthly* of April, 1956, carried a proposal by Averell Harriman for a multilateral soft lending institution.[74] The one feature of Monroney's proposal which might be regarded as original was the suggestion that the United States provide the IDA with local currencies generated by its agricultural disposal and soft loan programs for the IDA to lend to underdeveloped nations. Yet this was one aspect of his original idea which never was implemented. The bill authorizing United States membership in the IDA, as enacted in 1960, does not permit the executive to transfer to the IDA local currencies either as a grant or a loan.[75] Nor is there any prospect that this part of Monroney's original idea will be implemented. Thus, we must conclude that insofar as his idea was original it was not implemented; and insofar as it was implemented it was not originated by Monroney but had been prominent in public debate for a decade or more.

There are also reasons for doubting Robinson's conclusion that the executive branch would not have taken the initiative for an institution similar to the IDA. They are as follows: (1) Since 1954 the State Department had been trying to increase the amount of money available for economic aid to underdeveloped nations. In the 1958 Mutual Security hearings Senator Kennedy asked Dulles whether he thought the economic aid request was big enough. Dulles replied, "I think that we would certainly like to have more money."[76] (2) The executive branch wanted to circumvent the annual authorization-appropriation process. In 1957 Dulles told a Congressional committee: "I can assure you, Senator, that there would be nothing but enthusiasm in the executive branch of Government for any proposal which reduced the number of authorization and appropriation actions."[77] The IDA proposal provided the executive with a means of increasing economic

[73] See above, pp. 88–96, 108–10. See also Stringfellow Barr, *Citizens of the World* (Garden City, N.Y.: Doubleday & Co., 1952).

[74] Averell Harriman, "The Soviet Challenge and American Policy," *Atlantic Monthly*, April, 1956, pp. 42–47.

[75] On this point see Metzger, *Georgetown Law Journal*, XLIX, 32–36.

[76] U.S., Congress, Senate, Committee on Foreign Relations, *Hearings, Mutual Security Act of 1958*, 85th Cong., 2d sess., 1958, p. 181.

[77] U.S., Congress, Senate, Special Committee to Study the Foreign Aid Program, *Hearings, The Foreign Aid Program*, 85th Cong., 1st sess., 1957, p. 412.

aid through multiyear appropriations. (3) The executive branch was under pressure from the less developed nations in the United Nations to join a multilateral soft lending organization. (4) The administration was not opposed to multilateral aid per se. It approved of the IBRD and had even hinted that a compromise on the SUNFED might be reached by affiliating it with the IBRD. (5) Eugene Black was supporting the idea of soft lending if it were closely co-ordinated with the IBRD. He was known to have access to influential government officials in Washington. (6) The executive branch was looking for a way to induce Europe and Japan to contribute more public capital an easier terms. An organization such as the IDA provided a useful way to do this. (7) Proposals for multilateral soft lending agencies had been suggested many times, and the executive branch must have had this alternative under continual review. (8) Subsequent events indicated that the executive was interested in expanding economic aid through multilateral institutions. The IADB was suggested in 1958, and the IBRD was enlarged. For the above reasons we can conclude that, contrary to Robinson's assertion, it is quite likely that the executive branch would have proposed a similar idea within one or two years if Senator Monroney had not done so in 1958.

Robinson contends that the Department of State actively opposed the Monroney resolution as it was first broached. Although this is true insofar as it implies that the original proposal was not completely satisfactory to the State Department, it is misleading to the extent that it obscures State Department approval of parts of the proposal. Douglas Dillon told the Senate committee which conducted hearings on the Monroney resolution: "I am not opposed, neither is the State Department, to this development association, this proposed International Development Association. We see no reason why it cannot operate in conjunction with our own Development Loan Fund. We do not think that they are mutually exclusive."[78]

As originally suggested by Senator Monroney, the IDA proposal had two fundamental aims. First, the local currencies that were building up in accounts owned by the American government would be lent to underdeveloped nations via the IDA.

[78] Senate Committee on Banking and Currency, *IDA Hearings*, 1958, p. 129.

According to the senator, "Much of the usable capital of the IDA would come [from] local currencies which are now frozen and of little or no use to any country."[79] Second, the IDA was initially proposed by Monroney as a substitute for the DLF. He was proposing to give dollars and soft currencies to the IDA instead of appropriating dollars for the DLF. In his original speech on the Senate floor in February, 1958, the following interchange occurred:

MR. GORE: Would it not be possible, since we possess more than $2 billion of foreign currency, representing good international exchange, to substitute the use of international currency for the appropriation of American dollars, at least to some extent?

MR. MONRONEY: The Senator is reading my mind, because that is a part of the proposed program.[80]

Monroney later made it even clearer that he believed his plan would reduce the need for foreign aid appropriations:

We are now selling farm surplus for foreign currencies we cannot use, and appropirating [sic] more dollars for foreign aid. If these foreign currencies can be used for loans through a multilateral association, it will help in the economic development of underdeveloped countries, and reduce the need for undesirable unilateral aid.[81]

In order to assess the significance of the modifications subsequently made in the Monroney proposal, we must identify those features that he regarded as important in the proposal. Monroney made it quite clear that the lending of local currencies was an essential part of his plan. During the 1958 hearings he stated:

If it was contemplated that IDA would make all of its loans in hard currencies, I would be against the IDA. I think an essential of this thing is to put these currencies to some use and to find ways of intermixing a larger proportion of local currencies with the hard dollars. If it requires all dollars, then I am against the principle of the IDA.[82]

The IDA which came into being in 1960 was not expected to lend soft currencies and has not done so; therefore we must conclude that the output of the policy making process was an IDA which

79 *Ibid.*, p. 8.

80 Reprinted from *Congressional Record* in *ibid.*, p. 10.

81 *Ibid.*, p. 15.   82 *Ibid.*, p. 172.

Senator Monroney was on record as opposing. Monroney had also made it clear that he viewed his proposal as a substitute for the DLF. In this respect he also failed to attain his goal. In view of the fact that Monroney had to abandon completely his two most important objectives, it is difficult to agree with Robinson's description of the process as compromise in order to achieve "fundamental aims."[83] It was precisely his fundamental aims that were forsaken.

The executive branch position was consistent from the beginning. They argued that there was no objection to creating a multilateral soft loan agency if certain conditions were met, namely, that (1) it should be affiliated with the IBRD; (2) it should not be a substitute for the DLF; (3) it should be given dollars to lend instead of inconvertible currency. On each point Senator Monroney acquiesced to executive branch desires; yet Robinson refers to the State and Treasury Departments as having "altered their positions."[84] What really happened was that the executive branch looked more favorably on the Monroney proposal after he altered his position.

The process by which the IDA was created can be described as follows: A senator formally proposed the establishment of an international agency to promote economic development. Although the executive branch opposed specific aspects of the proposal, it was seeking ways to increase economic aid. The executive viewed the Monroney proposal as a potentially useful tool for prying additional dollar appropriations for economic aid out of Congress. Although the senator disagreed with the executive, he was willing to acquiesce to major substantive changes in the proposal if the executive would support it and give him the credit for the legislation. From the administration's point of view, a congressman was offering to help them with the difficult task of getting more foreign aid money from Congress. Giving the credit (or blame) for the legislation to Senator Monroney was a small price to pay. In effect, then, Senator Monroney offered to help the executive branch do something it wanted to do anyway, that is, to increase the amount of soft lending for economic development. If Robinson, Montgomery, and Mikesell want to call this taking the initiative in for-

[83] Robinson, *Congress and Foreign Policy-Making*, p. 85.
[84] *Ibid.*, p. 102.

eign policy making, that is their privilege; but the above discussion suggests that there are more fruitful ways to describe the birth of the IDA—ways that emphasize the political history of foreign aid since World War II.

PERCEPTION OF THE SITUATION AND SELECTION OF AN ALTERNATIVE

The techniques of reliance on domestic effort and stimulating the flow of private capital were selected for many of the same reasons as they were in the 1954–57 period. The main difference was that the economic reconstruction in Europe and the American balance of payments problem increased the appeal to American policy makers of techniques which did not call for the movement of American public capital. Of course, American private capital moving abroad would cause just as great a strain on the balance of payments as public capital, but a deficit due to private capital outflow was not so unpopular in terms of domestic politics. Since the main changes in American policy for promoting economic development concerned public capital movements, the discussion will focus on them in this section.

PUBLIC CAPITAL

During the 1958–62 period there was a significant shift in emphasis from grants to soft loans. Grants had been getting increasingly unpopular in terms of domestic politics, and the shift to soft loans was one indication of this.

Hard loans were given a boost by expansion of the Export-Import Bank and the IBRD and by creation of the IADB. None of these moves, however, involved much in the way of an immediate appropriation from Congress. This meant that the executive branch did not have to fight so hard in order to get legislative approval.

The major emphasis in the 1958–62 period was on soft lending as a technique for promoting economic growth. On the basis of perceptions relating to the importance of the goal of economic growth, the political feasibility of soft loans, and the efficacy of alternative techniques the executive chose to place increased emphasis on soft loans.

Importance of Economic Growth

The American policy makers' conception of the importance of promoting economic growth relative to other foreign policy goals was influenced by the Communist activity in the economic sphere, the pressure being applied by the less developed nations themselves, and the arguments presented in several studies appearing during the 1958–62 period.

The continuance of Communist efforts to strengthen economic relations with the less developed nations made American policy makers attach increasing importance to the goal of promoting economic development. As Secretary of State Dulles put it in 1958, "I have heard it said that 'we must not enter into a competition' with the Soviet bloc in this field. My reply is that we are not entering into a competition with them. They are entering into competition with us."[85] On numerous occasions spokesmen for the executive branch indicated that they perceived soft lending as a response to the Soviet challenge in the field of economic development.[86]

A second factor which caused the policy makers to increase their concern for promoting growth was the pressure by the governments of the less developed nations. Executive branch spokesmen did not conceal the fact that both the IDA and the United Nations Special Fund were, at least in part, responses to the pressure for the SUNFED that had been building up for several years in the United Nations.[87] And in 1959 President Eisenhower indicated that he was beginning to view the problem of economic development as having importance apart from that given it by the cold war:

[85] House Committee on Foreign Affairs, *Mutual Security Hearings,* 1958, p. 182. For State Department perceptions of Soviet bloc activities, see U.S. Department of State, Bureau of Intelligence and Research, *The Sino-Soviet Economic Offensive through June 30, 1962,* Research Memorandum RSB-145, September 18, 1962 (processed).

[86] See the following: House Committee on Foreign Affairs, *Mutual Security Hearings,* 1958, pp. 722–28, 738; *New York Times,* January 8, 1958, p. 1; Willis C. Armstrong, "Soviet Economic Challenge to U.S. Policy," *Department of State Bulletin,* February 10, 1958, pp. 203–10; Christian Herter, "Statement on Mutual Security Program," *Department of State Bulletin,* March 7, 1960, p. 377.

[87] See: Walter H. Judd, Statement before General Assembly, reprinted in *Department of State Bulletin,* January 13, 1958, pp. 60–65; and Christopher H. Phillips, Statement in Second Committee of General Assembly, reprinted in *Department of State Bulletin,* November 3, 1958, pp. 704–7.

I believe in a sense that the problem of the underdeveloped nations is more lasting, more important, for Western civilization than is this problem of the Soviet-Western differences.

There are 1,700,000,000 people that today are living without sufficient food, shelter, clothing, and health facilities. Now they are not going to remain quiescent. They are learning something about their own lot, and they are comparing their lot with ours. . . . They are just going to have an explosion if we do not help.[88]

The policy makers' perceptions of the importance of economic development in less developed areas were also influenced by a number of public studies. The most notable of these was the Draper Report (*Composite Report of the President's Committee to Study the United States Military Assistance Program*) in 1959. This report pointed out that economic conditions in underdeveloped nations constituted "both a threat and a challenge to every nation of the free world."[89] Other studies written in the 1958–62 period also stressed the desirability of making promotion of economic development abroad a high-priority foreign policy objective.[90]

Political Feasibility of Soft Loans

Congressional confusion.—The feasibility of soft lending in terms of domestic politics was enhanced by the lack of Congressional understanding of the nature of soft loans. In a study prepared for the State Department by Professor Edward S. Mason

---

[88] Transcript of Television Appearance of Eisenhower and Macmillan in London, reprinted in *Department of State Bulletin,* September 21, 1959, p. 406.

[89] *Composite Report of the President's Committee to Study the United States Military Assistance Program,* I, August 17, 1959, 65. Cited hereafter as the Draper Report.

[90] *Foreign Economic Policy for the Twentieth Century,* Report of the Rockefeller Brothers Fund Special Studies Project (Garden City, N.Y.: Doubleday, 1958) (cited hereafter as Rockefeller Report, *Foreign Economic Policy for the Twentieth Century*); U.S., Congress, Senate, Committee on Foreign Relations, *United States Foreign Policy,* "Economic, Social, and Political Change in the Underdeveloped Countries and Its Implications for United States Policy," a study prepared by the Center for International Studies, Massachusetts Institute of Technology, 86th Cong., 2d sess., 1960, Committee Print (cited hereafter as Senate Committee on Foreign Relations, *MIT Study,* 1960); U.S., Congress, Senate, Committee on Foreign Relations, *United States Foreign Policy,* "Worldwide and Domestic Economic Problems and their Impact on the Foreign Policy of the United States," a study prepared by the Corporation for Economic and Industrial Research, 86th Cong., 1st sess., Committee Print, 1959 (cited hereafter as Senate Committee on Foreign Relations, *CEIR Study,* 1959).

and others, it was noted that "when considering suggested changes in legislation or when interpreting existing provisions, Executive Branch officials customarily err on the side of conservatism in order to be certain not to antagonize the Congress. This is especially true when the program or concept is one which is highly controversial, as is the case with all aspects of foreign assistance."[91] This is an understated way of saying that the executive often misleads Congress regarding foreign aid. Regarding soft loans the executive contributed to Congressional confusion in at least three ways.

First, the executive tended to treat governmental policies in underdeveloped nations as fixed. When discussing the soft lending agencies, such as the IDA, the IADB, or the DLF, the executive stressed prohibitions on competition with private capital but rarely (if ever) pointed out that such prohibitions have little meaning unless one specifies a time period and defines "reasonable terms." Nor did executive branch spokesmen mention why private capital might not be available in certain situations.[92] Congress probably would have taken a less charitable view of soft lending if the private capital situation had been described as follows:

Private capital will not be forthcoming for investment in Ruritania on X terms because the potential private investors do not like the attitude of the Ruritanian government. The Ruritanian government does not like foreigners—especially white foreign businessmen. The government does not want big American corporations to come into their country because they fear something called "exploitation." Furthermore, the government is not enthusiastic about the idea of a private enterprise economic system. The government sometimes harasses foreign investors by expropriating their holdings in order to demonstrate to the domestic citizenry that it is not "soft on foreigners."

If such an explanation had been given, many legislators would probably have concluded that giving such countries soft loans would weaken the incentive of the governments to treat private

[91] Consultants on International Finance and Economic Problems, *The Problem of Excess Accumulation of U.S.-Owned Local Currencies: Findings and Recommendations Submitted to the Under Secretary of State*, April 4, 1960 (processed), pp. 12–13. (Cited hereafter as the Mason Report.)

[92] See for example: Senate Committee on Banking and Currency, *IDA Hearings*, 1958, pp. 316–20; Senate Committee on Foreign Relations, *Mutual Security Hearings*, 1959, pp. 1234–35; Senate Committee on Foreign Relations, *IDA Hearings*, 1960, p. 10.

foreign capital better. The executive branch, however, tended to treat governmental policies in recipient nations as constants. This implicit assumption that governmental policies were fixed under-lay the executive branch case for soft loans. Thus soft loans, it was argued, would not compete with private capital, because soft loans would not be made in situations in which private capital would be available [within X years] on reasonable terms—given certain governmental policies. The executive did not point out that the with-holding of soft loans might induce a change in governmental poli-cies which would increase the availability of private capital within X years on Y terms. This would have raised an issue which the executive did not want to raise, that is, that soft lending always competes with private capital on some terms and over some time period.

The executive branch treatment of governmental policies as fixed also underlay the argument that less developed nations needed soft loans because they had a limited "capacity to repay" (debt-servicing capacity) conventional loans, public or private.[93] The executive ignored the fact that governmental policies and debt-servicing capacity are in fact interdependent. A nation's bal-ance of payments is not something over which the government has no control; and given a degree of control over its balance of pay-ments, a government could increase or decrease its debt-servicing capacity, at least to some extent, and could thus increase or de-crease its "ability" to qualify for soft loans. A government could, for example, increase capacity to repay by reducing imports of luxuries by the rich or by refusing to permit the rich to take their money out of the country and put it in Swiss banks. Needless to say, the executive branch spokesmen did not point out to Congress the existence of such interdependence between governmental policies and debt-servicing capacity.[94]

[93] See for example: Douglas Dillon, "Department Urges U.S. Participation in Inter-American Bank," *Department of State Bulletin*, June 22, 1959, pp. 928–30; Senate Committee on Foreign Relations, *IDA Hearings*, 1960, pp. 10–11; Senate Committee on Foreign Relations, *Mutual Security Hearings*, 1959, p. 1235; Senate Committee on Foreign Relations, *International Development and Security Hearings*, 1961, p. 69.

[94] It is hard to determine whether the executive actually believed that capacity to repay was independent of government policy or not. We suspect that they were aware of the interdependency; yet the confusion even in academic circles on this point makes us wonder. See my critique of the concept of "capacity to repay" as used

A second way in which the executive contributed to legislative misunderstanding of soft loans, besides treating governmental policies as fixed, was by failing to differentiate between administrative earmarking of funds and the net impact on the economy of the aid recipient. Thus, when asked by a senator whether IDA funds would be loaned to a nation because of an internal governmental deficit in its budget, an administration spokesman gave a reply that indicated that IDA funds would be lent for specific projects *instead of* for financing deficits.[95] He did not point out that lending for specific projects and financing deficits are not mutually exclusive alternatives. If a project is financed which would have been financed even in the absence of IDA aid, the net effect would be to help finance a budget deficit (or surplus). There is no intent here to say that this failure to clarify was "bad," but merely to observe it. If we wanted to moralize, we would probably conclude that Congress got what it deserved, since it was constantly hounding the executive with criticisms of the foreign aid program based on the administrative earmarking fallacy. Congressmen wanted to believe that their insistence on administrative earmarking of funds was a means of "controlling" the use of foreign aid funds.[96]

A third way in which the executive contributed to Congressional confusion was by exaggerating the usefulness of local currency. The Mason Report summarized the situation as follows:

The pretense that local currencies always are of substantial value to us leads to a certain amount of hypocrisy in the relations between the Executive Branch and the Congress. When surplus agricultural crop

---

by the influential MIT group: David A. Baldwin, "International Development Aid for Underdeveloped Countries: A Comment," *Review of Economics and Statistics,* XLIV (May, 1962), 213. See also F. Machlup, "Three Concepts of the Balance of Payments and the So-Called Dollar Shortage," *Economic Journal,* LX (March, 1950), 46–68. The issues are reminiscent of the famous "Keynes-Ohlin" debate over whether Germany had the "capacity" to pay reparations in the 1920's. See John M. Keynes, "The German Transfer Problem," *Economic Journal,* XXXIX (March, 1929), 1–7; and Bertil Ohlin, "The Reparation Problem: A Discussion," *Economic Journal,* XXXIX (June, 1929), 172–73.

[95] Senate Committee on Foreign Relations, *IDA Hearings,* 1960, pp. 17–18.

[96] For example, see: U.S., Congress, House, Committee on Government Operations, *Hearings, Operations of the Development Loan Fund,* 86th Cong., 2d sess., 1960; and U.S., Congress, House, Committee on Government Operations, *Operations of the Development Loan Fund,* 86th Cong., 2d sess., 1960, Report No. 1526.

disposal is under discussion, it is emphasized that this is no giveaway. These surplus crops are being sold for local currencies which, if not dollars, are at least money. The same rationale applies to DLF loans, where the Executive Branch emphasizes that we are not giving away the dollars because we receive local currency in repayment. When, however, the Mutual Security Program is under discussion and the need for dollar appropriations is raised, it is properly pointed out that U.S.-held local currencies are no substitute for dollars, and their usefulness is, in most cases, quite limited.[97]

Having exaggerated the value of local currencies during the hearings on the DLF in 1957, the executive found it difficult to disabuse the legislators of their concept of the value of local currency in later hearings on foreign aid. For example, in the 1958 Mutual Security hearings the executive explained that local currencies could not be substituted for dollars because the local currency is to its home country "the same as a checkbook is to an individual bank account; writing more checks does not create more resources in the bank."[98] Although this analogy was used to illustrate the limited usefulness of local currencies, the committee report indicated that the legislators had missed the point. It noted: "As pointed out during the current hearings, the possession of such [currencies] constitutes what is, in effect, a checking account held by the United States by means of which we can draw on the resources of these countries."[99] The legislators' misunderstanding of the nature of local currency probably increased the political feasibility of soft lending from the administration point of view. Given the hostility of Congress to grants, the legislators would probably have looked less favorably on soft loans repayable in local currency had they realized the extent to which such loans resembled grants.

In sum, Congress misconceived the nature of soft lending with specific regard to (1) the relationship between governmental policies in the recipient nations and (a) debt-servicing capacity and

[97] Mason Report, p. 16.

[98] House Committee on Foreign Affairs, *Mutual Security Hearings*, 1958, p. 247.

[99] U.S., Congress, House, Committee on Foreign Affairs, *Mutual Security Act of 1958*, 85th Cong., 2d sess., 1958, Report No. 1696, p. 12. On Congressional confusion regarding local currencies see also C. David Hartmann, "Local Currency Programs and United States Foreign Policies" (Ph.D. dissertation, Columbia University, 1962), pp. 222–28.

(*b*) competition with private and public hard lending; (2) the relationship between administrative earmarking and actual net impact of aid; and (3) the value of inconvertible currency.

Congressional help.—With regard to the IDA the administration found that the political feasibility of the project was increased by the willingness of a senator to take charge of the proposal. The executive could describe the IDA as a product of legislative initiative and thereby appeal to the legislators' pride in a fellow congressman's accomplishment. It could also avoid much of the criticism by Congress of the executive's "spendthrift ideas" and its "excessive power." In the eyes of some congressmen a vote for the IDA was almost a way of snubbing the executive branch.[100]

Legitimacy.—In the eyes of the American business community the legitimacy of soft loan operations by the IDA was increased by affiliation of the IDA with the International Bank. John J. McCloy, chairman of the Chase Manhattan Bank and former president of the IBRD, recalled that when he was with the IBRD, "it was absolutely essential to fight a vigorous battle against so-called soft loans."[101] He then remarked that the present concern for rapid economic development had led him to conclude that soft lending could be useful if properly administered. "I keep emphasizing this identity between the International Bank and the IDA as one of the important reasons for my belief that we should support this new venture. Indeed, I would be opposed to it if this were not so."[102] During the early years of its existence, the IBRD had to concentrate on legitimizing its own activities; in 1960 it could pass some of its respectability on to the IDA, thus increasing the political feasibility of this soft loan agency.

"Sharing the burden."—During the 1958–62 period two developments increased the appeal of soft lending. First, the balance of payments difficulties of the United States intensified the desire of Congress and the executive to get Europe and Japan to furnish more public capital to the less developed areas. Second, the economic recovery of Europe and Japan from World War II made such actions more practical than before since Europe and Japan were more capable of giving foreign aid than they had been at any

---

[100] See, for example: Senate Committee on Foreign Relations, *IDA Hearings,* 1960, p. 8.

[101] *Ibid.,* p. 52.   [102] *Ibid.,* pp. 53–54.

time since the war. The IDA was featured in the 1958–60 period as a means of inducing Europe and Japan to give more aid. Secretary of the Treasury Anderson commented in 1960:

I should like to stress the importance of this contribution by other countries. The United States is scheduled to pay in $320 million of the initial subscriptions, while the more-developed countries are scheduled to provide $443 million. These 16 countries have recovered from the effect of the war, they have expanded their trade, and they have acquired adequate, or more than adequate, monetary reserves. Hitherto, capital on flexible terms of repayment has been provided almost entirely by the United States through the Development Loan Fund. In the International Development Association, other countries will provide a larger share of the convertible currency resources than will the United States.[103]

The local currency "problem."—In 1958 the United States had outstanding loans repayable in local currency amounting to more than $2 billion. In the Mutual Security hearings of that year ICA Director James H. Smith, Jr., noted that he was "particularly concerned about the ever-increasing balances of local currencies accruing from the mutual security program and Public Law 480."[104] A report prepared for the ICA in August, 1958, observed that rates of soft lending then current would bring United States local currency holdings to $10 billion equivalent within five years. The report concluded that future accumulations would be a serious problem and that "continued unrestricted accumulations of local currencies by the U.S. should be avoided."[105] And in 1960 the Mason Report, also prepared at the behest of the State Department, reached similar conclusions with respect to the desirability of augmenting local currency holdings. The Mason Report pointed out that "contrary to general assumptions, the excess accumulation of local currencies by the United States is a political as well as an economic problem." The report emphasized three political aspects of the problem: (1) Congressional misconceptions of the nature of local currency encouraged attempts to substitute such

[103] *Ibid.*, p. 11. See also *ibid.*, pp. 5, 17, 44.

[104] House Committee on Foreign Affairs, *Mutual Security Hearings*, 1958, p. 390.

[105] Robert L. Berenson, William M. Bristol, and Ralph I. Straus, *Accumulation and Administration of Local Currencies: A Special Report to James H. Smith, Jr., Director, International Cooperation Administration*, August, 1958, p. iv (processed). See also pp. 1–77 in this report.

currency for dollar appropriations. (2) The huge American holdings of local currency constituted a standing threat from the viewpoint of the country of origin. Since the less developed nations tend to be hypersensitive with respect to their independence, this problem was especially ticklish. (3) Attempts by American officials to get the local currency "off the books" by lending it back to the country of origin often resulted in political friction because of the reluctance of the government in the home country to borrow its own currency from the United States at 3 or 4 per cent interest when it could borrow from its central bank at 1 per cent.[106] One of the authors of this report, Professor Edward S. Mason, summarized it in a magazine article and concluded:

> All things considered, the best disposition of the vast bulk of local currency accumulations would be for us to grant them back for debt retirement or any other purpose deemed proper by the receiving country. Alternatively, we could burn them, though this would involve the country in the additional expense of printing new currency notes. A recent suggestion by Undersecretary Dillon that U.S. counterpart in Greece be used for debt reduction met with a storm of protest. Why, it was implied, should currencies held or controlled by the United States be used for debt retirement abroad when the American government is forced continually to add to its debt at home? The attitude is one of the consequences of treating local currency holdings or counterpart as something of value, as real money. Whether the Greek government uses American counterpart to retire debt or not, the American debt position remains the same.[107]

Thus, by 1961 the executive branch had become aware of several disadvantages of the type of soft loan repayable in inconvertible currency. And in his first foreign aid message to Congress President Kennedy announced that the DLF would henceforth make no soft loans repayable in local currency but would confine itself to soft loans repayable in dollars over periods of up to fifty years at low or zero rates of interest.[108]

Summary.—During the 1958–62 period the feasibility of soft lending as an instrument of statecraft for promoting economic

[106] All quotes are from Mason Report, pp. 1–16.

[107] Edward S. Mason, "Foreign Money We Can't Spend," *Atlantic Monthly*, May, 1960, p. 84.

[108] *Department of State Bulletin*, April 10, 1961, pp. 507–14.

growth was enhanced by the following factors: (a) congressional confusion as to the nature of soft loans, (b) increased legitimacy of soft lending in the eyes of businessmen as a result of affiliation of the IDA with the IBRD, (c) a desire to induce others to make soft loans by encouraging them to join the IDA with the United States, and (d) the help of Senator Monroney in getting approval for the IDA. An additional factor made a shift from soft loans repayable in local currency to soft loans repayable in dollars feasible; that factor was the increasing awareness of the "local currency problem."

Effectiveness of Other Techniques

The policy makers' perceptions of the efficacy of alternative techniques of statecraft also affected the decision to emphasize soft loans more. With respect to trade liberalization as an alternative technique the Eisenhower administration's position had been since 1953 one favoring "trade not aid." Secretary of State Rusk indicated that the Kennedy administration also viewed trade and aid as alternatives. He summarized his perception of the situation as follows:

In short, the situation facing many developing countries is this: Import requirements will increase as industrialization progresses; export earnings from primary commodities cannot be expected to meet these growing needs; if development is to continue these nations must receive more aid or export more processed and manufactured goods.

The industrialized nations, and especially the United States and our chief European allies, face three choices. We can ignore the problems and aspirations of the less developed nations, at one stroke denying our faith in freedom and the dignity of man and leaving most of the world to the Communists. We can make even larger donations of foreign aid indefinitely. Or we can progressively widen our import markets to manufactured goods from developing countries.[109]

Although policy makers bluntly pointed out that "the less developed countries will need fewer loans or grants if they can export more,"[110] it was fairly obvious to all that Congress was unlike-

---

[109] Dean Rusk, "Trade, Investment, and United States Foreign Policy," *Department of State Bulletin*, November 5, 1962, p. 686.

[110] Joseph D. Coppock, "The United States in a Competitive World Economy," *Department of State Bulletin*, March 12, 1962, p. 428.

ly to permit a degree of trade liberalization which would be sufficient to permit reliance on hard lending altogether—if at all. Policy
makers' perceptions of limitations on hard lending—either public
or private—were probably sharpened by the publication in 1960 of
an IBRD study pointing out that international indebtedness of
low income countries had increased 60 per cent in the 1956–58
period.[111] In short, the failure to liberalize trade in earlier years
made reliance on local effort, reliance on private investment, and
reliance on hard loans less efficacious in the 1958–62 period because it was more difficult for the underdeveloped nations to earn
foreign exchange than it would have been if the United States had
reduced tariffs more in the early postwar period.

The American policy makers were also beginning to decrease
their estimates of the probability that governments in less developed nations could be induced to change their "investment
climates" enough to allow them to attract enough private capital
to sustain a rate of growth judged satisfactory. This was explained
in part by increased understanding of the nature and importance
of the nationalism in underdeveloped areas. During the 1958–60
period we find increasingly frequent references in policy statements to such concepts as "the great force of change, this 'new nationalism.'"[112] There were warnings that the United States must
"satisfy its [the new nationalism's] legitimate aspirations, and . . .
guide its developing influence into channels consistent with the
welfare and peace of the world as a whole, as well as with the
prosperity and freedom of the new nations themselves."[113] Spokesmen for the Kennedy administration also referred to the "new understanding of the forces that motivate the burgeoning masses of
the lesser developed areas."[114]

The policy makers were also aware that the existence of the
Soviet Union as an alternative source of capital weakened the bargaining position of the United States in its attempts to get foreign

[111] Dragoslav Avramovic and Ravi Gulhati, *Debt Servicing Problems of Low-
Income Countries, 1956–1958* (Baltimore: Johns Hopkins Press, 1960), p. 59.

[112] John W. Hanes, Jr., "The Citizen and Foreign Policy," *Department of State
Bulletin,* May 16, 1960, p. 793.

[113] *Ibid.*

[114] Carl T. Rowan, "New Directions in Foreign Policy," *Department of State Bulletin,* March 5, 1962, p. 379.

governments to improve their "investment climates." Veteran diplomat Charles E. Bohlen observed in 1960 that "so long as the uncommitted countries are aware that the West is willing to provide a timely alternative to dependence on the bloc, they can resist any improper pressures that the Soviets may seek to apply."[115] It was equally obvious that the willingness of the Soviets to provide a "timely alternative" encouraged the uncommitted nations to resist "improper pressures" from the United States.

The policy makers' perceptions of the efficacy of relying on domestic effort and private investment were probably also affected by the appearance of several public studies during the 1958–62 period. Although they differed in the degree of emphasis they put on private enterprise, all agreed that private enterprise and domestic efforts would not be enough and that substantial amounts of public capital in the form of grants or soft loans should be forthcoming.[116]

SUMMARY

In the 1958–62 period the policy makers faced a situation in which they wanted to stimulate economic development abroad at a faster rate. The past reluctance of the United States to lower trade barriers increase the difficulty of earning foreign exchange for less developed nations and thus made it harder for them to service conventional loans. The existence of the Soviet aid program as well as the strength of internal nationalist feelings in most nations, reduced the likelihood that governments in less developed countries would be willing to change their policies to attract more private capital. Given the continued hostility of Congress to grants, soft loans once more appeared to offer the best combination of political feasibility and effectiveness.

IV. EFFECTIVENESS OF POLICY: 1958–62

Many of the techniques of statecraft and the corresponding limitations on those techniques remained the same in the 1958–62

[115] Charles E. Bohlen, "Economic Assistance in United States Foreign Policy," *Department of State Bulletin*, March 28, 1960, p. 498.

[116] Draper Report, pp. 73–74 *et passim;* Senate Committee on Foreign Relations, *MIT Study*, 1960, pp. 57–58 *et passim;* Senate Committee on Foreign Relations, *CEIR Study*, 1959, pp. 52–63; Rockefeller Report, *Foreign Economic Policy for the Twentieth Century*, pp. 23, 43–60.

period as in the 1954–57 period. Since mere repetition of what has been discussed previously is pointless, this discussion of the efficacy of policy will concentrate on the new developments in the 1958–62 period. We should bear in mind, however, that these new developments should be taken as a supplement to the section on effectiveness in the previous chapter.[117]

SOVIET AID

In the first place, the efficacy of American attempts to induce governments in less developed nations to change their policies so as to attract more private investment and so as to qualify for more hard loans from the IBRD was reduced by the growing aid program of the Soviet bloc. The existence of this alternative source of capital decreased the opportunity cost to the less developed nations of failure to comply with American desires.

Besides affecting the willingness of governments in underdeveloped nations to submit to American pressure, the Soviet bloc aid program directly affected the rate of economic growth in such nations. Charles Wolf, Jr., a RAND Corporation economist, has aptly pointed out that Americans too often assume that effects of aid from the Communists must be undesirable from the American viewpoint.[118] Insofar as the Soviet bloc provides additional resources to less developed nations, however, it is quite possible that such aid will spur economic growth as much as a comparable amount of dollar aid. Thus, Soviet bloc aid may actually help the United States to attain its goal of promoting economic development in less developed areas.[119] This is not to say that the Soviet Union would not also benefit from such a situation. "Competitive coexistence," as Wolf notes, "is a non-zero-sum game."[120]

On the other hand, we should recognize the possibility that Soviet bloc aid (or American aid, for that matter) could retard the rate of economic development.

[117] See above, pp. 181–90.

[118] Charles Wolf, Jr., *Foreign Aid: Theory and Practice in Southern Asia* (Princeton, N.J.: Princeton University Press, 1960), pp. 383–400.

[119] Note that it is also possible that Soviet bloc aid could help the United States attain the objective of promoting economic growth while simultaneously hindering the attainment of other goals, such as the minimization of Communist influence in less developed areas.

[120] Wolf, p. 392.

... Soviet aid might be directed toward less essential projects that a particularly interested ministry in the recipient country had been unable to retain in the country's development plan. By giving foreign exchange credits for such projects, on condition that their local currency costs be borne by the recipient country, Soviet aid might contribute to inflation and to the diversion of internal resources from more to less essential uses, thereby actually slowing down growth in the "aided" country. It is by no means impossible, for example, that some of the Soviet aid projects in Burma, such as the sports stadium, hotel, and theater, may have this effect.[121]

CREDIBILITY OF THREAT

The credibility of the American threat to withhold public capital was undermined in several ways. First, there were, as there had been throughout the 1950's, a number of public studies which argued for an increase in the amount of American economic aid. Second, the launching of more new aid programs, such as the IDA and the IADB, gave the underdeveloped nations more reasons for believing that the United States aid policy was subject to change. Third, the less developed nations had more reason than ever before to believe that the United States was interested in them as a result of the cold war. The numerous references to communism in public statements by policy makers made this clear. The awareness of the American interest in their fate led many governments to believe that the United States would hesitate to withhold aid. A fourth factor which limited the credibility of the American threat was the failure to secure long-term financing for aid. The Eisenhower administration tried and failed in 1957, and the Kennedy administration did likewise in 1961. The Kennedy program emphasized self-help measures by recipient nations and long-range social and economic development, but these goals depended on long-term financing. The executive could hardly give a credible threat to withhold aid when the governments in less developed nations were aware of the Congressional pressure on the executive to commit all aid funds. This pressure resulted from the bureaucratic desire to maintain or increase its level of appropriations and

[121] *Ibid.*, p. 393. Political scientists often ignore the possibility that aid could retard economic growth. Professor Hans Morgenthau, for example, refers to the American refusal to pave the streets of Kabul in Afghanistan as an "error." He does not acknowledge the possibility of any ill effects from such a project. "A Political Theory of Foreign Aid," *American Political Science Review*, LVI (June, 1962), 304.

from the standing implied threat of Congress to use failure to commit funds as justification for cuts in future appropriations— "You didn't use all the money we gave you last year, and so on." These governments were also aware that if the executive failed to commit all of its aid funds, Congress might conclude that too much had been appropriated and cut (as opposed to threatening to cut) the following year's appropriation; thus they could not be sure that funds would be available to the executive if and when they did comply with the desires of the executive. In short, failure to put aid on a long-term financing basis undermined the credibility of both threats to withhold aid and of promises to give it.

PRIVATE INVESTMENT

Between 1957 and 1962 United States direct private investment in foreign countries rose from $25.4 billion to $37.1 billion. Private capital, however, was reluctant to go to those areas of the world which, in terms of American foreign policy goals, needed it most. More than two-thirds of the increase in private investment between 1957 and 1962 went to Europe and Canada.

CO-ORDINATION

The efficacy of stimulating private capital and of public hard loans was curtailed by the proliferation of soft lending agencies. Although all of the soft loan agencies supported by the United States were supposed to refrain from competing with private capital or with public hard lending, the implementation of this restriction was difficult. There were so many sources of public funds that co-ordination of their efforts in order to prevent competition among them was more difficult than it would have been if all hard loans, soft loans, and grants were disbursed by a single agency.

TIED LOANS

The announcement in 1959 that recipients of DLF loans must spend them in the United States also limited the effectiveness of American aid. Since the usefulness of money depends on what the money will buy, the dollars borrowed from the DLF after 1959 were less useful to underdeveloped nations than they were before. They could be used to buy fewer things. To take a hypothetical example, if Britain sold tractors for $100 and the United States sold them for $200, an underdeveloped nation could get two tractors from Britain for the price of one in the United States. Thus, the tying of American aid would make the aid less effective as a means of promoting economic growth because it would buy only one tractor instead of two.

DOLLAR-REPAYABLE SOFT LOANS

It is difficult to compare the efficacy of soft loans repayable in dollars with those repayable in local currency because the efficacy of the latter type depends on what is eventually done with the local currency. During the period in which the local currency is being held and the repayment has not yet begun on dollar-repayable soft loans, the effect of each is about the same; that is, resources have been transferred from A to B, with no resources being transferred from B to A. But how should we evaluate the long-term, low-interest, dollar-repayable loan? We could define economic aid in terms of the difference between the amount of aid received at a given price and the amount which would have been received at a similar price in the commercial market. Thus, the price of a grant is zero; since we can get nothing from the commercial capital market for zero, a grant is 100 per cent aid. The price of a dollar-repayable loan for $100 at no interest is $100 over X years. The amount of aid in this transaction is represented by the difference between $100 and what the recipient would have had to pay in order to get a $100 loan repayable over X years from the commercial capital market. Although such a definition would give us a good measure of the recipients' benefits from aid, it involves a practical difficulty—it is difficult to determine the free-market rate for international lending. Thus, we must turn to a less accurate, but still useful, measure. Such a measure has been suggested by John Pincus. He has proposed a definition of economic aid in terms of the donor country's sacrifice of real resources.[122] Using this definition, Pincus estimates that AID loans at three-fourths of 1 per cent for forty years include about a 75 per cent

[122] John A. Pincus, *Economic Aid and International Cost Sharing* (Baltimore: Johns Hopkins Press, 1965), pp. 113–45. Pincus' exact definition is as follows: Aid is "the present value of aid disbursements minus the present value of repayments, discounted at an appropriate rate of interest reflecting domestic opportunity cost of public capital" (p. 115).

TABLE 1

Less Developed Countries

Annual growth rate of gross national product, population,
and per capita gross national product
(1957–58 average to 1963–64 average)

Countries	Annual GNP growth rate* (per cent)	Annual population growth rate† (per cent)	Annual per capita GNP growth rate (per cent)
Latin America:			
Argentina	0.6	1.7	−1.1
Bolivia	3.5	2.3	1.2
Brazil	5.3	3.1	2.2
Chile	3.3	2.3	1.0
Colombia	4.6	2.8	1.8
Costa Rica	4.1	4.0	.1
Ecuador	4.3	3.2	1.1
El Salvador	5.7	2.9	2.8
Guatemala	4.5	3.0	1.5
Honduras	3.6	3.1	.5
Jamaica	3.9	2.0	1.9
Mexico	5.3	3.1	2.2
Nicaragua	5.3	2.9	2.4
Panama	4.9	3.0	1.9
Paraguay	2.2	2.2	0
Peru	6.4	2.3	4.1
Trinidad and Tobago	6.0	3.0	3.0
Venezuela	4.5	3.8	.7
Far East:			
China (Taiwan)	7.1	3.1	4.0
Korea	4.7	2.9	1.8
Malaya, States of	5.9	3.1	2.8
Philippines	4.9	3.2	1.7
Thailand	7.4	3.0	4.4
Vietnam	3.5	2.8	.7
Near East:			
Cyprus	3.6	1.2	2.4
Greece	6.2	.7	5.7
Iran	4.7	2.4	2.3
Israel	10.5	3.6	6.9
Jordan	9.5	2.9	6.6
Turkey	4.0	2.9	1.1
South Asia:			
Ceylon	3.5	2.5	1.0
India	4.4	2.3	2.1
Pakistan	4.5	2.5	2.0
Africa:			
Ethiopia	4.5	1.4	3.1
Ghana	5.1	2.5	2.6
Kenya	3.5	2.9	.6
Malawi	2.1	3.0	− .9
Morocco	2.0	3.1	−1.1
Nigeria	3.3	2.0	1.3
South Rhodesia	3.6	3.3	.3
Sudan	4.5	2.9	1.6
Tunisia	4.7	2.6	2.1
Uganda	3.4	2.5	.9
Zambia	4.7	2.9	1.8

Source: U.S. Senate, Committee on Foreign Relations, *Hearings, Foreign Assistance 1965*, 89th Cong., 1st sess., 1965, p. 113.

* GNP growth rates are AID estimates based largely on official national statistics.

† Population growth rates are based on AID country, U.N., and other source data.

subsidy element. This figure is useful as a rough approximation of the degree to which such loans should be considered aid.

TOTAL AMOUNT

In 1960 Paul Hoffman reported that, despite the efforts of the United States and other nations, economic growth in the less developed areas had proceeded at a rate of only 1 per cent per year during the 1950's. He proposed that the developed nations try to promote growth in underdeveloped nations at 2 per cent annually in the 1960's. After allowing for increases in private investment and in the resources of existing public aid agencies, Hoffman estimated that about $20 billion over and above that which was likely to be available from these sources would be needed to attain his goal.[123] As of the end of 1962, there was no indication that additional public capital on the order of magnitude of $2 billion per year was likely to be forthcoming. The small size of the total amount of capital flowing to less developed nations continued to be a major obstacle to economic development.

POPULATION

In addition to the other obstacles to economic growth was the rapid multiplication of mouths to be fed. As Table 1 shows, the benefits of a growth in GNP can easily be canceled by a population increase. For example, Venezuela's GNP growth rate of 4.5 per cent resulted in a mere .7 per cent addition to per capita GNP.

[123] Hoffman, pp. 44–47.

VI

Concluding Remarks

ECONOMIC GROWTH AS A FOREIGN POLICY GOAL: SPECULATION

At the beginning of the discussion of soft loans it was noted that determination of whether or not promotion of economic development in less developed nations was "really" a goal of American foreign policy was not a topic of major interest in this study. Although some evidence of the existence of such a goal was cited, its existence was assumed for most of the analysis. Some speculation on the arguments for and against believing in the existence of such an objective is in order. One of the main reasons this writer has refrained from addressing himself to the task of identifying "real" goals is that he is not quite sure how to go about it. The members of the so-called "realist" school of international politics encounter little difficulty in this task because they "know" what goals statesmen seek based on their understanding of "first principles of statecraft."[1] This writer has to rely on more mundane empirical approaches.

Hans Morgenthau asserts that international bribery often appears in the guise of aid for economic development and that aid for economic development often appears in the guise of military assistance.[2] Although this writer intuitively suspects that Morgenthau is correct, he does not know how to prove it; and Morgenthau gives little help since he provides no evidence but merely asserts. In fact, Morgenthau further confuses the issue by setting up a

[1] Cf. George Liska, *The New Statecraft* (Chicago: University of Chicago Press, 1960), pp. 35 *et passim.*

[2] Hans Morgenthau, "A Political Theory of Foreign Aid," *American Political Science Review*, LVI (June, 1962), 303.

taxonomy for analyzing foreign aid based on motivation. His six categories are: (a) humanitarian foreign aid; (b) subsistence foreign aid; (c) military foreign aid; (d) bribery; (e) prestige aid; and (f) foreign aid for economic development.[3] Morgenthau specifically points out that the categories are not based on the function performed by the aid. Humanitarian aid, he observes, is "*per se* nonpolitical," but it can "perform a political function when it operates within a political context."[4] Morgenthau thus implies that humanitarian aid may or may not perform a political function, but it is nonetheless humanitarian aid. Later in the article, however, his argument implies that the function actually performed determines the category of aid: "Foreign aid professed and accepted for purposes of economic development *may turn out to be* something different from what it was intended to be. . . . Most likely, it will turn out to be a bribe or prestige aid. . . ."[5] Now, either the categories are based on *intended* function or they are based on *actual* function, but Morgenthau cannot have it both ways. If the categories are determined by actual function, then it is unwise for Morgenthau to speak of humanitarian aid as being "nonpolitical" and, at the same time, performing a political function.

Even if Morgenthau had been more consistent, his taxonomy would have been limited in its usefulness for analyzing foreign aid. This is because his categories are not mutually exclusive. It is quite possible that a given foreign aid transaction might be motivated by a desire to promote economic development, increase the prestige of the giver, and strengthen the military posture of the recipient. It is also possible, of course, for a given amount of aid to actually perform all of these functions simultaneously. The approach taken in the foregoing discussion of soft loans does not attempt to identify the single motivating factor behind an aid

[3] *Ibid.*, p. 301.   [4] *Ibid.*

[5] *Ibid.*, pp. 307–8. Italics mine. On page 303 Morgenthau notes a situation in which military aid is "really in the nature of a bribe." This statement gives us the impression that military aid can perform the function of bribery but still retain its status as military aid. The next paragraph, however, notes a situation in which "what appears to be military aid may also be actually in the nature of prestige aid." Now the reader is confronted with differentiating between "military aid" and "what appears to be military aid." Morgenthau's failure to distinguish clearly between actual and intended aid functions seems to be an example of what the Sprouts see as a tendency among foreign policy analysts to confuse undertakings and outcomes. See Harold Sprout and Margaret Sprout, *The Ecological Perspective on Human Affairs: With Special Reference to International Politics* (Princeton, N.J.: Princeton University Press, 1965), pp. 10–11.

transaction. Instead, it assumes that policy makers usually pursue multiple goals. Thus, it was not argued that promotion of economic growth was the *only* goal of various techniques of statecraft but merely that it was one among others. It was also pointed out that the existence of other goals and their relative importance affected the selection of techniques for promoting growth. Instead of thinking in terms of "either-or" categories, we can fruitfully conceive of the importance of a given goal as ranging along a continuum from zero to infinity. Thus, we would not say "either economic growth was a goal or it was not," but rather, "the relative importance of economic growth was X."

Despite the inadequacy of the arguments of those who would deny that economic growth was a foreign policy objective, we cannot ignore the difficulty which confronts the foreign policy analyst. Let us consider the arguments for and against accepting public policy statements as evidence of the existence of such a goal.

In the first place, there is good reason to suspect that executive branch spokesmen would hesitate to be candid about the goals of foreign policy because they know that they might be overheard by foreign governments. They would, therefore, be tempted to describe objectives in terms that would not offend such governments.

Secondly, the mass public as well as Congress have shown very little ability or readiness to understand the relatively subtle reasoning which underlies many foreign policy decisions. Robert Dahl noted with respect to the British loan in 1946 that:

> In 1946, while Congress was debating the loan to Britain, very few people in a nation-wide polling sample understood that the loan was anything more than a generous gift. Its relation to our own trade and security was not commonly grasped. The gap between the economist's argument for the loan and the ordinary citizen's understanding of it was fully as great as the differences between expert and amateur evaluation of means in the case of atomic energy.[6]

A third reason for skepticism regarding public policy statements designating economic growth as a goal of foreign policy is that, from the viewpoint of the executive, it is easier to tell Congress what Congress wants to hear in defending a given course of action. Congress might frown on the idea of bribing a foreign dic-

---

[6] Robert A. Dahl, *Congress and Foreign Policy* (New York: Norton, 1950), p. 75.

tator but be receptive to a proposal for stimulating economic growth in the dictator's nation.

We might also argue that in politics short-range objectives are usually more important than long-range ones; therefore, it is improbable that the President would be much concerned with promoting a goal which could only be realized twenty or thirty years hence. It is, after all, well known that professional diplomats tend to think of foreign relations in very short-range terms.

Let us now consider the arguments in favor of accepting public statements as evidence of the United States desire to promote economic development in low-income nations. First, there is the substantiating evidence furnished by the private views of those planning postwar foreign policy in the Department of State during World War II. It was noted in Chapter II that several documents and private communications expressed an interest in economic development of less developed areas.[7] Why would Leo Pasvolsky and others have indicated such an interest in economic growth at that time? There was no United Nations, no cold war; yet, in private documents they seriously discussed foreign economic growth as a policy objective.

A second reason for believing policy statements is that many people have argued the same way in private life as they did when playing the role of policy advisor. The best examples of this are furnished by the numerous scholars, such as Willard Thorp, Clair Wilcox, Stanley D. Metzger, Raymond F. Mikesell, W. W. Rostow, and Robert Asher, to cite only a few, who have moved from positions as government advisers to academia without any sudden change in their views on economic growth as a foreign policy goal.

A third argument in favor of accepting public statements is simply that we can make a plausible case for the desirability of such a goal. Some, including Morgenthau, claim that "the opinion is widely held that foreign aid is an end in itself, carrying its own justification, both transcending, and independent of, foreign policy."[8] Assuming we could give a precise meaning to such a position, it is doubtful that any reasonable man would subscribe to it. This writer knows of none who do; and, since Morgenthau and

[7] United States, Department of State, General Policy Series No. 15, *Postwar Foreign Policy Preparation 1939–1945* (Washington: U.S. Government Printing Office, 1949), pp. 141, 241, 468, 560–61.

[8] Morgenthau, *American Political Science Review*, LVI, 301.

the others purporting to see such a position as widely held rarely cite a specific example, we cannot take their claims very seriously.[9] The fact that many scholars believe that stimulating economic growth should be a foreign policy objective is proof enough of the plausibility of the case for it. Note that this is not to say that such scholars are correct, but merely that they are not patently ridiculous in their arguments.

The fourth argument relates to the nature of bureaucracy. Bureaucracies find it difficult to keep secrets; thus, even if it were true at one time that economic development was merely a façade hiding other goals, it would be difficult to preserve such a state of affairs for twenty years. Communications theorists describe a phenomenon they call "feedback." If we may speculate regarding its applicability to bureaucracies, it seems that such organizations begin to believe their own propaganda after a time. It is, therefore, possible for the goal of economic development to have sneaked in through the "back door" of the policy makers' office.

All of this, we must remember, has been in the nature of speculation. In the end this writer must admit that he favors the arguments in favor of accepting public statements, despite the formidable arguments against such a position. The arguments on each side are so strong that we almost have to flip a coin.

TECHNIQUES OF STATECRAFT AND ECONOMIC GROWTH

The foregoing chapters have described several techniques of statecraft employed by the United States in order to promote economic development abroad between 1943 and 1963. The techniques described are not the only ones which were used; they were, however, the most important ones. In the 1958–62 period a new technique appeared which was not discussed; that is the technique of controlling population growth. This technique may well prove to be the most effective one of all in the future.

The primary goal of the above discussion was to determine how

[9] Positions similar to that of Morgenthau are taken by John D. Montgomery, *The Politics of Foreign Aid* (New York: Praeger, 1962), pp. 83–84; and Edward C. Banfield, "American Foreign Aid Doctrines," in *Public Policy, 1961* (Cambridge, Mass.: Harvard University, 1962), p. 46.

and why the United States came to adopt soft loans as a technique for promoting growth. The approach taken examined various alternative techniques available to policy makers in four time periods in an effort to describe the process whereby the United States came to place major emphasis on the technique of soft lending. The techniques were discussed in terms of three major categories: (a) reliance on domestic effort, (b) stimulation of private foreign investment, and (c) furnishing capital through public channels.[10]

During the 1943–48 period reliance on domestic effort and stimulation of private investment were emphasized more relative to the alternative of public capital than they were in later periods. Public capital was furnished on conventional loan terms via the International Bank and the Export-Import Bank. The basic assumption of the rationale for selecting such a combination of techniques was that the world was entering a new era of extensive trade liberalization. Later events, of course, proved this assumption false. With respect to soft lending, the 1943–48 period can be described as one in which it was rejected with a vengeance. It was not just that the government would not bother to make soft loans but that it would work especially hard to avoid making them. The adoption of a policy of strategic nonlending by the IBRD was an instance of energetic avoidance of soft lending. If we are to comprehend the degree of change in American policy represented by adoption of soft loans, we must realize that the 1943–48 period was one of outright rejection of them.

If the 1943–48 period is characterized by rejection of soft loans, then the 1949–53 period can be described as one of reconsideration. Although reliance on domestic effort, stimulating private capital flow, and provision of hard loans through public channels remained the basic techniques of statecraft, there were indications

[10] It has been called to my attention that the analysis of techniques follows lines of inquiry recommended by Harold Lasswell: "The fourfold division of policy instruments is particularly convenient when the external relations of a group are considered: information, diplomacy, economics, force (words, deals, goods, weapons)." Postscript (1958) added to Politics: Who Gets What, When, How (New York: Meridian, 1958), pp. 204–5. No conscious effort was made to follow Lasswell's scheme; the similarity probably results from the impact of Lasswell's writing on the discipline of political science in general.

that the policy makers were seeking more effective techniques. Launching of the technical assistance program and later the Mutual Security program were examples of the policy makers' willingness to use public grants to spur economic growth. Although soft loans were still taboo throughout most of the period, the year 1953 marked the beginning of attempts to dispose of surplus agricultural commodities in such a way that the United States might end up holding I O U's payable in inconvertible currency.

In the 1954–57 period the United States expanded its use of both grants and soft loans. Soft lending was carried on through such institutions as the DLF, PL 480, and sections 505 and 402 of the Mutual Security Act of 1954. The type of soft loan made during this period was usually that repayable in local currency. During this period the United States was experimenting with soft lending as a technique of statecraft.

Soft lending finally took its place as a legitimate technique of American statecraft in the 1958–62 period. If the 1954–57 period was one of experimentation, then the 1958–62 period was one of adoption and refinement of the technique. The DLF activities were expanded, and two new multilateral soft lending channels were created—the IDA and the IADB. Although soft loans of the local currency type continued to be made, primary emphasis was placed on dollar-repayable soft loans.

Two trends are discernible in the way American policy makers have selected techniques for promoting foreign economic development since World War II. First, increasing emphasis has been placed on furnishing capital through public channels relative to the techniques of relying on domestic effort and stimulating private investment. Since 1943 the guiding principles of American policy on public capital movements have been: (1) Keep it small. (2) Keep it under American control. (3) Avoid offending private investors.

The second trend has been that toward more emphasis on a particular type of public capital movement—the soft loan.[11] Al-

[11] For evidence that future foreign aid debates are likely to focus on the appropriate size, nature, and allocation of soft loans see Agency for International Development, *Loan Terms, Debt Burden and Development,* April, 1965.

though grants and hard loans have not been abandoned, their importance relative to soft loans has diminished.

Let us summarize now the reasons put forth in foregoing chapters which explain why policy makers changed the policy of the United States toward economically underdeveloped nations.

The foregoing chapters have argued that the United States came to place growing emphasis on soft lending as a result of the decision makers' perceptions of: (a) the importance of promoting foreign economic growth relative to other foreign policy objectives, (b) the feasibility of various techniques in terms of domestic politics, and (c) the relative effectiveness of various techniques.

RELATIVE IMPORTANCE OF PROMOTING GROWTH

The following factors affected the judgment of the policy makers regarding the relative importance of promoting economic development in low-income areas as a goal of foreign policy: (1) The reconstruction of Europe reduced the importance of this goal of policy and thereby boosted the importance of promoting growth. In the 1943–48 period the United States policy makers were too busy with promoting the recovery of Europe to worry much about the less developed areas. (2) The onset of the cold war and the subsequent expansion of the Soviet economic aid program stimulated increased interest in the less developed areas on the part of American policy makers. (3) The fall of Nationalist China and the rise of a sense of rivalry between India and Communist China sharpened the policy makers' perception of the world situation as one in which two ways of life were being offered to the developing nations. One way held open the possibility of economic development without resort to totalitarian methods; the other did not. (4) The policy makers' perceptions of the "population explosion" in the underdeveloped nations increased their estimate of the job to be done. Economic growth, they realized, was a bigger problem than they had first thought. (5) The underdeveloped nations continually pressed the United States for more public capital on terms more lenient than those offered by the IBRD or the Export-Import Bank. The United Nations provided a forum in which American representatives had to face the representatives of poorer nations day after day. The less developed nations thus had a permanent, institutionalized setting within which to voice their demands. Between 1946 and 1962 the vast majority of new members in the United Nations were low-income nations, thus augmenting their influence in that organization.

DOMESTIC POLITICAL FEASIBILITY

Factors affecting the domestic political feasibility of soft lending as seen by the policy makers included the following: (1) The executive believed that it would be easier to secure Congressional approval for a soft loan program than for one based on grants.[12] In the first place, Congress had indicated a preference for any kind of loan program as opposed to any kind of grant program. And secondly, the fact that many congressmen were confused about the nature of soft loans made it easier to convince them that soft lending was "sound" and "business-like."[13] (2) Between 1945 and 1960 the World Bank acquired respectability in the eyes of both Congress and the American business community. Eugene Black's endorsement of soft lending and the affiliation of the IDA with the Bank served to reduce some of the domestic opposition to soft loans. (3) The split in the business community meant that some business leaders held a more favorable view of public capital movements in the 1958–62 period than they had in the 1940's. The fact that more businessmen were participating in the making and administering of foreign policy in the 1950's than in the 1940's also mitigated the traditional business hostility to public capital movements as a technique of statecraft. (4) The change in the balance of payments situation of the United States reduced domestic objections to the IDA because the executive could argue that joining the IDA was a way of shifting some of the foreign aid "burden" to Europe and Japan. (5) The desire of American farmers and of Congress to get rid of surplus agricultural commodities meant that domestic opposition to PL 480 was virtually

[12] In 1965 there were signs of the executive's lingering preference for grants coupled with a realistic recognition of Congressional attitudes. The AID argued that "if the sole objective were to do the job as quickly as possible with the least expenditure of funds, all aid would be on a grant basis." "But this is not a practical alternative," it added and went on to a discussion of soft loans. Agency for International Development, *Summary Report of a Study on Loan Terms, Debt Burden and Development*, April, 1965, p. 7.

[13] No definition, of course, was assigned to these all-purpose terms. It rarely is.

nonexistent. (6) The growth of the GNP from $297 billion (1954 dollars) in 1943 to $475 billion in 1962 without a commensurate growth in population in the United States increased the capacity of the nation to provide economic instruments of statecraft. Had this not been so, the domestic feasibility of launching a soft loan program would have been less.

EFFECTIVENESS OF TECHNIQUES

The following factors affected the decision makers' estimates of the relative effectiveness of the various techniques of statecraft available to them: (1) The decrease in the debt-servicing capacity of the low-income nations curtailed the effectiveness of public lending on conventional terms and of stimulating private investment. The policy makers sought ways to transfer capital to developing nations in forms that would cause little strain on the recipient's balance of payments. Grants and soft loans were more effective in this respect than hard loans and private investment, which would require either repayment or repatriation of profits in foreign exchange. (2) The frequent contacts of American representatives with those of the less developed nations facilitated an increase in American understanding of the strength of nationalism in these nations. The policy makers' estimates of the degree of probability that governments in less developed nations would radically change their policies toward private investors were diminished. (3) The failure to establish the International Trade Organization and the subsequent American reluctance to lower trade barriers made it more difficult than it otherwise would have been for less developed nations to attract private capital and service loans from the IBRD and the Export-Import Bank. The executive branch realized this and pointed out many times between 1943 and 1962 that the effectiveness of stimulating private capital, of reliance on domestic efforts, and of public lending via the IBRD and Export-Import Bank depended to a large degree on lowering of American trade barriers.[14] (4) The growth of a body of academic literature on economic development which utilized

[14] The reluctance of Congress to lower trade barriers affected the policy makers' estimates of future debt-servicing capacities in low-income nations. This should be distinguished from their perceptions of actual debt-servicing capacity. Cf. points No. 1 and 3.

concepts such as "capacity to repay" and "absorptive capacity" also contributed to the policy makers' estimates of the relative effectiveness of grants and soft loans vis-à-vis other techniques. It does not matter here whether such arguments were valid or not; what matters is that a substantial body of academic literature on economic development recommended the use of public grants and soft loans as techniques for spurring growth. (5) The effectiveness of joining the IDA as a means of inducing other nations to make soft loans was increased by the economic recovery of Europe and Japan. Such a move would have been useless in 1948, for instance.

SOME HYPOTHESES CONSIDERED

The discussion of the evolution of American policy for promoting economic development presented above facilitates testing of numerous hypotheses about foreign aid and foreign policy. Six such hypotheses will be examined.

HYPOTHESIS NO. 1

Hypothesis: *The establishment of the IDA and the DLF provided examples of Congressional initiative in foreign policy making.*[15] Those who have put forth this hypothesis have used it to buttress their arguments to the effect that Congress can, under appropriate circumstances, exercise initiative in the realm of foreign policy. Thus, rejection of the hypothesis would have broad implications for recommendations regarding the "proper" role of Congress in policy making. Robert Dahl has argued that: "Perhaps the single most important fact about Congress and its role in foreign policy . . . is that it rarely provides the initiative."[16] Dahl's statement sufficiently establishes the importance of any hypothesis purporting to have discovered exceptions to the rule.

It was noted in discussion of the DLF and the IDA that proponents of the hypothesis do not define "initiative," but we may

[15] The hypothesis receives its fullest statement in James A. Robinson, *Congress and Foreign Policy-Making* (Homewood, Ill.: Dorsey Press, 1962), pp. 61, 62, 68, 192, *et passim.* See also Montgomery, pp. 219–21. For a more detailed examination of this hypothesis, see David A. Baldwin, "Congressional Initiative in Foreign Policy," *Journal of Politics,* XXVIII (November, 1966).

[16] Dahl, p. 58. Roger Hilsman follows a similar line of argument in "Congressional-Executive Relations and the Foreign Policy Consensus," *American Political Science Review,* LII (September, 1958), 729–30, 740.

infer from the contexts that they were thinking in terms of the "influence" of Congress in the foreign policy making process. Dahl has defined influence in terms of the extent to which A gets B to do something that B would not otherwise do.[17] If we use this definition of influence, and if we accept the evidence presented in the preceding chapters, we must conclude that the creation of the DLF and the IDA came about as a result of Congressional influence—but not in the sense which Robinson and Montgomery believe. The executive, were it not for Congress, would probably have preferred to rely on trade liberalization and grants. Over a period of years Congress, in effect, vetoed the use of these techniques. The executive branch move toward soft loans can thus be accurately described as B doing something he would not otherwise have done. But Robinson and Montgomery are not taking such a long-range view; they argue that Congressional initiative "occurred" in 1957 (the DLF) and 1958 (the IDA). As of 1957 and 1958 there was good reason to believe that the executive branch had already realized that Congress was likely to veto grants and trade liberalization and had resigned itself to soft loans. For reasons enumerated in the discussion of these institutions, it is probable that the executive branch would have proposed the DLF and the IDA—or reasonable facsimiles—within a year or two even in the absence of Congressional "initiative."

Let us assume, for the moment, that the DLF and the IDA *were* in some sense "initiated" by Congress. If we were to summarize the progress in the study of public administration since World War II in one sentence, it would probably read thus: It consisted of the discovery that policy making and administration are inseparable and that policy making is about 90 per cent administration. The implication of this for foreign aid policy is that it is almost impossible for Congress to influence policy except through the appropriation process. Given the appropriation, the executive branch can usually interpret the legislative authority in such a way as to do whatever it wants to do. For example, Congress has been credited with furnishing the initiative in the shift from "balance-of-payments loans" to "project loans";[18] yet this is a perfect illus-

[17] Robert A. Dahl, *Modern Political Analysis* (Englewood Cliffs, N.J.: Prentice-Hall, Inc., 1963), p. 40.

[18] Montgomery, pp. 220–21.

tration of the futility of Congressional attempts to control the use of aid. The executive branch could easily tie a loan to a specific project in an administrative sense while knowing all along that the real reason for, and net impact of, the loan would be to relieve a balance of payments problem. The implication of all this is that one question is paramount in the eyes of the executive branch: How much money is Congress giving us? If we treat this as the single most important consideration in executive branch planning, then we will be even more skeptical about the degree to which A (Congress) got B (executive) to do something (the DLF and the IDA) which he would not otherwise have done. Both the DLF and the IDA were proposals for increasing the amount of dollar appropriations available to the executive; there was evidence that the executive wanted more money for foreign aid; thus, Congress was helping the executive to do something it wanted to do anyway—get more money from Congress. Since the primary obstacle to the appropriation of more foreign aid funds was Congress itself, it would be misleading to describe the expansion of appropriations as a case of Congressional initiative. If B is beating on a door, and A is holding the door shut, we probably would hesitate to attribute initiative to A if he stopped holding the door shut and B opened it and came in.

HYPOTHESIS NO. 2

Hypothesis: *Foreign aid as an issue is peculiarly serviceable to the President.* This hypothesis has been advanced by Professor Edward C. Banfield.[19] He argues that because the issue of foreign aid concerns "principles much more than interests,"[20] it is useful to the President in gathering "enough informal influence to mitigate the extreme decentralization of formal authority inherited from the Founding Fathers."[21] It is difficult to say much about this hypothesis since Banfield presents little evidence to support it. Suffice it to say that the above survey of the development of American economic aid policy gives no confirmation to the Banfield position. There is little evidence that Presidents have thought of foreign aid as anything but a "headache" insofar as domestic politics are concerned. President Eisenhower, for example, used to get quite upset at being accused of endorsing a "giveaway." In

[19] *Public Policy, 1961,* p. 89.   [20] *Ibid.*   [21] *Ibid.*

December, 1962, President Kennedy summarized the Presidential view of foreign aid: "I would like to cut out foreign aid. It is very unpopular. It is a hard fight every year. President Eisenhower had the same struggle, and so did President Truman."[22] And in 1964 when President Johnson presented the smallest foreign aid request in fifteen years, it was widely rumored that the reason was his belief that the repeated rebuffs given the President on foreign aid were seriously eroding the prestige of the Presidency. In short, the preceding discussion casts considerable doubt on the validity of Banfield's hypothesis.

HYPOTHESIS NO. 3

Hypothesis: *Inefficient administration of the foreign aid program is responsible for Congressional hostility to foreign aid.* This hypothesis is put forth by a number of public commentators and by legislators themselves, especially those who vote against foreign aid. A typical statement of the position is contained in *Where Did Your Money Go?*, a journalistic exposé of supposed malpractice in the administration of foreign aid.[23] The above survey of American policy making provides a fairly good test of this hypothesis. Assuming that the many agencies devoted to moving public capital abroad—the IBRD, the FOA, the ECA, the ICA, the DLF, the IDA, and so on—have operated with varying degrees of efficiency, the hypothesis would indicate that Congressional hostility should have varied accordingly. Yet Congressional hostility to foreign aid was made manifest in each of the four time periods examined, and no substantial degree of variation in the intensity of such hostility was noticable. Few people today remember the hostility expressed by many legislators to such programs as the Marshall Plan, the IBRD, and Point Four.

If the hypothesis were correct, we would have expected that the recommendations of the Clay Committee in 1963,[24] which pur-

[22] Speech before Economic Club in New York in December 1962, quoted in Andrew Tully and Milton Britten, *Where Did Your Money Go? The Foreign Aid Story* (New York: Simon and Schuster, Inc., 1964), p. 28. For a description of President Eisenhower's foreign aid frustrations, see Sherman Adams, *Firsthand Report* (New York: Harper & Bros., 1961), pp. 374–80.

[23] *Ibid.*, pp. 196–97.

[24] Report to the President from the Committee to Strengthen the Security of the Free World, *The Scope and Distribution of United States Military and Economic Assistance Programs*, March 20, 1963.

ported to increase the efficiency of the aid program, would have been met with a decrease in legislative hostility. Instead, Congress reacted by slashing the aid request more vigorously than it ever had before—despite the executive's endorsement of the Clay report.

The hypothesis would also have made it difficult to predict the attitude of the House of Representatives toward a proposal for expanding the IDA put forth in early 1964. Not even the sternest foe of foreign aid has ever accused Eugene Black or his successor of inefficient administration in the IBRD or the IDA. When the matter was debated in the House in February 1964, no reference was made by anyone to inefficient administration of the IDA, but the proposal to expand the resources of the IDA was nevertheless voted down.[25] Regarding this vote on the IDA, the proponents of the hypothesis could say that it is past inefficiency in other programs that is responsible for present hostility to all foreign aid. If the hypothesis is thus qualified, it is not very useful for prediction because future reactions of Congress are indeterminate.

The examination of American foreign aid policy as it unfolded between 1943 and 1962 suggests an alternative hypothesis: Any proposal by the executive branch calling for increased dollar appropriations from Congress for the purpose of giving those dollars to foreigners will be met with strong Congressional opposition compared to the opposition encountered on appropriations for military expenses and domestic expenditures.

HYPOTHESIS NO. 4

Hypothesis: *Congressional support for foreign aid has gradually stabilized.*[26] Professor Montgomery, in his widely read book, *The Politics of Foreign Aid*, contends that Congressional support for foreign aid has been "stabilized at an adequate level."[27] Montgomery fails to answer the question, Adequate for what? He also ignores the fact that although votes on authorizing legislation may

[25] U.S., *Congressional Record*, 88th Cong., 2d sess., 1964, 110, 3421–22, 3458–70, 3499–3517. The request was subsequently approved.

[26] The fullest statement of this hypothesis is in Montgomery, pp. 199–202. Such a hypothesis is also implicit in the Banfield argument, *Public Policy, 1961*, pp. 45–92. Cf. also Harlan Cleveland, "The Fits and Starts of Foreign Aid," *The Reporter*, April 16, 1959, p. 25.

[27] P. 200.

have leveled off at an average of some 70 per cent in favor of passage, these votes have been in favor of a steadily declining amount of foreign aid measured as a percentage of the GNP. (See Table 2.) Montgomery adds that "if foreign aid has had no consistent body of supporters in Congress, it has also had few self-acknowledged enemies. It has not been 'foreign aid' that has lacked support, but rather its specific programs."[28] Likewise, we could say that it is not world federalism that lacks support but

TABLE 2

TOTAL U.S. AID AS A PERCENTAGE OF GNP: 1946–64*

Fiscal Year	GNP†	Aid‡	Aid as Per Cent of GNP
1946–48.........	704	15.1	2.1
1949–52.........	1,219	22.4	1.8
1953–57.........	1,988	29.2	1.5
1958...........	445	5.4	1.2
1959...........	483	5.7	1.2
1960...........	503	5.2	1.0
1961...........	518	5.8	1.1
1962...........	556	6.6	1.2
1963...........	584	6.9	1.2
1964...........	623	6.2	1.0

* Calculated from Agency for International Development, Statistics and Reports Division, *U.S. Overseas Loans and Grants and Assistance from International Organizations*, Special report prepared for the House Foreign Affairs Committee, March 3, 1965.

† Billions of current dollars.

‡ Billions of current dollars. Includes military assistance, Export-Import Bank long-term loans, capital subscriptions to international organizations, and other forms of aid. See Table 3.

specific programs; it is not civil rights that lacks support—even in the deep South—but those specific programs; it is not free speech that lacks support but specific attempts to exercise it. This lip service "support" for something vaguely identified as the "principle of mutual security (or foreign aid)" is typical of statements by the American Farm Bureau or United States Chamber of Commerce on behalf of the aid program. Such statements usually include a recommendation that the specific administration request —which has already been cut by the executive branch to a "bare minimum"—be cut by a substantial amount, by about one-third or so. This tendency to treat support for principle and support for appropriations requests as separate questions can be highly mis-

[28] *Ibid.*, p. 199.

TABLE 3

SUMMARY BY FISCAL YEAR AND PROGRAM
(U.S. Fiscal Years—Millions of Dollars)

U.S. OVERSEAS LOANS AND GRANTS—NET OBLIGATIONS AND LOAN AUTHORIZATIONS

PROGRAM	Post-War Relief Period	Marshall Plan Period		Mutual Security Act Period				Foreign Assistance Act Period			Total	REPAYMENTS AND INTEREST	TOTAL LESS REPAYMENTS AND INTEREST
	1946–48	1949–52	1953–57	1958	1959	1960	1961	1962	1963	1964	1946–64	1946–64	1946–64
A.I.D. and predecessor agencies—total	....	*14,505*	*9,140*	*1,620*	*1,916*	*1,866*	*2,012*	*2,508*	*2,297*	*2,136*	*38,004*	*1,490*	*36,514*
Loans	(—)	1,577	868	417	626	564	707	1,331	1,343	1,328	8,761	1,490	7,271
Grants	(—)	12,928	8,272	1,203	1,291	1,302	1,305	1,178	954	808	29,243	.....	29,243
Social Progress Trust Fund	....	....	....	....	....	....	....	226	127	42	396	5	390
Food for Peace—Total	(—)	*83*	*2,672*	*794*	*889*	*1,106*	*1,251*	*1,575*	*1,717*	*1,762*	*11,849*	*330*	*11,519*
Title I—(Total Sales Agreements)	(—)	(—)	(2,036)	(720)	(817)	(1,109)	(1,061)	(1,308)	(1,202)	(1,248)	(9,501)	(—)	(9,501)
Less: (Planned for U.S. Uses)	(—)	(—)	(569)	(312)	(216)	(237)	(289)	(239)	(188)	(231)	(2,280)	(—)	(2,280)
Title I—Planned for Loans and Grants	....	....	*1,467*	*408*	*601*	*872*	*772*	*1,069*	*1,014*	*1,017*	*7,220*	*324*	*6,896*
104c—Grants for Common Defense	....	....	240	71	34	20	66	136	113	138	818	.....	818
104e—Grants for Economic Development	....	....	210	25	100	317	226	282	254	252	1,666	.....	1,666
104e—Loans to Private Industry	....	....	2	73	116	88	62	88	62	60	552	43	509
104g—Loans to Government	....	....	1,016	239	350	447	418	563	585	566	4,185	280	3,905
Title I—Ass't from other country sales agreements	....	....	37	5	....	....	....	....	15	....	57	1	56
Title II—Emergency relief and economic development	....	....	317	87	48	63	239	183	287	236	1,460	.....	1,460
Title III—Voluntary relief agencies	....	83	850	295	240	172	240	271	325	391	2,866	.....	2,866
Title IV—Dollar credit sales	....	....	....	....	....	....	....	52	76	118	246	5	241
Export-Import Bank Long-Term Loans	2,096	904	1,510	516	710	294	943	503	502	568	8,545	5,316	3,229
Other U.S. Economic Programs	12,553	4,049	526	23	19	97	88	234	363	254	18,205	4,013	14,192
Total Economic	*14,649*	*19,541*	*13,847*	*2,953*	*3,534*	*3,363*	*4,294*	*5,046*	*5,008*	*4,762*	*76,999*	*11,154*	*65,845*
Loans	8,063	3,458	3,455	1,247	1,802	1,396	2,130	2,779	2,775	2,707	29,814	11,154	18,660
Grants	6,586	16,082	10,392	1,706	1,732	1,967	2,164	2,268	2,232	2,055	47,186	.....	47,186

SOURCE: Agency for International Development, Statistics and Reports Division, *U.S. Overseas Loans and Grants and Assistance from International Organizations*, Special report prepared for the House Foreign Affairs Committee, March 3, 1965.

NOTES FOR TABLE 3

AGENCY FOR INTERNATIONAL DEVELOPMENT

The data cover commitments for economic and technical assistance made by A.I.D. and its predecessor agencies. Commitments may be defined as development loans authorized and obligations of other A.I.D. funds. All annual commitment data as well as the cumulative totals are on a "net" basis, that is, new obligations from funds appropriated for that fiscal year, plus or minus reobligations or deobligations of prior year funds. Data for FY 1949 cover 15 months, from the start of the Marshall Plan, April 3, 1948, to June 30, 1949.

Commitments made by A.I.D. and its predecessor agencies are shown separately for loans and grants. The loan total covers development loans, Alliance for Progress loans, supporting assistance loans, and any other loans from A.I.D. or predecessor agency funds. The loans made from the Social Progress Trust Fund by the Inter-American Development Bank are not included here, but are shown separately.

SOCIAL PROGRESS TRUST FUND

The data represent loans authorized by the Inter-American Development Bank from the $525 million Social Progress Trust Fund which the Bank administers; they also include minor amounts of technical assistance grants from the Trust Fund. This fund was established in FY 1961 as part of the Alliance for Progress program and is available for Latin American countries only.

OTHER ECONOMIC ASSISTANCE

Food for Peace: PL 480—Agricultural Trade Development and Assistance Act of 1954 and Amendments thereto.

TITLE I—SALES FOR FOREIGN CURRENCY

Title I of the Act provides for the sale of surplus agricultural commodities for foreign currency, and in Section 104, specifies the ways in which these currencies may be used.

The figures for sales agreements shown as a parenthetical item, not added into total assistance, represent the export market value of sales agreements signed during each year with minor adjustments for subsequent shortfalls in deliveries. An additional parenthetical item, "Planned for U.S. Uses," is also shown. These figures represent the portion of the sales proceeds planned for U.S. uses such as payment of U.S. obligations or for special foreign currency programs to develop agricultural markets, provide military family housing, promote trade fairs, and the like. They include any amounts used under Section 104(d) to purchase aid goods for other countries. (See below.) The "Total Sales Agreements" amount less the "Planned for U.S. Uses" represents the country aid portion of the sales agreements and is equal to the entries shown on the line "Title I—Planned for Loans and Grants."

The figures for "Planned for Loans and Grants" represent those portions of the foreign currency proceeds of the sales which are planned as loans or grants to the recipient country under Sections 104(c), (e), and (g), or as "Cooley Amendment" loans to private industry in the foreign country under Section 104(e). The portion of each sales agreement which is "Planned for Loans and Grants" is included in the assistance totals in the year the sales agreement was signed. A few agreements are more than a year's requirement. These have been prorated. In addition, adjustments have been made for actual shortfall of deliveries from annual agreements.

Under "Title I—Assistance from Other Country Sales Agreements" are shown the Section 104(d) Triangular Trade transactions whereby a third country receives, on a loan or grant basis, foreign currency generated by a surplus commodity sales agreement between the United States and another foreign country.

TITLE II—FAMINE RELIEF AND OTHER EMERGENCY ASSISTANCE

Title II authorizes funds for the transfer of commodities held in stock by the Commodity Credit Corporation to help friendly foreign people to meet famine or other urgent

NOTES FOR TABLE 3—*Continued*

or extraordinary relief requirements or to promote economic development. The data represent commodities authorized at CCC cost, plus ocean freight distributed by country.

TITLE III—DONATIONS FOR VOLUNTARY RELIEF AGENCIES

The data included under Title III cover only the donations of surplus commodities to Voluntary Relief Agencies such as CARE, National Catholic Welfare Conference, Lutheran World Relief, etc., for distribution to needy people abroad. Barter transactions are not included. The figures represent authorizations for voluntary relief agency donations, valued at CCC cost. For years prior to Fiscal Year 1955, the data represent transfers authorized under Section 416 of the Agricultural Act of 1949 (Public Law 81-439). The data for Fiscal Year 1952 represent transfers during fiscal years 1950–52. Ocean freight is not distributed by country but is included in the Non-Regional table.

TITLE IV—DOLLAR CREDIT SALES

Title IV, added to the Act in September 1959, provides for dollar credit sales of surplus agricultural commodities, repayable within twenty years. The data shown represent the export market value of the credit sales agreements signed. Some agreements have covered more than one year's program and these have been prorated.

EXPORT-IMPORT BANK LONG-TERM LOANS

These data were compiled from the semiannual reports of the Export-Import Bank. They represent authorizations for loans of five years or more maturity, by the Export-Import Bank or by private financial institutions if the loan is guaranteed by the Export-Import Bank. They exclude short-term exporter credits and those loans or parts of loans bought by private banks and other institutions at their own risk. Cancellations and terminations are deducted from loans authorized. Repayments have not been taken into account. The fiscal year data have been constructed so that if a loan made in one year is increased in a later year, the increase is included at the time it occurred; but if the loan is decreased or cancelled in a later year, the loan has been decreased in the year originally authorized.

OTHER NON-A.I.D. ECONOMIC PROGRAMS

In general, the programs included here predated the Mutual Security Program. The major programs included are "UNRRA," "Civilian Supplies (including Government and Relief in Occupied Areas)," "Surplus Property Credits," "Civilian Relief in Korea," "Greek-Turkish Aid," and "Philippines Rehabilitation." A few programs are also included which ran concurrently with MSP, such as "Inter-American and Related Highways" and "Elimination of Foot and Mouth Disease in Mexico." "Occupied Areas Commodity Credits" are not included since these were short-term credits generally not over 15 months.

To the extent possible, these early programs have been presented on an obligations basis. Programs obligated prior to June 30, 1945, such as Lend Lease, have been excluded even though expenditures continued in 1946 and later. For UNRRA, Civilian Supplies and certain minor programs, obligations by fiscal year were not available. For these programs, therefore, it was necessary to present data on an expenditures basis, and to include an unknown portion obligated prior to July 1, 1945, but delivered in fiscal years 1946 and subsequently.

In recent years, the principal programs in this category have been capital subscriptions to the Inter-American Development Bank and the International Development Association; the Peace Corps; Philippine War Damage Claims; and the United Nations bond issue.

TIME PERIODS

The commitment data for all programs are shown by U.S. fiscal years arranged in four broad groupings: Post-War Relief Period (1946–48); Marshall Plan Period (1949–52); Mutual Security Act Period (1953–61); and Foreign Assistance Act Period (1962–64).

NOTES FOR TABLE 3—*Continued*

The Agency for International Development has been in existence only during the latter period.

REPAYMENTS AND INTEREST

The "Repayments and Interest" column shows the cumulative principal repaid and interest collected for the period 1946–64 against loans made during that period. It excludes any repayments or interest collections against loans made prior to July 1, 1945.

These data include repayments and interest collections in dollars and in foreign currencies; the latter are expressed in dollar equivalents.

For loans fully or largely repaid on which interest has been collected for a number of years, the total repayment and interest figure will frequently be in excess of the original loan.

NOTE: Details may not add to totals due to rounding.

leading. In the 1958 Mutual Security hearings even that arch enemy of foreign aid, Eugene W. Castle, author of such studies as *Billions, Blunders, and Baloney*[29] and *The Great Giveaway*,[30] supported the "principle" of foreign aid. All he wanted was to cut about $2 billion from the appropriation.[31]

Attempts to identify the nature and magnitude of opposition to foreign aid have been generally unsatisfactory. In the first place, although Montgomery is correct in noting that the avowed enemies of foreign aid have been few, he fails to point out that these few have often held strategic positions in Congress (e.g., Otto Passman). He also overlooks the fact that these "few" are highly energetic in their efforts against aid. Roger Hilsman observes that "it takes only a short political experience to learn that a minority who hold a view with great intensity will have more political effect than a diffuse majority who believe the opposite, but not very forcefully."[32] Where is that foreign aid supporter who can match the enthusiasm of Otto Passman? We should modify the Hilsman thesis to account for the fact that the American legislative process is such that it is much easier to hinder than promote action on a bill.

A second aspect of foreign aid opposition which has been often overlooked is that relating to the lack of interest-group support.

[29] New York: Devin, 1955.

[30] Chicago: Regnery, 1957.

[31] U.S., Congress, House, Committee on Foreign Affairs, *Hearings, Mutual Security Act of 1958*, 85th Cong., 2d sess., 1958, pp. 1394–95.

[32] *American Political Science Review*, LII, 727.

To be sure, the League of Women Voters and various church groups are ardent defenders of foreign aid, but no one has ever seriously contended that such groups wield much power on issues involving large appropriations. There is, in fact, "widespread agreement that the most influential interest groups in the foreign policy field, as in the domestic arena, are economic interest groups."[33] And no economic interest group is very enthusiastic in its support for foreign aid. The AFL-CIO is probably the most enthusiastic, but congressmen can easily perceive that the issue is not a vital one for labor. The National Association of Manufacturers rarely bothers to show up for foreign aid hearings; neither did the United States Chamber of Commerce in 1960. The latter group, however, usually does appear and gives a half-hearted, highly qualified statement supporting a cut-down version of the foreign aid request.

A third respect in which discussion of the nature and magnitude of opposition to foreign aid has been unsatisfactory is in considering, or rather failing to consider, seemingly unrelated issues such as taxation. It is quite possible for groups to oppose foreign aid effectively without actually desiring to do so or even perceiving that they are doing so. Because of the nature of the federal budgetary process, the net result of advocacy of cuts in government spending, lower taxes, and a balanced budget may well be a reduction in the foreign aid appropriation.[34] Yet we are continually encountering the proposition that American "public opinion" favors foreign aid, as measured by a series of questions relating directly to foreign aid.[35] It may well be, however, that we could better understand the nature of the opposition to aid if we were to ask, "Would you like to pay higher taxes?"

Roger Hilsman notes that there are many publics (the Almond thesis), including one for fiscal policy and one for foreign policy.[36] He also notes that they may overlap, but he fails to account

[33] Bernard C. Cohen, *The Influence of Non-governmental Groups on Foreign Policy-Making* (Boston: World Peace Foundation, 1959), p. 6.

[34] See Arthur Smithies, *The Budgetary Process in the United States* (New York: McGraw-Hill, 1955), pp. 10–11.

[35] See for example, Barbara Ward, "Foreign Aid *Has* Succeeded," *New York Times Magazine,* July 12, 1964, p. 9.

[36] *American Political Science Review,* LII, 730–32.

for interrelated issues. In other words, he cannot account for a situation in which the fiscal policy public and foreign policy public are completely separate but in which the views of the fiscal policy public govern Congressional behavior on foreign policy. Because money is the common denominator of both foreign aid and fiscal policy, any scheme for analyzing opposition to foreign aid must consider opinions on fiscal policy also. In short, many of those studying the nature and magnitude of opposition to foreign aid have been looking in the wrong places; or, more accurately, they have failed to look in enough of the right places.

The examination of the development of American policies for promoting economic growth presented in preceding chapters provides scant evidence of stable support for foreign aid. If anything, it provides support for veteran diplomat George F. Kennan's hypothesis that the American governmental system is unsuitable "for the promulgation of any sustained administrative program (particularly one calling for the annual appropriation of sizeable sums of money) that . . . [is] not supported at all times by the enthusiasm of some interested domestic pressure group."[37]

A variation of Hypothesis No. 4 has a deterministic tinge. This variation describes foreign aid as "necessary,"[38] "inevitable,"[39] or as "impelled"[40] by external events. Paradoxically, advocates of this position often find themselves arguing, as Montgomery has, that although, on the one hand, "foreign aid as a political instrument of U.S. policy is here to stay because of its usefulness and flexibility," on the other hand we must increase the understanding of, and support for, the program in order that its permanence may be "more solidly based."[41] The problem, of course, is that faced by every determinist; that is, why is further effort necessary if the outcome is inevitable?

HYPOTHESIS NO. 5

Hypothesis: *Building a consensus in favor of foreign aid is basically a matter of "educating" Congress and the public with re-*

[37] "The Future of Our Professional Diplomacy," *Foreign Affairs*, XXXIII (July, 1955), 566.

[38] Charles Wolf, Jr., *Foreign Aid: Theory and Practice in Southern Asia* (Princeton, N.J.: Princeton University Press, 1960), p. 412.

[39] Montgomery, p. 19.   [40] *Ibid.*, p. 254.   [41] *Ibid.*, p. 9.

spect to the nature and purpose of foreign aid. Probably no hypothesis about foreign aid is more generally accepted than this one. Although the form varies, the point is always that if only we could "clarify" the issues and clear up some of the confusion in the minds of congressmen and the public, the effectiveness of foreign aid as a technique of statecraft would be improved.[42] Regarding soft loans, Peter Kenen rhetorically asks, "Why not be frank? Let us return to grants instead of obscuring the distinction between bankable loans and development assistance."[43] The prevalence of this view is probably largely explained by the emphasis in democratic theory on the desirability of rational discussion of issues. Unfortunately, what is "desirable" and what is "effective" do not always coincide. On the basis of the survey of American policies for promoting economic growth from 1943–62, this writer suggests an alternative hypothesis, which is that a certain amount of vagueness with respect to the nature and purpose of a foreign aid proposal may actually facilitate the building of a consensus in support of that proposal.[44] For example, Congress would, we suspect, have dealt more harshly with soft loan proposals in the 1950's if they had understood more clearly the extent to which such loans resembled grants. The question "Why not be frank?" is a relevant one, but it should not be asked rhetorically. There may be valid political reasons for not being frank.

The hypothesis that a little confusion may grease the cogs in the policy making machinery accords well with long-standing American practice of concealing subsidies to domestic groups from the public eye. Although people do not commonly think of them as such, tariffs are subsidies to domestic producers; price supports are subsidies to farmers; requirements that foreign aid

---

[42] Various statements of this hypothesis can be found in the following works: William Adams Brown, Jr., and Redvers Opie, *American Foreign Assistance* (Washington: Brookings Institution, 1953), p. 394; Stanley D. Metzger, "The New International Development Association," *Georgetown Law Journal*, XLIX (Fall, 1960), 41; Raymond F. Mikesell (ed.), *U.S. Private and Government Investment Abroad* (Eugene: University of Oregon Press, 1962), pp. 345–46; Wolf, pp. 256–57, 412–13; and Montgomery, pp. 212–13, 236, 241, 267, 270–71.

[43] *Giant Among Nations* (Chicago: Rand McNally, 1963), p. 192.

[44] For a discussion of the strategies developed by the executive branch to win Congressional approval for foreign aid, see David A. Baldwin, "The Congressional Politics of Foreign Aid," *Challenge*, September–October, 1965, pp. 22–25.

be shipped in American bottoms are subsidies to the American shipping industry; and various forms of special treatment in taxation constitute a subsidy to other groups. We might even say that clear and open acknowledgment of the existence of subsidies is the exception rather than the rule in American politics.

Hypothesis No. 5 implies a view of Congressional behavior as the outcome of intellectual analysis, but there are good reasons to be wary of such a view. Are we to believe, for example, that the reason congressmen are relatively enthusiastic about defense spending is because they "understand" the program better than they do foreign aid? We suspect that the fact that defense employment constitutes 10 per cent or more of the manufacturing employment of fifteen states might have something to do with Congressional behavior on defense appropriations.[45] Likewise, we suspect that the vote of a senator from Oklahoma in favor of an oil depletion allowance is not primarily a result of his superior "knowledge" about the oil industry. The point, of course, is that although political scientists may regard the observation that foreign aid lacks a domestic constituency as a cliché, it contains an element of truth which the student of foreign aid ignores at his peril. If we had to choose between two extreme positions, one which explained Congressional behavior in terms of intellectual processes and the other which explained it in terms described by Henry Adams, we would do well to stick with Adams: "You can't use tact with a Congressman! A Congressman is a hog! You must take a stick and hit him on the snout!"[46]

We need not, however, adopt an extreme position. The hypothesis to the effect that vagueness may be helpful in forming a consensus accords well with the view of foreign policy making put forth by Hilsman. He points out that building a consensus requires persuading and bargaining in addition to education and that "sales gimmicks are no final solution."[47] He further notes that deciding as little as possible with respect to a given issue often facilitates building a consensus on that issue.[48] Thus, soft

[45] Cf. New York Times, April 13, 1964, p. 18.

[46] The Education of Henry Adams (New York: Modern Library, 1931), p. 261.

[47] American Political Science Review, LII, 738–39 et passim. See also Roger Hilsman, "The Foreign Policy Consensus: An Interim Research Report," Journal of Conflict Resolution, III (December, 1959), 361–82.

[48] American Political Science Review, LII, 738–39.

loans could be considered as useful in achieving a consensus in favor of foreign aid, since there was general confusion as to what had been decided when a soft loan proposal had been approved. Given the continuing hostility of Congress toward foreign aid proposals between 1943 and 1962, the advocate of Hypothesis No. 5 would do well to heed the following parable: A nearsighted duck hunter is dangerous from the duck's point of view since he might hit a duck with one of his wild shots. It does not necessarily follow, however, that it is in the duck's best interest to "clarify" the situation for the hunter by furnishing him with eyeglasses.

Montgomery has argued that none of the suggestions for long-term financing of foreign aid could be adopted as law "without reaching a degree of congressional consensus about foreign aid that has not yet been achieved for far more modest proposals."[49] This is a good example of a conception of consensus building as an intellectual rather than a political problem. If President Johnson, for example, had been willing to abandon the Civil Rights Bill in 1964, he probably could have mustered enough support from Southern Democrats to get a long-term financing proposal approved. We can better understand the consensus-building process if we think in terms of the political costs of bargaining than if we think in terms of educational processes.[50]

HYPOTHESIS NO. 6

Hypothesis: *Foreign aid can be fruitfully studied by treating allocation of a given amount of aid and determination of that amount as separate questions.*[51] Charles Wolf, Jr., has achieved a high degree of mathematical precision in his treatment of foreign aid, but he has done so only by addressing himself to the problem of allocating a given amount of aid.[52] It will be argued that the degree of precision attained by Wolf was purchased at the price

[49] P. 212.

[50] On the concept of political costs see Aaron Wildavsky, *The Politics of the Budgetary Process* (Boston: Little, Brown & Co., 1964), p. 158.

[51] This hypothesis, in the form of an assumption, underlies the influential RAND Corporation Study by Charles Wolf, Jr., *Foreign Aid: Theory and Practice in Southern Asia.* See especially pp. vii, 3, 412–16. In 1955 Thomas C. Schelling scolded his fellow economists for treating aid levels and allocation decisions independently, thus indicating the prevalence of the hypothesis at that time. "American Foreign Assistance," *World Politics,* VII (July, 1955), 612–13.

[52] Cf. Wolf, pp. 296–382.

of irrelevancy as far as improving the effectiveness of policy is concerned, and since Wolf was trying to improve policy, he must be judged to have failed. Separation of the questions of aid levels and allocation promotes a relatively mechanical view of the foreign policy process, and it hinders consideration of the bargaining aspects of executive-legislative relations and of the executive's relations with foreign governments. These bargaining aspects involved in the relationship between *how* aid is allocated and *how much* is allocated may well be the most important variables from the point of view of the government official responsible for developing foreign aid policy. Recommendations to government officials based on Wolf's analysis would be at best irrelevant and might even damage the aid program. No foreign aid administrator or policy planner can afford to forget for a moment that the way aid is allocated today may well affect the amount of next year's aid appropriation—few ever do. No foreign policy maker in the United States has ever faced the problem of how to allocate a given amount of aid because he has never been able to take future appropriations for granted. In fact, we suspect that the problem of how to maximize next year's appropriation is the single most important question from the viewpoint of the foreign aid official. If this is true, Wolf has assumed away the most important problem facing the foreign aid administrator.

Consider the following specific examples of interdependence between determination of aid levels and aid allocation. First, the decision to give aid in the form of surplus agricultural commodities and soft loans repayable in local currency is a decision on aid allocation; yet the history of foreign aid as discussed in previous chapters clearly indicates that the amount of dollar appropriations made available by Congress was affected by the form of allocation. Congress tended to be more generous in appropriating funds for the purchase of CCC commodities to be distributed as foreign aid. On the other hand, Congress tended to be more niggardly than it otherwise would have been when appropriating dollars for soft loans repayable in local currency, pointing out that fewer dollars were needed because the executive had all of that "good" local currency at its disposal. Thus, in 1958, 1959, and 1960 the amount of dollar appropriations was affected by Congressional perceptions of local currency stocks which had accumulated as a result of past decisions on how to allocate aid.

On several occasions in the 1950's Congress scolded the executive for having asked for more foreign aid funds than it needed and proceeded to cut the appropriation under consideration. Congress often cited the existence of uncommitted funds as evidence of past exaggeration of needs by the excutive branch. This in turn gave the foreign aid administrators an incentive to allocate aid funds more rapidly than they otherwise would have done. Foreign aid officials could easily perceive the effect of allocation of this year's funds on the size of next year's appropriations.[53]

Between 1957 and 1961 executive branch proposals often emphasized methods of allocating aid which would allow circumvention of the annual authorization-appropriation process, for example, the IDA, IBRD expansion, the IADB, the DLF, and expansion of the Export-Import Bank. Such decisions affected the channels through which, and the terms on which, public capital would move to less developed nations; yet we suspect that the executive would have put forth different proposals if the amount of funds available for such activities had been fixed. Robinson has pointed out that in discussion of proposals for long-term financing of aid "most of the argument in Congress revolves around whether one procedure means bigger or lesser foreign aid programs."[54]

Evidence was presented in foregoing chapters that the executive turned to the soft loan method of allocating aid partially from the belief that Congress would appropriate more money for allocation this way than for allocation in the form of grants. Wolf objects to the use of ambiguous concepts in foreign aid legislation on the grounds that it confuses the problem of aid allocation; but he fails to consider the possibility that ambiguous formal criteria for aid allocation, such as those relating to soft loans, may facilitate building a consensus for a larger total amount of foreign aid appropriations. It has been argued above that the

[53] This is a rather typical behavior pattern for any governmental agency dependent on year to year appropriations. See Robert A. Dahl and Charles E. Lindblom, *Politics, Economics, and Welfare* (New York: Harper & Bros., 1953), pp. 459–60. Mikesell notes that "the ICA administrators not only could not give foreign governments assurance of a continuous flow of assistance to carry out long-range development plans, but in addition, they have been unable to exert maximum influence on development programs because of the necessity of committing all of the funds appropriated before the close of the fiscal year." Mikesell, p. 565.

[54] Robinson, p. 210.

misunderstanding of soft loans by many legislators did in fact lead to an increase in the total amount relative to what that amount would have been in the absence of confusion.

Why should aid be allocated via many agencies, as is now the case, instead of through a unified aid administration? There are probably many reasons, including institutional jealousy; but the above discussion of American policy from 1943–62 would suggest that one reason might be in order to impede efforts by a hostile Congress to curtail total appropriations for public capital movements. Mikesell has noted that "a further multiplication of aid agencies may prove to be the most expeditious means of obtaining funds for economic development."[55] The point is that allocation and aid levels are so closely related that we often suspect that what appears superficially to be an allocation decision is primarily a decision on the total amount of aid.

The amount of time that foreign aid administrators can devote to studying allocation problems is diminished by the need to prepare arguments for next year's confrontation with Otto Passman. "It has been reliably estimated," according to Montgomery, "that one-third of the time of all ICA personnel, both in Washington and overseas, was spent preparing materials for presentation to Congress."[56] And when Representative Otto Passman "visited Viet-Nam for two days in September 1958, the aid mission devoted 328 man-days to preparing staff papers and making other arrangements."[57] Assuming that the way foreign aid administrators allocate aid when they have much time differs from the way they allocate it when they have little time, we must conclude that concern for next year's total amount affects this year's allocation procedure.

One of the essential elements in allocating economic aid is the estimation of aid "requirements" in terms of some over-all plan. Such "requirements," however, are not independent of estimates of the amount of aid likely to be available.[58] Soft lending programs, for example, usually relate allocation of soft loans to the balance of payments situation of the borrower. The concept of the balance of payments which underlies such planning is what Professor

[55] Mikesell, p. 576.   [56] Montgomery, p. 218.   [57] *Ibid.*, p. 219.

[58] Cf. Schelling, *World Politics*, VII, 612–13.

Machlup calls a "programme balance."[59] Although Machlup is addressing himself to the problem of the "dollar gap" in the early postwar period, we can easily see the applicability of his reasoning to the determination of "requirements" for soft loans:

... One should really not speak of policies of "dealing" with a deficit in a programme balance of payments. For this is not a deficit which first "exists," and then is "dealt with." Instead, it is a deficit which is programmed when there is a chance to finance it. There is no sense in drawing up a programme balance with a dollar deficit when there is no hope of finding the funds required to carry out the programme. The entire programme is built around the potentialities of finding the foreign finance for the deficit.[60]

Likewise, any development plan "requiring" a given amount of aid in the form of soft loans would quickly be changed if it became obvious that such aid would not be forthcoming.

In sum, although simplification is necessary for social analysis, some factors can be ignored only at the price of a high degree of irrelevancy. With regard to foreign aid, the interdependence between aid levels and aid allocation is one of those factors. Wolf goes even further, and argues that "the problem of increasing the effectiveness of the Mutual Security Program, is thus, synonymous with the problem of improving the allocation of aid funds."[61] We should be wary of this conclusion, however; it is quite possible to conceive of the problem of increasing the over-all effectiveness of foreign aid in the following ways: (*a*) more efficient allocation of a given amount of funds, (*b*) less efficient allocation of a greater amount of funds, (*c*) allocation of a greater amount of funds at a given level of efficiency, and (*d*) more efficient allocation of a smaller amount of funds. One of these alternatives—less efficient allocation of greater amounts—is rarely considered by foreign policy analysts. This writer suspects that this alternative is the most feasible way to increase the total effectiveness of the economic aid program. This is especially true since, as was pointed out above, too much efficiency in allocation may encourage a cut in appropriations.[62] Furthermore, there is no reason to assume,

[59] F. Machlup, "Three Concepts of the Balance of Payments and the So-Called Dollar Shortage," *Economic Journal*, LX (March, 1950), 46.

[60] *Ibid.*, p. 58.

[61] Wolf, p. 412.   [62] Cf. Dahl and Lindblom, p. 459.

a priori, that total effectiveness would vary in direct proportion to effectiveness per foreign aid dollar.

IMPLICATIONS FOR FURTHER RESEARCH

The preceding analysis of the evolution of American soft loan policy is part of a long-term project which will include a comprehensive critique of the academic literature on foreign aid. The goal is to clarify what the author believes to be the confused state of public debate on the issue of foreign aid in the United States.

This study can be considered as a case study or as four case studies involving the comparative method. By comparing the four time periods we can get a better idea as to which factors tend to be fixed and which tend to vary. We can, for example, detect such elements of continuity as (a) substantial Congressional hostility, (b) lack of enthusiasm for foreign aid by American businessmen, (c) a tendency to treat aid and trade as separate problems, (d) substantial dissatisfaction by recipients and a desire for more aid, and (e) a lack of long-range planning and financing. Thus, considered as a single case study, the above analysis can serve to generate hypotheses; or, considered as four case studies, it can facilitate the testing of hypotheses about the development of American policies for promoting economic growth.

It is anticipated that the foregoing chapters will be useful to students of foreign policy investigating the way nations go about selecting techniques of statecraft, the role of the United Nations and the International Bank in affecting the selection of techniques of statecraft by various nations, the role of Congress in the formulation of American foreign policy, the role of blackmail in international politics, the general topic of political aspects of financial activities by governments, the problem of making foreign policy under a system of separation of powers, the extent to which nations pursue contradictory policies and thus fail to make use of their potential power, the role of political culture (e.g., beliefs about the role of government in the economy) in the formulation of foreign policy, and the degree to which various techniques of statecraft are likely to be effective in promoting economic development under various conditions.

Selected Bibliography

Systematic studies of foreign policy techniques for promoting economic development are rare. A useful framework for conducting such studies is presented by Harold and Margaret Sprout, *Foundations of International Politics* (Princeton, N.J.: Van Nostrand, 1962). More specific problems of analyzing foreign aid strategies are discussed perceptively in Thomas C. Schelling, *International Economics* (Boston: Allyn & Bacon, 1958). Stimulating insights regarding how the subject should be approached are provided by Jacob Viner, *International Trade and Economic Development* (Glencoe, Ill.: Free Press, 1952).

Although there are many books on foreign aid, few approach the subject in a systematic and rigorous way. Among the more serious scholarly works on foreign aid and foreign policy, the following are especially valuable: Robert E. Asher, *Grants, Loans, and Local Currencies: Their Role in Foreign Aid* (Washington: Brookings Institution, 1961) is a good introduction to terminology and basic policy problems. The definitive early history of American foreign aid policies is William Adams Brown, Jr., and Redvers Opie, *American Foreign Assistance* (Washington: Brookings Institution, 1953). Especially strong on the economic aspects of foreign aid, but rather weak on political aspects, are two RAND Corporation studies, Charles Wolf, Jr., *Foreign Aid: Theory and Practice in Southern Asia* (Princeton, N.J.: Princeton University Press, 1960) and John A. Pincus, *Economic Aid and International Cost Sharing* (Baltimore: Johns Hopkins Press, 1965). An interesting discussion of political aspects of foreign aid is contained in John D. Montgomery, *The Politics of Foreign Aid* (New York: Praeger, 1962). The best study of foreign aid and American domestic politics is Michael K. O'Leary, tentatively entitled *Ameri-*

can Politics and Foreign Aid (New York: Atherton, forthcoming).

The most useful primary sources for the study of evolving American strategies for stimulating economic growth are as follows: The *New York Times* is indispensable, not only because of its factual reliability but also because it provides the vast majority of foreign policy makers with an image of reality. Likewise, the weekly *Department of State Bulletin* is useful because it is both authoritative and believed to be authoritative by foreign policy makers in various parts of the government.

The legislative-executive debate can be observed in hearings on foreign aid and trade. The committees on foreign relations, banking and currency, agriculture, appropriations, and ways and means frequently publish relevant hearings. In addition, Congress often publishes studies that have been prepared at the request of various committees. Such studies can provide both sophisticated analysis and an indication of the kinds of information being fed into the policy making process. Especially useful are U.S. Congress, House, Committee on Foreign Affairs, *Staff Memorandum on International Lending and Guaranty Programs,* 88th Cong., 2d sess., Committee Print, 1964; U.S., Congress, Senate, *Foreign Aid Program: Compilation of Studies and Surveys,* prepared under the direction of the Special Committee to Study the Foreign Aid Program, 85th Cong., 1st sess., 1957, Senate Doc. 52; and U.S., Congress, Senate, *United States Foreign Policy: Compilation of Studies,* prepared under the direction of the Committee on Foreign Relations, 87th Cong., 1st sess., 1961, Senate Doc. 24.

The executive branch has also commissioned a number of studies on foreign policy and economic growth. The most noteworthy of these are Advisory Committee on Underdeveloped Areas, *Economic Strength for the Free World,* a Report to the Director for Mutual Security by the Advisory Committee on Underdeveloped Areas, May, 1953; Commission on Foreign Economic Policy, *Staff Papers* (Washington: U.S. Government Printing Office, 1954); Consultants on International Finance and Economic Problems, *The Problem of Excess Accumulation of U.S.-Owned Local Currencies: Findings and Recommendations Submitted to the Under Secretary of State,* April 4, 1960 (processed); Gordon Gray, *Report to the President on Foreign Economic*

Policies (Washington: U.S. Government Printing Office, 1950); International Development Advisory Board, *Partners in Progress, a Report to the President by the International Development Advisory Board*, March, 1951.

Annual Reports and *Summary Proceedings* of annual meetings of the International Bank for Reconstruction and Development and its affiliates provide background on the activities of these agencies. Development of United Nations attitudes toward financing economic development can be traced in United Nations Secretariat, Department of Economic Affairs, *Methods of Financing Economic Development in Under-developed Countries* (United Nations Publication Sales No.: 1949.II.B.4); United Nations Secretariat, Department of Economic Affairs, *Measures for the Economic Development of Underdeveloped Countries* (United Nations Publication Sales No.: 1951.II.B.2); United Nations, *Report on a Special United Nations Fund for Economic Development* (United Nations Publication Sales No.: 1953.II.B.1); United Nations General Assembly, Tenth Session, *Official Records*, Supplement No. 17, "Special United Nations Fund for Economic Development," Report Prepared in Pursuance of United Nations General Assembly Resolution 822 (IX), A/2906, 1955; United Nations General Assembly, Ninth Session, *Official Records*, Supplement No. 19, "Special United Nations Fund for Economic Development," Final Report by Raymond Scheyven, Prepared in Pursuance of United Nations General Assembly Resolution 724B (VIII), A/2728, 1954.

BOOKS

Adams, Henry. *The Education of Henry Adams.* New York: Modern Library, 1931.

Agarwala, A. N., and Singh, S. P. (eds.). *The Economics of Underdevelopment.* New York: Oxford University Press, 1958.

Almond, Gabriel A. *The American People and Foreign Policy.* Revised ed. New York: Praeger, 1960.

Asher, Robert E. *Grants, Loans, and Local Currencies: Their Role in Foreign Aid.* Washington: Brookings Institution, 1961.

Asher, Robert E., et al., *The United Nations and Economic and Social Co-operation.* Washington: Brookings Institution, 1957.

Avramovic, Dragoslav, assisted by Gulhati, Ravi. *Debt Servicing Ca-*

pacity and Postwar Growth in International Indebtedness. Baltimore: Johns Hopkins Press, 1958.

Avramovic, Dragoslav, and Gulhati, Ravi. *Debt Servicing Problems of Low-Income Countries, 1956–1958.* Baltimore: Johns Hopkins Press, 1960.

Bauer, Raymond A., Pool, Ithiel de Sola, and Dexter, Lewis Anthony. *American Business and Public Policy.* New York: Atherton, 1963.

Benham, Frederic. *Economic Aid to Underdeveloped Countries.* New York: Oxford University Press, 1961.

Berliner, Joseph S. *Soviet Economic Aid.* New York: Praeger, 1958.

Black, Eugene R. *The Diplomacy of Economic Development.* Cambridge, Mass.: Harvard University Press, 1960.

Brown, William Adams, Jr., and Opie, Redvers. *American Foreign Assistance.* Washington: Brookings Institution, 1953.

Cairncross, Alec. *The International Bank for Reconstruction and Development.* ("Essays in International Finance," No. 33.) Princeton, N.J.: Princeton University Press, 1959.

Castle, Eugene W. *Billions, Blunders, and Baloney.* New York: Devin, 1955.

———. *The Great Giveaway.* Chicago: Regnery, 1957.

Chandler, Lester V. *The Economics of Money and Banking.* 4th ed. revised. New York: Harper & Row, 1964.

Coffin, Frank M. *Witness For Aid.* Boston: Houghton Mifflin, 1964.

Cohen, Bernard C. *The Influence of Non-governmental Groups on Foreign Policy-Making.* Boston: World Peace Foundation, 1959.

Crabb, Cecil V., Jr. *American Foreign Policy in the Nuclear Age.* Evanston, Ill.: Row, Peterson and Co., 1960.

Dahl, Robert A. *Congress and Foreign Policy.* New York: Norton, 1950.

———. *Modern Political Analysis.* Englewood Cliffs, N.J.: Prentice-Hall, Inc., 1963.

Dahl, Robert A., and Lindblom, Charles E. *Politics, Economics, and Welfare.* New York: Harper & Bros., 1953.

Eisenhower, Milton S. *The Wine Is Bitter: The United States and Latin America.* Garden City, N.Y.: Doubleday, 1963.

Elder, Robert E., and Murden, Forrest D. *Economic Co-operation: Special United Nations Fund for Economic Development.* New York: Woodrow Wilson Foundation, 1954.

Elliott, William Y., *et al. The Political Economy of American Foreign Policy.* New York: Henry Holt, 1955.

Engler, Robert. *The Politics of Oil.* New York: Macmillan, 1961.

Feis, Herbert. *Foreign Aid and Foreign Policy.* New York: St. Martin's, 1964.

Harrod, R. F. *The Life of John Maynard Keynes*. London: Macmillan, 1951.

Heilbroner, Robert L. *The Great Ascent: The Struggle for Economic Development in Our Time*. New York: Harper Torchbooks, 1963.

Higgins, Benjamin. *United Nations and U.S. Foreign Economic Policy*. Homewood, Ill.: Irwin, 1962.

Hoffman, Paul G. *One Hundred Countries and One and One Quarter Billion People*. Washington: Albert D. and Mary Lasker Foundation, 1960.

Jackson, Robert G. A. *The Case for an International Development Authority*. Syracuse, N.Y.: Syracuse University Press, 1959.

Knorr, Klaus, and Patterson, Gardner (eds.). *A Critique of the Randall Commission Report on United States Foreign Economic Policy*. Princeton, N.J.: International Finance Section and Center of International Studies, Princeton University Press, 1954.

Lasswell, Harold. *Politics: Who Gets What, When, How*. New York: Meridian, 1958.

Liska, George. *The New Statecraft*. Chicago: University of Chicago Press, 1960.

Mason, Edward S. *Foreign Aid and Foreign Policy*. New York: Harper & Row, 1964.

Matecki, B. E. *Establishment of the International Finance Corporation and United States Policy*. New York: Praeger, 1957.

Mikesell, Raymond F. (ed.). *U.S. Private and Government Investment Abroad*. Eugene: University of Oregon Press, 1962.

————. *United States Economic Policy and International Relations*. New York: McGraw-Hill, 1952.

Millikan, Max F., and Rostow, W. W. *A Proposal: Key to an Effective Foreign Policy*. New York: Harper & Bros., 1957.

Montgomery, John D. *The Politics of Foreign Aid*. New York: Praeger, 1962.

Morris, James. *The Road to Huddersfield*. New York: Pantheon, 1963.

Myrdal, Gunnar. *Economic Theory and Underdeveloped Regions*. London: G. Duckworth, 1957.

Patterson, Gardner, and Behrman, Jack N. *Survey of United States International Finance, 1950*. Princeton, N.J.: Princeton University Press, 1951.

Patterson, Gardner, Gunn, John M., Jr., and Swerdlove, Dorothy L. *Survey of United States International Finance, 1953*. Princeton, N.J.: Princeton University Press, 1954.

Robinson, James A. *Congress and Foreign Policy-Making*. Homewood, Ill.: Dorsey Press, 1962.

Robinson, James A. *The Monroney Resolution: Congressional Initiative in Foreign Policy Making.* New York: Eagleton Foundation Studies in Practical Politics, Henry Holt, 1959.

Rubinstein, Alvin Z. *The Soviets in International Organizations: Changing Policy Toward Developing Countries, 1953–1963.* Princeton: Princeton University Press, 1964.

Salter, Arthur. *Foreign Investment.* ("Essays in International Finance," No. 12.) Princeton, N.J.: Princeton University Press, 1951.

Schelling, Thomas C. *International Economics.* Boston: Allyn & Bacon, 1958.

———. *The Strategy of Conflict.* Cambridge, Mass.: Harvard University Press, 1960.

Smithies, Arthur. *The Budgetary Process in the United States.* New York: McGraw-Hill, 1955.

Snider, Delbert A. *Introduction to International Economics.* Homewood, Ill.: Irwin, 1954.

Snyder, Richard C., and Furniss, Edgar S., Jr. *American Foreign Policy: Formulation, Principles, and Programs.* New York: Rinehart, 1954.

Spanier, John W. *American Foreign Policy since World War II.* Revised ed. New York: Praeger, 1962.

Sprout, Harold, and Sprout, Margaret. *Foundations of International Politics.* Princeton, N.J.: Van Nostrand, 1962.

Staley, Eugene. *War and the Private Investor.* Garden City, N.Y.: Doubleday, 1935.

Tully, Andrew, and Britten, Milton. *Where Did Your Money Go? The Foreign Aid Story.* New York: Simon & Schuster, Inc., 1964.

Viner, Jacob. *International Trade and Economic Development.* Glencoe, Ill.: Free Press, 1952.

Westerfield, H. Bradford. *The Instruments of America's Foreign Policy.* New York: Crowell, 1963.

Whitman, Marina von Neumann. *The United States Investment Guaranty Program and Private Foreign Investment.* ("Princeton Studies in International Finance," No. 9.) Princeton, N.J.: Princeton University Press, 1959.

Wilcox, Clair. *A Charter for World Trade.* New York: Macmillan, 1949.

Wolf, Charles, Jr. *Foreign Aid: Theory and Practice in Southern Asia.* Princeton, N.J.: Princeton University Press, 1960.

ARTICLES AND PERIODICALS

Baldwin, David A. "The International Development Association: Theory and Practice," *Economic Development and Cultural Change,* X (October, 1961), 86–96.

————. "International Aid for Underdeveloped Countries: A Comment," *Review of Economics and Statistics*, XLIV (May, 1962), 213.

Bauer, P. T. Review of Benjamin Higgins, *Economic Development: Problems, Principles, and Policies* in *Economic Development and Cultural Change*, X (October, 1961), 97–101.

Cleveland, Harlan. "The Fits and Starts of Foreign Aid," *The Reporter*, April 16, 1959, pp. 25–29.

Fenno, Richard F., Jr. "The House Appropriations Committee as a Political System: The Problem of Integration," *American Political Science Review*, LVI (June, 1962), 310–24.

Fetter, Frank Whitson. "The Need for Postwar Foreign Lending," *Papers and Proceedings of the Fifty-fifth Annual Meeting of the American Economic Association*, 1943, pp. 342–46.

Harriman, Averell. "The Soviet Challenge and American Policy," *Atlantic Monthly*, April, 1956, pp. 42–47.

Haviland, H. Field, Jr. "Foreign Aid and the Policy Process: 1957," *American Political Science Review*, LII (September, 1958), 689–724.

Hilsman, Roger. "Congressional-Executive Relations and the Foreign Policy Consensus," *American Political Science Review*, LII (September, 1958), 725–44.

————. "The Foreign-Policy Consensus: An Interim Research Report," *Journal of Conflict Resolution*, III (December, 1959), 361–82.

Johnston, Bruce F. "Farm Surpluses and Foreign Policy," *World Politics*, X (October, 1957), 1–23.

Kennan, George F. "The Future of Our Professional Diplomacy," *Foreign Affairs*, XXXIII (July, 1955), 566–86.

Kindleberger, Charles P. "United States Economic Foreign Policy: Research Requirements for 1965," *World Politics*, XI (July, 1959), 588–613.

Machlup, F. "Three Concepts of the Balance of Payments and the So-Called Dollar Shortage," *Economic Journal*, LX (March, 1950), 46–68.

Mason, Edward S. "Foreign Money We Can't Spend," *Atlantic Monthly*, May, 1960, pp. 79–86.

McLellan, David S., and Woodhouse, Charles E. "Businessmen in Foreign Policy," *Southwestern Social Science Quarterly*, XXXIX (March, 1959), 283–90.

————. "The Business Elite and Foreign Policy," *Western Political Quarterly*, XIII (March, 1960), 172–90.

Metzger, Stanley D. "The New International Development Association," *Georgetown Law Journal*, XLIX (Fall, 1960), 23–43.

Morgenthau, Hans. "A Political Theory of Foreign Aid," *American Political Science Review*, LVI (June, 1962), 301–9.

New York Herald Tribune. February 20, 1947.

New York Times. 1943–62.

Pincus, John A. "The Cost of Foreign Aid," *Review of Economics and Statistics,* XLV (November, 1963), 360–67.

"Point IV," *Fortune Magazine,* February, 1950, pp. 89–96, 176, 178, 181, 182.

Rao, V. K. R. V. "An International Development Authority," *India Quarterly,* VIII (July–September, 1952), 236–69.

Rosenstein-Rodan, P. N. "International Aid for Underdeveloped Countries," *Review of Economics and Statistics,* XLIII (May, 1961), 107–38.

Schelling, Thomas C. "American Foreign Assistance," *World Politics,* VII (July, 1955), 606–26.

Singer, H. W. "International Aid for Economic Development: Problems and Tendencies," *International Development Review,* VI (March, 1964), 16–21.

Ward, Barbara. "Foreign Aid *Has* Succeeded," *New York Times Magazine,* July 12, 1964, pp. 9, 18–19.

X. [Kennan, George F.] "Sources of Soviet Conduct," *Foreign Affairs,* XXV (July, 1947), 566–82.

UNITED STATES GOVERNMENT PUBLICATIONS

Advisory Committee on Underdeveloped Areas. *Economic Strength for the Free World,* A Report to the Director for Mutual Security by the Advisory Committee on Underdeveloped Areas, May, 1953.

Berenson, Robert L., Bristol, William M., and Straus, Ralph I. *Accumulation and Administration of Local Currencies: A Special Report to James H. Smith Jr., Director, International Cooperation Administration,* August, 1958. (Processed.)

Commission on Foreign Economic Policy. *Report to the President and the Congress.* Washington: U.S. Government Printing Office, 1954.

Commission on Foreign Economic Policy. *Staff Papers.* Washington: U.S. Government Printing Office, 1954.

Commission on Organization of the Executive Branch of the Government. *Overseas Economic Operations,* A report to the Congress, June, 1955.

Composite Report of the President's Committee to Study the United States Military Assistance Program. 2 vols., August 17, 1959.

Consultants on International Finance and Economic Problems. *The Problem of Excess Accumulation of U.S.-Owned Local Currencies:*

Findings and Recommendations Submitted to the Under Secretary of State, April 4, 1960. (Processed.)

Department of State Bulletin. 1943–62.

Gray, Gordon. *Report to the President on Foreign Economic Policies*. Washington: U.S. Government Printing Office, 1950.

International Development Advisory Board. *A New Emphasis on Economic Development Abroad: A Report to the President of the United States on Ways, Means and Reasons for U.S. Assistance to International Economic Development*, March, 1957.

International Development Advisory Board. *Partners in Progress*, A Report to the President by the International Development Advisory Board, March, 1951.

President's Materials Policy Commission. *Resources for Freedom*. 5 vols. Washington: U.S. Government Printing Office, 1952.

Report to the President by the President's Citizen Advisers on the Mutual Security Program, March 1, 1957.

The Scope and Distribution of United States Military and Economic Assistance Programs, Report to the President from the Committee to Strengthen the Security of the Free World, March 20, 1963.

Straus, Ralph I. *Expanding Private Investment for Free World Economic Growth*, A special report prepared at the request of the Department of State, April, 1959.

U.S. Bureau of Foreign Commerce. *Factors Limiting U.S. Investment Abroad (Part 2): Business Views on the U.S. Government's Role*. Washington: U.S. Government Printing Office, 1954.

U.S. Congress, Committee on Foreign Affairs and Committee on Foreign Relations. *Legislation on Foreign Relations: With Explanatory Notes*. Joint Committee Print, 86th Cong., 2d Sess., 1960.

U.S. Congress, Joint Economic Committee. *Dimensions of Soviet Economic Power*. Joint Committee Print, 87th Cong., 2d Sess., 1962.

U.S. *Congressional Record*. Vol. CX. 88th Cong., 2d Sess., 1964.

U.S. Department of State. *Postwar Foreign Policy Preparation 1939–1945*. General Policy Series No. 15. Washington: U.S. Government Printing Office, 1949.

U.S. Department of State. *The Sino-Soviet Economic Offensive in the Less Developed Countries*. European and British Commonwealth Series, No. 51, 1958.

U.S. House of Representatives, Committee on Appropriations. *Hearings, Mutual Security Appropriations for 1960*. 86th Cong., 1st Sess., 1959.

U.S. House of Representatives, Committee on Appropriations. *Mutual Security Appropriation Bill, 1958*. Report No. 1172, 85th Cong., 1st Sess., 1957.

U.S. House of Representatives, Subcommittee of the Committee on Appropriations. *Hearings, Mutual Security Appropriations for 1958*. 85th Cong., 1st Sess., 1957.

U.S. House of Representatives, Committee on Banking and Currency. *Hearings, Increase of Lending Authority—Export-Import Bank*. 82d Cong., 1st Sess., 1951.

U.S. House of Representatives, Committee on Banking and Currency. *Hearings, International Development Association Act*. 86th Cong., 2d Sess., 1960.

U.S. House of Representatives, Committee on Foreign Affairs. *Background Material on Mutual Defense and Development Programs: Fiscal Year 1965*. Committee Print. 88th Cong., 2d Sess., 1964.

U.S. House of Representatives, Committee on Foreign Affairs. *Expropriation of American-Owned Property by Foreign Governments in the Twentieth Century*, report prepared by the Legislative Reference Service, Library of Congress. Committee Print. 88th Cong., 1st Sess., 1963.

U.S. House of Representatives, Committee on Foreign Affairs. *Hearings, International Technical Cooperation Act of 1949*. 81st Cong., 1st Sess., 1949.

U.S. House of Representatives, Committee on Foreign Affairs. *Hearings, Mutual Security Act Extension*. 82d Cong., 2d Sess., 1952.

U.S. House of Representatives, Committee on Foreign Affairs. *Hearings, The Mutual Security Act of 1954*. 83rd Cong., 2d Sess., 1954.

U.S. House of Representatives, Committee on Foreign Affairs. *Hearings, Mutual Security Act of 1957*. 85th Cong., 1st Sess., 1957.

U.S. House of Representatives, Committee on Foreign Affairs. *Hearings, Mutual Security Act of 1958*. 85th Cong., 2d Sess., 1958.

U.S. House of Representatives, Committee on Foreign Affairs. *Mutual Security Act of 1951*. Report No. 872, 82d Cong., 1st Sess., 1951.

U.S. House of Representatives, Committee on Foreign Affairs. *Mutual Security Act of 1954*. Report No. 1925, 83rd Cong., 2d Sess., 1954.

U.S. House of Representatives, Committee on Foreign Affairs. *Mutual Security Act of 1955*. Report No. 912, 84th Cong., 1st Sess., 1955.

U.S. House of Representatives, Committee on Foreign Affairs. *Mutual Security Act of 1956*. Report No. 2213, 84th Cong., 2d Sess., 1956.

U.S. House of Representatives, Committee on Foreign Affairs. *Mutual Security Act of 1957*. Report No. 776, 85th Cong., 1st Sess., 1957.

U.S. House of Representatives, Committee on Foreign Affairs. *Mutual Security Act of 1958*. Report No. 1696, 85th Cong., 2d Sess., 1958.

U.S. House of Representatives, Committee on Foreign Affairs. *Regional and Other Documents Concerning United States Relations With Latin America.* Committee Print, 87th Cong., 2d Sess., 1962.

U.S. House of Representatives, Committee on Foreign Affairs. *Report on Foreign Policy and Mutual Security.* Report by James P. Richards. Report No. 551, 85th Cong., 1st Sess., 1957.

U.S. House of Representatives, Committee on Government Operations. *Hearings, Operations of the Development Loan Fund.* 86th Cong., 2d Sess., 1960.

U.S. House of Representatives, Committee on Government Operations. *Operations of the Development Loan Fund.* Report No. 1526, 86th Cong., 2d Sess., 1960.

U.S. House of Representatives, Committee on Government Operations. *Review of the Budget Formulation and Presentation Practices of the International Cooperation Administration.* Report No. 449, 85th Cong., 1st Sess., 1957.

U.S. House of Representatives, Committee on Ways and Means. *Foreign Trade Agreements.* Report No. 594, 79th Cong., 1st Sess., 1945.

U.S. House of Representatives, Special Committee on Post-War Economic Policy and Planning. *The Post-War Foreign Economic Policy of the United States.* Report No. 541, 79th Cong., 1st Sess., 1945.

U.S. National Advisory Council on International Monetary and Financial Problems. *Semi-Annual Reports to Congress.* 1946–1954.

U.S. Senate, Committee on Agriculture and Forestry. *Hearings, Policies and Operations Under Public Law 480.* 85th Cong., 1st Sess., 1957.

U.S. Senate, Committee on Banking and Currency. *Hearings, International Development Association.* 85th Cong., 2d Sess., 1958.

U.S. Senate, Committee on Foreign Relations and Committee on Armed Services. *Hearings, Mutual Security Act of 1951.* 82d Cong., 1st Sess., 1951.

U.S. Senate, Committee on Foreign Relations and Committee on Armed Services. *The Mutual Security Act of 1951.* Report No. 703, 82d Cong., 1st Sess., 1951.

U.S. Senate, Committee on Foreign Relations. *Hearings, Act for International Development.* 81st Cong., 2d Sess., 1950.

U.S. Senate, Committee on Foreign Relations. *Hearings, International Development Association,* 86th Cong., 2d Sess., 1960.

U.S. Senate, Committee on Foreign Relations. *Hearings, International Development and Security.* 87th Cong., 1st Sess., 1961.

U.S. Senate, Committee on Foreign Relations. *Hearings, Mutual Security Act of 1953.* 83rd Cong., 1st Sess., 1953.

U.S. Senate, Committee on Foreign Relations. *Hearings, Mutual Security Act of 1954.* 83rd Cong., 2d Sess., 1954.

U.S. Senate, Committee on Foreign Relations. *Hearings, Mutual Security Act of 1955.* 84th Cong., 1st Sess., 1955.

U.S. Senate, Committee on Foreign Relations. *Hearings, Mutual Security Act of 1956.* 84th Cong., 2d Sess., 1956.

U.S. Senate, Committee on Foreign Relations. *Hearings, Mutual Security Act of 1957.* 85th Cong., 1st Sess., 1957.

U.S. Senate, Committee on Foreign Relations. *Hearings, Mutual Security Act of 1958.* 85th Cong., 2d Sess., 1958.

U.S. Senate, Committee on Foreign Relations. *Hearings, Mutual Security Act of 1959.* 86th Cong., 1st Sess., 1959.

U.S. Senate, Committee on Foreign Relations. *The Mutual Security Act of 1954.* Report No. 1799, 83rd Cong., 2d Sess., 1954.

U.S. Senate, Committee on Foreign Relations. *The Mutual Security Act of 1955.* Report No. 383, 84th Cong., 1st Sess., 1955.

U.S. Senate, Committee on Foreign Relations. *The Mutual Security Act of 1956.* Report No. 2273, 84th Cong., 2d Sess., 1956.

U.S. Senate, Committee on Foreign Relations. *United States Foreign Policy,* "Economic, Social, and Political Change in the Underdeveloped Countries and Its Implications for United States Policy," a study prepared by the Center for International Studies, Massachusetts Institute of Technology. Committee Print, 86th Cong., 2d Sess., 1960.

U.S. Senate, Committee on Foreign Relations. *United States Foreign Policy,* "Worldwide and Domestic Economic Problems and Their Impact on the Foreign Policy of the United States," a study prepared by the Corporation for Economic and Industrial Research. Committee Print, 86th Cong., 1st Sess., 1959.

U.S. Senate. *Foreign Aid Program: Compilation of Studies and Surveys,* prepared under the direction of the Special Committee to Study the Foreign Aid Program. 85th Cong., 1st Sess., 1957, Senate Doc. 52.

U.S. Senate, Special Committee to Study the Foreign Aid Program. *Foreign Aid.* Report No. 300, 85th Cong., 1st Sess., 1957.

U.S. Senate, Special Committee to Study the Foreign Aid Program. *Hearings, The Foreign Aid Program.* 85th Cong., 1st Sess., 1957.

UNITED NATIONS AND SPECIALIZED
AGENCIES PUBLICATIONS

International Bank for Reconstruction and Development. *Annual Reports.* 1946–1962.

International Bank for Reconstruction and Development. *The International Bank for Reconstruction and Development: 1946–1953.* Baltimore: Johns Hopkins Press, 1954.

International Bank for Reconstruction and Development. *Summary Proceedings* of the Annual Meetings of the Board of Governors. 1946–1962.

United Nations A/C.2/SR.613, November 9, 1959.

United Nations A/C.2/SR.618, November 13, 1959.

United Nations A/C.2/SR.370, November 8, 1955.

United Nations A/C.2/187, October 28, 1955.

United Nations A/C.2/SR.302, October 25, 1954.

United Nations A/C.2/SR.163, December 10, 1951.

United Nations A/C.2/SR.259, October 14, 1953.

United Nations A/C.2/SR.147, November 20, 1951.

United Nations E/CN.1/SR.111, May 17, 1951.

United Nations E/CN.1/80:E/CN.1/Sub.3/29, May 19, 1950.

United Nations General Assembly. *Comments of Governments on the report of the Committee of Nine, submitted in accordance with General Assembly resolution 724B (VIII)*. A/2646/Add.1. May 25, 1954.

United Nations General Assembly, Ninth Session. *Official Records,* Supplement No. 19, "Special United Nations Fund for Economic Development," Final Report by Raymond Scheyven, Prepared in Pursuance of United Nations General Assembly Resolution 724B (VIII). A/2728, 1954.

United Nations General Assembly, Tenth Session. *Official Records,* Supplement No. 17, "Special United Nations Fund for Economic Development," Report Prepared in Pursuance of United Nations General Assembly Resolution 822 (IX). A/2906, 1955.

United Nations. *Report on a Special United Nations Fund for Economic Development.* United Nations Publication Sales No.: 1953.II.B.1.

United Nations Secretariat, Department of Economic Affairs. *Measures for the Economic Development of Underdeveloped Countries.* United Nations Publication Sales No.: 1951.II.B.2.

United Nations Secretariat, Department of Economic Affairs. *Methods of Financing Economic Development in Under-developed Countries.* United Nations Publication Sales No.: 1949.II.B.4.

United Nations. *Yearbook of the United Nations.* 1947–62.

OTHER SOURCES

Banfield, Edward C. "American Foreign Aid Doctrines," in *Public Policy, 1961.* Cambridge, Mass.: Harvard University Press, 1962, pp. 44–94.

Campbell, John C. *The United States in World Affairs.* (Annual.) Volumes for 1945–1947, 1947–1948, 1948–1949. New York: Harper & Bros., 1947, 1948, and 1949, respectively.

Committee for Economic Development. *Economic Development Assistance,* 1957.

Foreign Economic Policy for the Twentieth Century, Report of the Rockefeller Brothers Fund Special Studies Project. Garden City, N.Y.: Doubleday, 1958.

Hufbauer, G. C. "United States Balance of Payments and Economic Aid," *Public Policy, 1961.* Cambridge, Mass.: Harvard University Press, 1962, pp. 139–51.

National Foreign Trade Convention. *Annual Reports.* 1949–62. New York: National Foreign Trade Council, 1949–63.

Schelling, Thomas C. "American Aid and Economic Development: Some Critical Issues," *International Stability and Progress.* New York: American Assembly, 1957, pp. 121–69.

Stebbins, Richard P. *The United States in World Affairs.* (Annual.) Volumes for 1949–1962. New York: Harper & Bros., 1950–63.

Index

Acheson, Dean, 21, 72–80 *passim*, 94, 105, 106
Act of Bogotá, 206
Act for International Development, 72, 74, 106
Adams, Henry, 266
Adams, Sherman, 77 n., 174 n., 176 n., 178 n., 217 n., 256 n.
Advisory Committee on Underdeveloped Areas, 109–10
AFL–CIO, 263
Agarwala, A. N., 63 n.
Agricultural Trade Development and Assistance Act, 101, 122, 124, 128, 131–32, 154–58, 187–90, 203, 206–7
Agriculture, and foreign aid, 100–101 130, 131 n., 144–45, 154–58, 206–7
Alliance for Progress, 203
Almond, Gabriel, 101, 105 n.
American Bankers Association, 57 n.
American Farm Bureau, 258
Analytical framework: approach, 11–13; capital channels, 2–3; definitions, 2–7 major questions, 11; need for interdisciplinary approach, vii–viii; statecraft and economic development, 1–2; time periods, 13
Anderson, Robert, 232
Armstrong, Willis C., 225 n.
Asher, Robert E., 5 n., 32 n., 74 n., 88, 95 n., 128, 184 n., 185, 204 n., 235 n., 246

Baldwin, David A., 180 n., 229 n., 253 n., 265 n.
Ball, George, 194 n., 200 n.
Banfield, Edward C., 247 n., 255–56, 257 n.
Barr, Stringfellow, 220 n.
Bauer, P. T., 94 n.
Bauer, Raymond A., 77 n.
Behrman, J. N., 67 n., 94 n.

Benham, Frederic, 193 n.
Berenson, Robert L., 232 n.
Berliner, Joseph S., 136 n.
Black, Eugene R., 32, 50, 96–100 *passim*, 141–44, 150, 151–52, 176, 212–13, 215, 251, 257
Bohlen, Charles E., 10, 25, 57, 236
Braden, Spruille, 20
Brand, Vance, 200 n., 205
Bristol, William M., 232 n.
British loan of 1946, 10, 60, 64
Britten, Milton, 256 n.
Brown, William Adams, Jr., 61 n., 69 n., 104 n., 265 n.
Business elite: and foreign aid, 64–65, 113, 149–52, 175–76, 231; and foreign policy, 53–57, 101–5, 146–52, 214–16; and IBRD, 56–57, 147, 151–52, 231; and private investment, 55, 104, 146–48; and public lending, 54–55, 101–3; split in, 148–49; and SUNFED, 143; and trade liberalization, 55–56, 104–5
Byrnes, James F., 14

Cairncross, Alec, 30 n., 32 n., 38 n., 44 n., 46 n.
Capehart, Homer, 157, 168, 177
Capital: channels, 22; defined, 12 n.
Carnett, George S., 208 n.
Castle, Eugene W., 262
Castro, Fidel, 209
Chamberlain, John, 195
China, 86
Clayton, William L., 23 n.
Cleveland, Harlan, 4 n., 45 n., 257 n.
Cohen, Bernard C., 263 n.
Cold war, 25, 62, 111
Collado, E. G., 89 n.
Colmer Committee. *See* House Special Committee on Postwar Economic Policy and Planning

Commission on Foreign Economic Policy, 105, 152–53, 168
Committee for Economic Development, 57, 148–49, 150, 152 n., 175, 214
Commodity Credit Corporation, 101, 131, 132, 154–57, 268
Congress: and foreign aid, 60–61, 64, 106–7, 111, 113, 129–30, 133, 143–44, 150–51, 154–67, 170–71, 176–78, 217–24, 253–55, 257–67; role in foreign policy, 12 n., 57; and trade liberalization, 58–60, 105–6, 152–54, 178, 216–17; and U.S. policy, 105–7, 216–24
Connally, Tom, 106
Cooper, John Sherman, 157
Coppock, Joseph D., 234 n.
Crabb, Cecil V., Jr., 6, 10
Crawford, Morris H., 208 n.

Dahl, Robert, 245, 253–54, 269 n., 271 n.
Development Loan Fund, 9, 10, 117, 122, 132–34, 158–67, 204–5, 253–55
Dexter, Lewis A., 77 n.
Dillon, Douglas, 172, 174, 184, 185, 191, 194, 200 n., 201 n., 221, 228 n., 233
Dodge, Joseph M., 173
Dollar gap, 87–88
Dulles, John Foster, 117, 119, 120 n., 121, 124, 129, 156, 163, 166–69 passim, 174, 176–77

Economic development: defined, 11 n.; as a foreign policy goal, 13–15, 72–75, 117–19, 191–92, 243–47; and peace, 13–15, 73–74; and prosperity, 13–15, 74–75
Economic growth, 11 n.
Eisenhower, Dwight D., 77, 79, 85, 105, 106, 117–21 passim, 125, 127, 128, 153, 165, 168–74 passim, 178, 192, 193, 216, 217, 225–26, 234, 238, 255–56
Eisenhower, Milton S., 8–9, 78, 172–73, 195, 206
Elder, Robert E., 102 n.
Elliott, William Y., 46 n.
Engler, Robert, 182 n.
Erhardt, Ludwig, 195
European Recovery Program, 21–22, 63, 65. See also Marshall Plan
Export-Import Bank, and U.S. policy, 20, 21, 23, 82, 127–28, 201–3

Fairless, Benjamin, 150, 153
Fenno, Richard F., Jr., 133 n.
Fetter, Frank W., 70
Firestone, Harvey S., Jr., 152 n.
Foreign Operations Administration, 124
Foreign policy: concept of, 2, 15 n., 16 n.; external setting, 24–50, 85–100, 134–44, 208–13; internal setting, 51–61, 100–107, 144–67, 213–24
Foreign policy techniques: described, 16–24, 75–85, 119–34, 192–208; effectiveness of, 65–71, 113–16, 181–90, 236–42; process of choosing, 24–65, 85–113, 134–81, 208–36
Friedrich, Carl J., 144 n.
Fulbright, J. W., 105 n., 150, 166

Garner, Robert L., 32, 127
General Agreements on Tariffs and Trade, 153
Grace, J. Peter, 152 n.
Gray, Gordon, 108–9
Greek-Turkish Aid Program, 64
Gulhati, Ravi, 184 n., 235 n.

Hanes, John W., Jr., 235 n.
Harriman, W. Averell, 83, 220
Harrod, R. F., 29, 33 n., 60
Hartmann, C. David, 155 n., 230 n.
Haviland, H. Field, Jr., 161 n.
Hays, Brooks, 140 n.
Hazlitt, Henry, 195
Heilbroner, Robert L., 5 n.
Herter, Christian, 60
Hickenlooper, Bourke, 105 n., 155 n.
Higgins, Benjamin, 171 n., 187 n., 202 n.
Hilsman, Roger, 253 n., 262, 263–64, 266
Hirschman, Albert O., 200
Hitler, Adolf, 53
Hoffman, Paul, 65 n., 150, 197, 242
Holland, Henry P., 128 n.
Hollister, John B., 129–30, 151, 157, 160–61, 169, 170, 185
Hoover, Herbert, Jr., 170
House Special Committee on Postwar Economic Policy and Planning, 58–59
Hufbauer, G. C., 214 n.
Hughes, Rowland R., 170
Humphrey, George M., 82, 105 n., 121–22, 169
Humphrey, Hubert, 155 n.

India, 86
Inter-American Development Bank, 201–3, 205–6

International Bank for Reconstruction and Development: attitudes toward, 28; and business, 56–57; and commercial banking, 33–35; imaginary limits on, 42–50; policies, 23, 32–50; and politics, 35–37; president, 30–32; and soft loans, 96–98, 143–44, 212–13, 231; and strategic nonlending, 37–42; and SUNFED, 139–40; and UNEDA, 98; and United Nations, 97–98; and U.S. policy, 20, 29–50, 82–85, 96–100, 125–26, 141–44, 201–2, 211–13; voting, 22. *See also* Business elite

International Cooperation Administration, 117, 129–30, 151, 185

International Development Advisory Board, 109, 152 n., 166

International Development Association, 110, 200–201, 205, 218–24, 225, 253–55, 257

International Development Authority, 91–96, 109, 113

International Finance Corporation, 103, 122, 124, 125, 126–27, 138, 171–72, 175, 201–2

International Monetary Fund, 54, 56, 57 n., 170

International Trade Organization, 18, 58, 60, 66, 76, 105, 109, 113

investment guaranties, 80–81, 115, 124, 197–98

Jackson, Robert G. A., 45 n.

Javits, Jacob, 108, 170 n., 219

Johnson, Lyndon B., 195 n., 256 n., 267

Johnson, U. Alexis, 191

Johnston, Bruce F., 101 n., 144 n.

Johnston, Clement, 146

Johnston, Eric, 150, 152 n., 166

Judd, Walter H., 60, 225 n.

Kellog, R. D., 55 n.

Kenen, Peter B., 9 n., 265

Kennan, George F., 62, 264

Kennedy, John F., 185, 193–99 *passim*, 204, 215, 217, 220, 233, 234, 238, 256

Keynes, John M., 33, 56, 229 n.

Khrushchev, N., 174

Knorr, Klaus, 153 n.

Labouisse, Henry R., 204 n.

Lasswell, Harold, 248 n.

League of Women Voters, 263

Lend-lease aid, 52

Lindblom, Charles E., 269 n., 271 n.

Liska, George, 243 n.

Local currency: definitions, 4–5; misunderstanding of, 162–63, 218, 226–31; and money, 4–5; problem of, 232–33; and soft loans, 4–7; uses of, 84, 129–34, 186–90, 206–7

Local currency loan, definitions, 4–5

Lubin, Isador, 82 n.

Luce, Clare Booth, 60

McCloy, John J., 31, 32 n., 65 n., 231

McGhee, George C., 78 n., 194 n.

McLellan, David S., 148 n., 150 n., 151 n.

McMahon, Brien, 108, 219

Machlup, F., 87 n., 229 n., 270–71

Maffry, August, 171–72

Magee, James S., 210 n.

Mann, Thomas C., 195

Marshall, George C., 22

Marshall Plan, 60–68 *passim*, 103, 106

Martin, Edwin M., 192 n.

Martin, William McChesney, 63, 65 n.

Marx, Karl, 63

Marxism, 53

Mason, Edward S., 4 n., 226–27, 233

Matecki, B. E., 32 n., 110–11, 125 n., 126, 172

Meany, George, 210 n.

Metzger, Stanley D., 218, 220 n., 246, 265 n.

Meyer, Eugene, 31

Mikesell, Raymond F., 5 n., 7 n., 9 n., 27 n., 30 n., 32 n., 36, 130 n., 171 n., 158–59, 218 n., 246, 265 n., 269 n., 270

Millikan, Max F., 179–80

Millikin, Eugene D., 152

Money, definition, 3–5. *See also* Local currency

Monroney, A. S. Mike, 218–24, 234

Montgomery, John D., 4 n., 35 n., 154–56, 164–67, 171 n., 218–24, 247 n., 253–55, 257–58, 262, 264, 265 n., 267, 270

Morgenthau, Hans, 238 n., 243–47

Morgenthau, Henry, Jr., 14 n., 15, 21, 26, 60

Morris, James, 29 n., 30 n., 41 n.

Murden, Forrest D., 102 n.

Mutual Defense and Development Program, 8

Mutual Security Act, 106

Mutual Security Program, 81, 83, 122, 124, 128, 129–31, 271

National Association of Manufacturers, 64, 104, 105, 214, 263
National Foreign Trade Convention, 56–57, 102, 103, 104, 147
National Foreign Trade Council, 64
New Deal, 51
Nixon, Richard, 169

Ohlin, Bertil, 229 n.
O'Leary, Michael K., 273–74
Opie, Redvers, 61 n., 69 n., 104 n., 265 n.
Organization for Trade Cooperation, 153

Paley Commission. See President's Materials Policy Commission
Passman, Otto, 166, 262, 270
Pasvolsky, Leo, 246
Patterson, Gardner, 94 n., 153 n.
Phillips, Christopher H., 225 n.
Pincus, John, 240–41
PL 480. See Agricultural Trade Development and Assistance Act
Pool, Ithiel de Sola, 77 n.
Population, 71, 116, 241–42
President's Materials Policy Commission, 75
Private investment: effectiveness of, 67–70, 113–15, 239; and European reconstruction, 21; stimulation of, 17–22, 76–81, 120–24, 193–98
Public capital: channels, 81–85, 125–26, 199–201; effectiveness, 114–16, 184–90, 236–42; furnishing of, 22–24, 81–85, 124–34, 198–207; guiding principles, 22, 125; portents, 84–85; terms, 23–24, 82–85, 126–34, 201–7. See also Soft loans

Randall, Clarence, 150
Randall Commission. See Commission on Foreign Economic Policy
Rao, V. K. R. V., 88–90, 98, 102
Reciprocal Trade Agreements Act, 58–59, 152–53, 216
Reciprocal Trade Agreements Program, 105
Reed, Daniel A., 152
Reston, James, 169, 173
Reuther, Walter, 108, 120, 219
Richards, James P., 161, 165
Robinson, James A., 153 n., 164–67, 218–24, 253–55, 269
Rockefeller, Nelson, 109, 150, 169, 173

Roosevelt, Franklin Delano, 13, 16, 18
Rosenstein-Rodan, P. N., 180 n.
Rostow, W. W., 179–80, 246
Rowan, Carl T., 235 n.
Rubinstein, Alvin Z., 136 n.
Rusk, Dean, 192, 197, 234

Salter, Arthur, 52 n., 115
Schelling, Thomas C., 34 n., 43, 44 n., 47 n., 48 n., 49 n., 101, 182 n., 183 n., 267 n., 270 n.
Scheyven, Raymond, 93, 137–40, 143
Schumpeter, J. A., 63
Simpson, Richard A., 152
Singer, H. W., 10 n.
Singh, S. P., 63 n.
Smith, Adam, 33, 195
Smith, H. Alexander, 175
Smith, James H., Jr., 232
Smithies, Arthur, 149, 263 n.
Snider, Delbert A., 44 n.
Social Progress Trust Fund, 206
Soft loans: arguments, 26–27, 90–92, 93–95, 143–44; and Congress, 158–67; definitions, 3–7; dollar repayable, 240; efficiency of, 186–90; legitimacy, 8–10, 231; misunderstanding of, 9–10; and money, 3–5; synonyms, 3–5; and U.S. policy, 62–65, 85, 107–13, 128–34, 172–81, 204–7
Soviet bloc aid, 237–38
Spanier, John W., 67 n.
Special United Nations Fund for Economic Development, 93, 95, 110, 113, 120, 122, 126, 137–41, 143–44, 175, 209–11, 225
Sprout, Harold, 2 n., 244 n.
Sprout, Margaret, 2 n., 244 n.
Staley, Eugene, 53 n.
Stalin, Joseph, 87, 134–35, 174
Stassen, Harold, 112, 124, 165, 169
Stebbins, Richard P., 74 n., 83 n., 164 n., 202 n., 216 n.
Stevenson, Adlai E., 195 n., 210 n.
Straus, Ralph I., 70 n., 232 n.
Straus, Roger W., 122 n.
Strausz-Hupé, Robert, 68 n.

Taft, Robert A., 60, 151
Thorp, Willard, 79 n., 246
Thumberg, Penelope H., 208 n.
Tinbergen, Jan, 138
Trade Expansion Act, 216
Trade liberalization, 17–19, 65–66, 76–79, 120–21, 181, 193–94

Truman, Harry S, 72, 73, 77, 85, 86,
    93, 108, 168, 256
Tully, Andrew, 256 n.

Underdeveloped countries, defined, 11 n.
United Nations: and development fi-
    nancing, 88–96, 136–41, 209–11; and
    IBRD, 91; and U.S. policy, 28 n.
United Nations Economic Development
    Administration, 89, 90, 93, 98, 102,
    110, 113
United Nations Expanded Program of
    Technical Assistance, 125, 128, 141,
    203
United Nations Monetary and Finan-
    cial Conference, 15
United Nations Special Fund, 125, 141,
    209–11, 225
United States Chamber of Commerce,
    56, 57 n., 104, 146, 215, 258, 263

Viner, Jacob, 94 n.
Von Mises, Ludwig, 195
Vorys, John, 60, 61, 107, 159, 160

Wadsworth, J., 60
Wallace, Henry A., 108
Warburg, James P., 108
Ward, Barbara, 263 n.
Webb, James, 76 n.
Westerfield, H. Bradford, 5 n.
White, William S., 163
Whitman, Marina von Neumann, 80 n.,
    81 n., 115
Wilcox, Clair, 18 n., 19 n., 21 n., 27,
    28 n., 62, 64, 69 n., 246
Wildavsky, Aaron, 267 n.
Wolf, Charles, Jr., 13, 14 n., 15 n.,
    136 n., 237–38, 264 n., 265 n., 267–72
Woodhouse, Charles E., 148 n., 150 n.,
    151 n.
Woods, George D., 215–16